MANUAL
of
JUDEO-SPANISH

STUDIES AND TEXTS

IN

JEWISH HISTORY AND CULTURE

The Joseph and Rebecca Meyerhoff Center
for Jewish Studies
University of Maryland

XVI

General Editor: Bernard D. Cooperman

UNIVERSITY PRESS OF MARYLAND

MANUAL
of
JUDEO-SPANISH
Language and Culture

Marie-Christine Varol
Professor at the Jewish Studies Department,
Institut National des Langues
et Civilisations Orientales (INALCO), Paris

∗

TRANSLATION AND ADAPTATION INTO ENGLISH BY
Ralph Tarica
Professor Emeritus, University of Maryland, College Park

∗

DRAWINGS BY
Gaëlle Collin

∗

95 PHOTOGRAPHS

UNIVERSITY PRESS OF MARYLAND
(United States)
L'ASIATHÈQUE
maison des langues du monde
(Europe)
2008

LIBRARY OF CONGRESS CATALOGING-IN-PUBLICATION DATA

Varol-Bornes, Marie-Christine.
  [Manuel de judéo-espagnol. English]
  Manual of Judeo-Spanish : language and culture / Marie-Christine Varol.
    p. cm. — (Studies and texts in Jewish history and culture ; 16)
  ISBN 978-1-934309-19-3
    1. Ladino language—Textbooks for foreign speakers—English. 2. Sephardim. I. Title.
  PC4813.2.V3713 2008
  467'.9496—dc22   2008010824

Cover: La Kanfafaná, a marketing area in the old Jewish quarter of Balat (Istanbul). Photo
          Viktor Yenibahar. All rights reserved.

Design and layout: Jean-Marc Eldin.

U.S.: ISBN 978-1-934309-19-3 (University Press of Maryland)
Europe: ISBN 978-2-915255-75-1 (L'Asiathèque – Maison des langues du monde)

CONTENTS

Originally published in French as *Manuel de Judéo-espagnol: langue et culture,* by Langues & Mondes–L'Asiathèque, Paris, 1998, with the support of Charles Danon, Izi Levi and Giuseppe Modiano. Our thanks to them for their generous contribution to saving the Judeo-Spanish language and culture. Thanks are also due to Lorenzo Salzmann, Paul Vesseyre, Maurice Hasson, Enrico Isacco, Gérard Lévy and others who supplied photographs for the original French edition, used again in this English version.

Jean Carasso, founder and editor of *La Lettre sépharade,* has vigorously promoted the need for an English version, following the UNESCO Conference on Judeo-Spanish/Ladino held in Paris in June 2002. Our thanks to him and to the financial sponsorship provided by the Fonds Emilia Valori pour la Sauvegarde des Traditions.

For their expert production of the English language version of the accompanying audio CD, very special thanks are due to Julie Subrin and David Tarica.

Translator's Preface

This book is a translation into English of a work that many of us thought might never appear. The common perception is that Judeo-Spanish[1] is rapidly disappearing as a "native" language. At the beginning of the 21st century the heirs to this language and its rich culture now live in many corners of the world and have adopted the languages of the countries in which they live, notably English, French, modern Spanish and Hebrew. Even in the heart of the nation that gave the Spanish Jews sanctuary after their expulsion from Spain in 1492 —the old Ottoman Empire—young people increasingly think of Turkish as their primary language.

And yet, as Marie-Christine Varol explains in her introduction, there are strong indications that many of the heirs to the Judeo-Spanish language and culture persist in wanting to keep the flame alive. This is a culture that has long cherished its heritage. How else can we explain that several hundred thousand people continued speaking their late Medieval Spanish through several centuries of cohabitation among Turks, Greeks, Slavs, Arabs and others, without relinquishing their particular language or specific identity? There has always been a strong pride in Judeo-Spanish history, rich in the cultural achievements of writers, thinkers and influential personages from the Spanish Middle Ages onward. In our own day, who can deny the deep sense of attachment still held for traditions as they were cultivated by the Spanish Jews throughout the Mediterranean world and especially the old Ottoman Empire?

Marie-Christine Varol's approach is to treat Judeo-Spanish as a distinct language, worthy of a full pedagogical treatment of grammatical structures and lexical terms, and not simply as a somewhat curious dialect of old Castilian Spanish. The addition of a compact disc to illustrate the actual speech of native and near-native speakers makes this a method that lends itself well both to individual study as well as group classroom instruction. Readers will be particularly grateful for the inclusion of a multitude of cultural readings, photographs and songs that are typical of Judeo-Spanish culture, revelatory of the world of their grandparents—and *their* grandparents—as well as the continuing existence of a specifically Judeo-Spanish presence in the modern world. Indeed, the book

---

1. Judeo-Spanish is frequently called *Ladino* despite the fact that, strictly speaking, *Ladino* refers to the close translations of Hebrew texts into a literary variety of Judeo-Spanish (see the author's introduction). In this book, the language and the culture are referred to as "Judeo-Spanish," and the heirs to that culture as "Spanish Jews."

7

may be seen not only as a pedagogical manual but as a compendium of linguistic and cultural information that makes it suitable as a basic reference work.

The original work by Marie-Christine Varol has been translated here as closely as possible. There are only a few features that have been adapted for a specifically English-speaking readership. In regards to spelling, the *Vidas Largas* style has been converted to the system used more commonly by English speakers, that of *Aki Yerushalayim,* with slight modifications. Those points of grammar that would be difficult to comprehend for the reader with no background in a Romance Language have been expanded somewhat—such structures as object pronoun placement, the various past tenses and the subjunctive. Occasional vocabulary items that have entered Judeo-Spanish from the French have also been added for further ease of comprehension.

There will undoubtedly be puzzlement, perhaps even protests, from readers who will recall that their particular families said things differently from what is represented here—*aguera,* perhaps (instead of *agora* or *aora*), *denpues* (and not *despues, dispues* or *duspues*), *shevdo* (and not *shavdo*), and so on and on. Readers are encouraged to read the author's introductory remarks on the practical need to select *one* particular dialect upon which to focus in a book such as this—specifically, here, that of most native Judeo-Spanish speakers of Istanbul—while leaving the field entirely open for people with regional variants to further utilize and cultivate their particular differences.

Various Judeo-Spanish centers throughout the world continue to maintain the old religious rites and the traditions associated with cooking, eating, family life and the celebration of the passages of life. There are people who still speak the language, many more who understand it to varying degrees, and possibly others who may want to learn it "from scratch." Indeed, there is abundant evidence of efforts underway in a number of countries—Argentina, France, Israel, Spain, Turkey, the United States, only to name the most obvious—to revitalize the study of Judeo-Spanish. With the publication of her book in French, Marie-Christine Varol has made an enormous contribution to that effort. It is our hope that the present book will further extend that contribution to an English-speaking readership.

RALPH TARICA

Acknowledgements

This manual is a collective work whose authors are so numerous that a list of their names and contributions would take up as many pages as the manual itself.

I would have to recognize all the informants I recorded during interviews in Turkey from 1974 to 1986, people whose lives I shared on a daily basis for nine years, those I heard afterwards, exchanges with so many others, belonging to diverse communities, those I have not ceased to see on my various trips, or those in France at the Vidas Largas Association, or in courses given at the INALCO (National Institute of Eastern Languages and Civilizations, Paris) or at the European Jewish University. Was it Yusuf Altıntaş or Klara Perahya who had me write *azete* instead of *azeyte?* Was it Dolly Benozio who had me put in a *y* or Sabetay Varol who had me remove it? I no longer know. Everyone expressed their opinions, added, removed, commented on, with good humor. There is only room here for me to thank those who recounted or sang the texts presented here, cited proverbs or gave an account of their memories. They are: Mss. Monique Adato, Matilda Algranti, Süzí Arditi, Bekí Bardavid, Gentille Behar, Rachel Bello, Rachel Benhabib, Ester Danon, Sará Elmaz, Klara Emanüel, Malka Moskatel, Mme Nassi, Lucie Tari-Nasi, Rika Varol, Mati Varon… and Messrs. Izak Arditi, Izak Azuz, Salomon Bardavid, Enrique Barzilay, Viktor Behar, Marko Danon, Robert Elmaz, …and still others.

I offer my thanks likewise to all the authors who gave me permission to reproduce their works and whose names are cited at the end of each excerpt and in the final bibliography.

This book would not have been so richly illustrated had it not been for the generosity of several contributors: Lorenzo Salzmann, who provided so many of his admirable photographs, Enrico Isacco who placed at my disposal the collections he assembled and recorded, including those gathered by Maurice Hasson and Gérard Lévy. It also owes much to Paul Veysseyre who, along with Victor Yenibahar, produced fine photographs of the Balat neighborhood. I shall not forget the kindness of those who agreed to have their photographs published. In addition to the informants cited above, they include Mss. Zafer Duşi, Elmaz Kumrulukuş, Ida Sarfati, Viktorya Emanüel, Djoya and Malka Moskatel, Perla and Matilda Algranti, Mathilde Behar, Marianne Saltiel, Joëlle Tiano-Moussafir, Vicky Tiano-Suléma, Işil Emanüel, Tracy, Iren and Idil Moskatel, Gabrielle Moussafir, Luna, Bianca and Shila Taka, Suzanne Varol and Messrs. Jak and Izzet Emanüel, Izak Moskatel, Elie Moussafir, Rubén Sarfati, Victor Behar. Jean-Marc Eldin patiently set these photos onto pages.

This book would have had no "voice" had it not been for Mss. Jessica Benlolo, Gaëlle Collin, Dolly Benozio, Esther Ifrah, Greta Liberge, Monique Simon, Isabelle Sarfati-Zaoui, and Messrs. Daniel Alcalay, Guy Amira, Daniel Bredel, Raphaël Elmaleh, Alain Gicquiaux and Sabetay Varol; or for Luiz Menase, who gave us advice, and for Mr. Roger Frénoy who helped us with the fine-tuning.

Thanks go to my students at the INALCO who were the first to take these courses and do the exercises and who actively participated in developing this manual.

Special thanks go to Gaëlle Collin who accomplished a wonderful job of page composition and setting, without ever complaining about this author's whims or spells of remorse. The book is further in debt to her for the drawings illustrating the work, the transcriptions from texts in Hebrew characters and numerous editorial corrections. Jeanne Laedlein read, edited, and double-checked the vocabulary entries and verbs, and picked out various inconsistencies and errors without concern for the time she spent. Joëlle Tiano-Moussafir reread the manuscript, particularly the grammar, and offered additional expressions from Rhodes.

I would like to thank Mr. André Bourgey, former Dean of the INALCO, and my colleagues and friends who gave me encouragement and advice such as Itzhok Niborski who shared with me his experience as a teacher of Yiddish. I owe a particular debt to Klara and Elie Perahya, who reread and wrote comments on the manuscript and helped me to define the limits to the possible ways of expression in regards to regional or individual variants.

My thanks to Mr. and Mrs. Thiollier for having stood by me and supported me in this undertaking. I would like to salute here the courage and scientific exactness of their publishing company, which resulted in this first published teaching manual of Judeo-Spanish.

This manual would not have existed had it not been for Jean Carasso, whose enthusiasm, energy and determination smoothed away many a problem and won out over my fleeting moments of discouragement.

I would not have written this manual had it not been for Haïm-Vidal Sephiha who directed my dissertation, had me partake of his passion and art of teaching in his courses and workshops, and who gave me the responsibility of carrying on his teaching at the university.

I give thanks to Judeo-Spanish for having helped me to live through a difficult moment in my life.

MARIE-CHRISTINE VAROL

*Jackie-Lynn Cohen deserves my thanks for having given me my first set of half-lens reading glasses needed for me to write this manual.

Introduction

Why, in 1998, publish a teaching manual of Judeo-Spanish? That is the question asked by most speakers of this language before adding that it is not a language, that it is going to disappear, that there is no longer any reason to speak it, that there are a thousand reasons not to speak it, and that, besides, it is not spoken anymore—all this explained in Judeo-Spanish.

Now what strikes the sociolinguist is precisely the persistence of this language despite a century and a half of intense disparagement and despite its loss of status and function. This perpetually announced death has still not taken place, to our greater delight. It would of course be foolhardy to say that this won't happen, and so the role of this manual is likewise to make this language known or discovered in order to contribute to its safeguarding.

Judeo-Spanish in fact constitutes an important and venerable heritage as attested to by its history.[2] It is the language brought by the Jews brutally expelled from Spain in 1492, some of whom reached North Africa, others northern Europe (Bordeaux, London, Amsterdam, etc.), still others Italy, while others, in great numbers, were accepted by Sultan Bajazet II to the lands of the Ottoman Empire: Sarajevo, Sofia, Constantinople, Smyrna, Rhodes, and especially Salonika, but also Cairo, Safed and Jerusalem—these are among the places where Sephardic Judaism flourished and its culture developed.

In Morocco, the Spanish of the expelled people evolved into a variety of Judeo-Spanish, *Haketiya,* with its own personality and flavor, influenced by Arabic and distinct from the Judeo-Spanish of the Ottoman Empire, even if a significant number of texts circulated between the communities, made comprehensible by a common Spanish base. From 1860 on, once Spanish presence was felt in Morocco, *Haketiya* became re-Hispanicized to a large extent. Spoken today by a very scattered community, it appears threatened. Given its particular features it is not possible to give a systematic study of this language here. This manual may nonetheless provide a basis for such a study.

In the vast territories of the Ottoman Empire, in the cities, brilliant Judeo-Spanish-speaking communities developed, absorbing bit by bit the Greek-speaking Romaniote (or Yavanite) communities that had been living there since the time of the Byzantine Empire. It was at the end of the 17th century that the two communities seem to have merged and that Judeo-Spanish became the language of almost all, even if Greek remained known and spoken. Despite the

---

2. On this subject, a useful work to be consulted is Haïm-Vidal Sephiha's *L'agonie des Judéo-Espagnols*, Paris: Entente, 1977.

existence of several regional variants (of which the main ones will be pointed out in this work) recognized by most of them and essentially fairly limited, this Judeo-Spanish, called by its speakers *espanyol, espanyoliko, ispanyolit, djudezmo,* and more frequently *djudyó* or *djidyó,* offered a remarkable cohesion that allowed widely separated communities to communicate, exchange news, and publish works aimed at a wide readership.

The area in which this language was spoken went beyond the Ottoman Empire. There was a Judeo-Spanish community in Bucharest and another in Vienna that saw a considerable development in the 19th century. Vienna even became one of the principal publishing centers of Judeo-Spanish at the beginning of the 20th century. Finally, France, North and South America became an emigration pole for Spanish Jews between the two world wars.

After the extermination of the Jews deported to Nazi camps, nothing was left of the prestigious community of Salonika, and the communities of Yugoslavia, Greece, France, Austria and Romania were decimated. The Bulgarian community managed to emigrate, mainly to Palestine, and the Turkish community was preserved. At the present time Judeo-Spanish is spoken sporadically in large European and American cities, and in a more consistent way in Turkey (in Istanbul and Izmir) and in Israel. Currently what remains of the Rhodes community can be found for a large part in Brussels, where a journal, *Los Muestros,* is published. The Turkish community includes about 25,000 persons; it is prosperous and active and produces a weekly newspaper and a magazine in Turkish and in Judeo-Spanish, *Şalom* and *Tiryaki.* Bilingual shows are put on and cassettes of songs are produced there.

In Israel the Judeo-Spanish community is principally concentrated in Tel Aviv, in the Batyam neighborhood, and in Jerusalem. Judeo-Spanish is the object of increasing interest there, with radio broadcasts, language and literature courses taught in high schools and at the university, and the publication of a magazine entirely in Judeo-Spanish, *Aki Yerushalayim.* It should be mentioned that, in France, thanks to the work accomplished by Haïm-Vidal Sephiha for the defense and promotion of his language, Judeo-Spanish is taught (at the INALCO), and there are weekly radio programs and workshops in language and oral literature given under the auspices of the *Vidas Largas* association as well as courses and cultural activities organized by the *Akí Estamos* association.[3] There likewise exists a French journal published by Jean Carasso, *La Lettre Sépharade* as well as an English-language version of the same journal published in the United States. In Mexico, the Sephardic community center has set up courses in Judeo-Spanish for young people.

---

3. Judeo-Spanish is recognized as a "Language of France" by the General Delegation for the French Language and the Languages of France.

A RICH AND COMPLEX LANGUAGE

Medieval Spanish

Judeo-Spanish is first of all the heir to Medieval Spanish of which it preserves numerous features, primarily phonetic and lexical. Its literature up to the 19ᵗʰ century can likewise be situated in the Medieval tradition. Many of the terms borrowed from contact languages possess a corresponding term of Spanish origin, which has sometimes become loaded with particular connotations that allow for puns, a playful style and meanings that make up the richness and infinite variety of this language. Speakers of Judeo-Spanish are experienced multilinguists, and as such know perfectly well how to Hispanicize their Judeo-Spanish when they find themselves in the presence of Spanish speakers. The passage from one language to the other is easy (although a few surprises sometimes lie in waiting). Acquiring Judeo-Spanish is easy for those who know Spanish and is relatively easy for speakers of a Romance language such as French. For English-speakers, a prior knowledge of one of these languages will of course facilitate the learning process for Judeo-Spanish.

Hebrew: the holy language, and Ladino: the liturgical language

We use "Hebrew" here in the broad sense of Hebrew/Aramaic sources as found in the Bible and the Mishnah. To those who would see in "Judeo-Spanish" a combination of Spanish plus Hebrew, we wish them good luck! The presence of Hebrew in this language is in fact a subtle one and the Hebrew lexicon is actually quite small, even when it is limited to the religious sphere—which it definitely is not. Hebrew terms often bear ironic connotations when compared with their equivalents having a Spanish origin. They are often used because they cannot be understood by the "Others," and this cryptic usage has given slangy, amusing and quick-witted connotations to a goodly number of terms. Thus, a *nekevá* is not just a "female" but can sometimes be a "matronly type" or sometimes a "pretty girl walking by on the street." Names for catastrophes that come from the Hebrew are frequently used and carry a load of irony and self-mockery that other terms do not have. The exaggerated and comic dejection they evoke comes from the fact that recourse to Hebrew defines them as the special fate of the Jewish people, unavoidable, as a catastrophe that could only happen to Jews. Using a large number of Hebrew words in Judeo-Spanish identifies the speaker as being of the male sex, a rabbi or learned man, quite conservative, even "overly religious," and this is not generally well thought of by others.

The influence of Biblical and Mishnaic Hebrew/Aramaic is present when there is frequent reference to texts, when using proverbs and biblical metaphors, and when figurative language is called for. It operates indirectly through the intermediary of *Ladino*. This term, which sometimes denotes Judeo-Spanish itself, refers in fact, as Professor Sephiha has shown,[4] to a linguistic calque, borne of a tradition of pedagogical translation, of rabbinic source, whose usage can already be attested to in writings of 13th century Spain. This artificial language, using solely the vocabulary of Spanish, follows word for word the syntax and even the morphology of Hebrew whenever the need is felt. Judeo-Spanish draws from this liturgical language certain stylistic effects and syntactic turns of expression. We shall see several examples in this work (Lesson 8B, *La Agadá de Pesah*), showing to what extent the resulting text appears strange, even though all the words are of Spanish origin. *Ladino* was an artifice aimed at more easily teaching the Hebrew of religious texts orally to children who knew Spanish in Spain and Judeo-Spanish in the Diaspora.

Turkish: The language of power, of work, of men, and subsequently of modernity

It is impossible to think of the Spanish Jews as strictly speaking only one language. If written texts reveal at best only a few Turkish borrowings, it seems reasonable to think that at least a passive knowledge of Turkish was the rule, at least as concerns the majority of the men. The Jews did not live self-sufficiently in their own state and, while they may have been in the majority in certain quarters of large towns, they were never the only inhabitants of those towns. The notion of a ghetto has no sense in this context. The Jewish habitat centered around synagogues; but if one looks at the Balat neighborhood in Istanbul—which everyone agrees in describing as one of the main Jewish quarters of Istanbul still at the beginning of the 20th century—one notes that the number of synagogues was just barely higher than the number of mosques and Greek churches, and that it was an important residential center for the Armenians, who had a large church and high school there. The bath was Turkish even if it had a *mikvé* for the ritual immersion of the Jews. The baker was Albanian, and the Turkish cabaret owners and oarsmen from the Black Sea were in fierce competition with the Jewish cabaret owners and oarsmen who complained about them.[5] This mixed habitat is not recent; the registers of the *Bostancı Başı* written in the 17th century, as well as more recent commercial directories testify to this same reality. In fact, I have never personally met a monolingual Spanish Jew, even among people born at the end of the 19th century, and even among the women who were reputed never to have left their environment. Their Turkish may have been

---

4. Haïm-Vidal Sephiha, *Le Judéo-Espagnol*, Paris: Entente, 1996, and *Le Ladino (judéo-espagnol calque): Structure et évolution d'une langue liturgique,* Paris: Vidas Largas, 1979 (2 vols.).

5. Marie-Christine Varol, *Balat faubourg juif d'Istanbul,* Istanbul: Isis, 1989.

faulty and their pronunciation highly accented, but they knew this language even if they only spoke it when they had to.

The fact that Salonika had a majority Jewish population may have limited their knowledge of Turkish, yet the texts from the beginning of the 20th century, especially the press, attest to a good knowledge of the publications in that language and show that Turkish is a source for borrowings and linguistic models. Before the Republic, in fact, Turkish was considered as the language of the men and a large number of slang terms, puns and jokes with double meanings could only be deciphered through a knowledge of that language. This allowed the ladies to pretend not to understand anything. Judeo-Spanish speech that was strongly "Turkicized" denoted a lower-class status and was the proof of an insufficient education. When teaching in Turkish became generalized, including in Jewish schools, and Turkish switched to the Latin alphabet, Turkish became the language of studies and of modernity. The name of a disease in Turkish would appear more scientific than its equivalent with a Spanish origin. At the present time, it is customary to comment on statements made in Judeo-Spanish by means of explanations, parenthetical remarks or assertions in Turkish.

French: The Alliance Israélite Universelle

From 1860 on, this institution founded modern schools in the Ottoman Empire, taking the place of local initiatives and bringing a major teaching system to the Jewish communities. Considered as a language of education, a language of modernity and progress, French was all the more accepted, learned and assimilated because of the closeness of its structure and lexicon to Judeo-Spanish. Ultimately to replace the latter, French coexisted easily with Judeo-Spanish, brought it the modern terminology that it was lacking and provided it with euphemisms. At the present time it is interesting to note that in Turkey it is the French speakers who have best preserved the use of Judeo-Spanish while the English speakers have made Turkish the main language at home. This has not prevented anyone there from knowing all three languages to various degrees and to choose to use them knowledgeably depending on the constraints or needs of the situation in which they are communicating. The use of "Judeo-Fragnol," the Judeo-Spanish strongly marked by French to use Professor Sephiha's term, is especially useful for writing, or when communicating with French people by whom they want to be sure they are understood! Spanish Jews are in fact convinced that no one other than themselves can understand this complex and moving code that is Judeo-Spanish, to the point that anyone who speaks it is often considered as an integral member of the community. The French spoken in the Levant in general, and that of the Turkish Jews in particular, is interesting in that it is fairly well marked by its contact with Turkish and Judeo-Spanish. Here is an interesting example: the exclamation *barminán!*, from the Hebrew/Aramaic stock of words, is also expressed in Judeo-Spanish as *leshos de mozós!*, frequently abridged to *leshos!*, but also translated into French as *loin de nous!* [far from us!] or *toujours loin!*— which is hard for a non-initiated French-speaker to understand in a conversation. We will refer in this work to certain particularities of this "French from Turkey"—as the Jews themselves call it—that will help in understanding how certain complex structures or expressions work.

Italian: The prestige language of Levantine ports of call

The Italian spoken by many Frankos or Levantines who settled in the Ottoman Empire to conduct business was also a language of prestige in the 19th and beginning of the 20th centuries. To take advantage of measures that were favorable to Levantines, many businessmen took on Italian nationality. There were Italian schools in the principal cities, but it appears that it was in Izmir and Salonika that its influence was the strongest. After the First World War, the presence of Italians contributed to its further reinforcement. Excessive Italianization of speech in Judeo-Spanish, as is the case with French-ifying, is branded as pretentious.

Greek: Language of the Romaniotes and language of the Greeks

Earlier we said that the Romaniote and Sephardic (that is, those expelled from Spain) communities most often merged into each other and adopted the same liturgical and linguistic practices. The main trace of this complex phenomenon in the 20th century is undoubtedly the good knowledge of Greek held by the Jews of Istanbul particularly until the 1950s. If Greek was considered as a funny and rather vulgar language—an opinion that strongly marks the borrowings into Judeo-Spanish—it was nonetheless a well-known language, although for varying reasons. For some it was the language of their Greek neighbors, in strong numbers in Istanbul before the 1950s and even more so in the preceding centuries. The Greeks were the minority with whom the Jews had the most relationships, on an equal footing since they were equally dependent upon the Turkish administration. Yet while their relationships could be smooth and without distrust, they could at the same time be in strong conflict for religious reasons at the heart of which could be found the slander of ritual murder, or the accusation of deicide by common Greek folk fanaticized by Orthodox popes who were poorly educated. The fights could degenerate into real confrontations that the higher authorities of the Jewish and Greek communities had to calm down or that had to be arbitrated by the Ottoman authorities.

Yet another current within the Jewish population cultivated Greek for completely different reasons, through family tradition, as a language of culture and they sometimes attended the Greek high school rather than the Jewish school. The Karaites of Istanbul, kept at a distance by Jews of the Rabbinical tradition, likewise preserve the use of Greek at home even though they know Turkish, of course, but also apparently Judeo-Spanish. There are therefore two competing attitudes towards Greek: the minority one that sees in Greek a language of prestige, and the majority one that looks down with condescension upon the language of their neighbors and rivals, thought of as common people, superstitious and poorly educated. It is this latter attitude that colors Judeo-Spanish borrowings from the Greek.

Castilian Spanish

By this term I mean the Spanish of present-day Spain, also called by the Spanish Jews *"el espanyol halís de la Spanya,"* "the genuine Spanish of Spain," which goes a long way in revealing how they consider their own. It was at the end of the 19th century that Castilian was "discovered" by the Jews, and Judeo-Spanish by the Spaniards. The effects would be felt on both sides. The Spaniards would want to reconquer this part of Spain in the East, whereas the champions of Judeo-Spanish as well as its detractors see Spanish as their standard of prestige, the benchmark for measuring the "degeneration" of their language. The Spaniards made plans to teach Spanish at these unhoped-for economic outposts and the Spanish Jews corrected their "jargon," as they said, their "defective Spanish," their "sloppy" or "dishwater" Spanish. But whereas Hispanists were stunned to hear this language that had been suspended in time for five hundred years, taking them back to words and sounds that they thought had disappeared forever, Castilian has ironically become one of the principal factors in the impoverishment of Judeo-Spanish today. Indeed, in the name of some mythical return to its origins, or of some "purity" to be regained, terms rich in connotations such as *byervo*, "word," have been replaced, in a thoroughly thoughtless manner, by the term used in Castilian, in this case *palavra*—if not *palabra*—thereby destroying whole networks of connections, of echoes and of meanings. *Palavra* in Judeo-Spanish means what the word "parole" means in French with the same connotations as the French term, including "to give one's word." Now this term, come into Turkish, means "a lie" in that language, thereby allowing for allusions and plays on language in Judeo-Spanish.

Dropping the term *byervo* on the sole pretext that modern Spanish has lost it takes little account of the history of the language. In some instances, even terms that only came into Spanish in recent times are proposed to replace some borrowing from the Turkish that can be found in texts as far back as the 18th century.

Multilingualism

There are those who would seek to purge Judeo-Spanish of its borrowings, but then it would not survive as Judeo-Spanish. Irony, distance, puns, the endless plays on meanings and stylistic nuances bouncing back and forth, make this language of quotations, double entendres, discreet jokes that seem undecipherable, of implied or overly-clear meanings, into an original and eternally renewed linguistic system steeped in a devastating sense of humor that can only be achieved through a knowledge of several languages—a knowledge that gives it its strength, its richness and its freedom.

We cannot insist enough on the fact that the preceding overview of languages should not be seen as anything more than a convenient summary. Judeo-Spanish is not a series of juxtapositions; it is a complex code one of whose constituent parts is multilingualism and the play on languages.

Doktor Maymunidis! is what one says to someone who poses and claims to be smart. One might think that this is some sort of deformation due to ignorance about the Cordoba philosopher Maimonides, which in Judeo-Spanish is *Maymonides*. But that would be quite wrong, for one also needs to hear in this name the Turkish *maymun,* of the same etymon, meaning "monkey," and the Greek *-idis* with which Greeks of the Black Sea area form family names. What these irreverent Spanish Jews are making fun of, then, at the first level, is not the great Maimonides but rather a monkey, furthermore Greek, who takes himself for a Maimonides. And tough luck if he didn't get it! Here is the essence of Judeo-Spanish and we will attempt in this work, whenever we can, to show this type of phenomenon at work.

Let us wager that Judeo-Spanish, which has already absorbed several languages without finding any of its dynamics altered, will deal with Castilian the same way it did with the others: by assimilating them and having recourse to them—that is, by integrating them into its multilingual code and using them however it pleases. If that is the only harm to befall it, no one will be the sadder.

Norm and variation

Most linguists in our time who want to teach a language that does not have fixed norms begin by setting up a central language, based on usage, for teaching purposes. Every regional usage is then taught by reference to this common code. Such an academic norm may tend to lock the practice of the language into outdated and restrictive forms that do not reflect actual practice, thereby impeding lexical creativity and rejecting borrowings. The absence of such a norm is currently thought to allow for freedom, an advantage for, and condition of the vitality of a language. Linguistic creativity that allows speakers to be free, to display their agility, humor, and poetry without fear of being criticized for making mistakes in the language, is in fact one of the mainsprings of Judeo-Spanish. Arlene Malinowski even noted in 1992 that this freedom of expression was one of the factors that have preserved Judeo-Spanish, a characteristic often advanced by its speakers to justify their attachment to the language. Because this language is cryptic it has also been a vehicle for expressing verbal revenge, through humor, in an oppressive society. This explains its wild sense of humor based on hilarious lexical creations and other linguistic traits (see words beginning with *m-* in Lesson 3B and ending with *-dero* in Lesson 2A in this manual).

The reverse side of this freedom, however, may be linguistic insecurity. Lost among the variations and fluctuations in the language, the speaker no longer knows which form to use and becomes afraid of speaking badly. Without going so far as to call for the creation of an "Academy of Judeo-Spanish," we believe nevertheless that the determination of a prescribed usage should be commonly defined, but without causing detriment to the teaching of variants. This is what may perhaps happen through the cooperative efforts of different groups within the *Otoridad Nasyonala para el Ladino* (High Authority for the defense of Judeo-Spanish) recently formed in Israel. A very useful agreement on writing conventions has been virtually completed. It is our hope that our manual will provide for further thought on this subject, as open and least restrictive as possible.

This leads to the question of the status of a language manual and the uses to which it is put by speakers of the language and by its learners. It would be hard for such a type of work to escape serving as a role model. People expect it somehow to choose and establish the norm on the basis of a variety of usages. That is not our goal here. We should probably explain, then, what our goal is.

The point of departure of this work, the primary reference in matters of linguistic usage, is the community of Turkey, which has preserved a fairly extensive living practice of Judeo-Spanish, identical to that of Israel, where the Judeo-Spanish speaking community came out largely from that of Turkey, as we have seen. The principal variants are indicated. For example, keeping the initial Spanish *f* in Salonika (the initial *h* in written Castilian) is well-known and will be commented on; likewise the closed vowels of Belgrade and Sarajevo. These particularities do not impede comprehension and readers are free to choose the usage they prefer.

The most problematic point concerns verb conjugations. On this subject, Judeo-Spanish has inherited the fluctuation prevalent at the end of the Middle Ages in Spain and which still persist there in certain regional practices. One should not see here the result of degeneration of the language, or of a weakening process, or of the absence of writing, an explanation erroneously offered for a language that has never stopped being written. One can find the same fluctuation in Medieval texts, as has been said, but also in Judeo-Spanish texts over time and in contemporary authors: *tenré, terné, teneré* and *tendré* ("I will have") can be found at random in many texts. All these forms that relate to a fragile time, the future, are understood by speakers, some of whom will readily even use two of them at times. As for the present manual, we recommend (in Lesson 7 and beyond) learning the simplest one, the regular form, while indicating the existence of other forms. This approach may make our verb charts heavy, but readers will be able to choose from among these very frequent forms, in speech and in writing, the one that comes closest to the idea they have of the language, provided they do not consider it the only valid form. For example, we give the dominant usage relating to the imperfect tense (Lesson 6A) while also indicating the dominant form in Bulgaria. Certain minority or particular forms, however, may have been omitted, for which we offer our apologies in advance. Such is the case for the form of the imperfect used by Marcel Cohen in his work *Lettre à Antonio Saura,* recomposed by adding imperfect endings onto the root of the past tense: *trushiya, dishiya,* etc.

We do not pretend to be exhaustive; this method cannot present the entirety of the language. We have had to content ourselves with a reasonable number of forms, expressions, terms and usages, in such a way as not to discourage learners. Supplements can be found in those priceless dictionaries that are being published and in works that remain yet to be published such as a complete work on verb conjugation in Judeo-Spanish and its variations which would be extremely useful to linguists, and a complete grammar that would go into greater depth for the points that are brought up here and would treat those points that are not.

The phonetic and writing systems of Judeo-Spanish

Vowels

The vowels are: *a, e, i, o, u.*

u also serves as a semi-consonant ([w] in phonetic notation), and *y* serves as a voiced fricative semi-consonant ([j] in phonetic notation).

The sounds ö [cf. French *professeur*] and ü [cf. French *tu*] exist in words borrowed from the Turkish or French. They will be noted, but they do not constitute phonemes in Judeo-Spanish. We have not indicated the fricatization of intervocalic *g* (for example, *agora* is pronounced *agora*) nor the fricative intervocalic *d* (for example, the *d* in *cada* sounds like the *th* in English *that*).

Consonants

		Labials	Dentals	Prepalatals	Palatals	Velars
Occlusives	Voiceless	p	t			k
	Voiced	b	d			g
Affricates	Voiceless			ch		
	Voiced		[d]	dj		
Fricatives	Voiceless	f	s	sh		h
	Voiced	v	z	j	y	
Trills	Voiced		r			
Laterals	Voiced		l			
Nasals	Voiced	m	n	ny		

Accentuation in Judeo-Spanish

♦ Most words are accentuated on the next-to-the-last (penultimate) syllable, with the voice descending on the last syllable. These are words ending with a vowel, as well as *-s*, *-sh* or *-n* which are indicators of the plural and of verbal forms. Other words are accented on the last syllable. For example, in the conjugation of the present tense, the accented syllable is shown here in bold: **kan**to, **kan**tas, **kan**ta, kan**tamos**, kan**tásh**, **kan**tan.

♦ When accentuation differs from this usage, the vowel that is accentuated is marked with the tonic accent sign. For example, in conjugating the imperfect or future tense, accentuation is marked as follows: *kantávamos, kantaré, kantarás*, etc.

Words borrowed from the Turkish, Hebrew and French often preserve their original accentuation and take an accent sign: *la menorá, la kavané, el kavé, el büró, la televizyón, el sinemá*, etc.

♦ The written accent is also a useful device to differentiate the interrogative form of a word from its non-interrogative form: *ké?* is the interrogative form of the relative pronoun *ke, kuándo?* as opposed to *kuando*, etc. The written accent is also used to distinguish between two meanings of the same word; for example: *tú/tu* = you/your; *él/el* = he/the, *sí/si* = yes/if, etc. These differences will be indicated in the course of the book. The pronunciation of these vowels does not change, but ambiguities in the written language can thus be avoided. **NB**: In the *Aki Yerushalayim* writing system, written accents are hardly ever used.

♦ To listen to pronunciation models, turn to page 28 and to the exercise (track 1) on the CD that accompanies this book.

Writing and graphic conventions

Until around 1925, the main writing system for printed Judeo-Spanish was the system of characters called "Rashi," based on the Hebrew alphabet. For handwriting, it was "Solitreo," a cursive system based on Hebrew. "Square" Hebrew characters were reserved for titles or for certain religious texts. However, several usages coexist, and from the middle of the 19th century on many people began using adaptations of the Latin alphabet with which to write Judeo-Spanish, particularly in correspondence. Here they used spelling styles imitated from the French or transcriptions from the *Rashi*, and sometimes Spanish graphic conventions. Examples of *solitreo* will be found in this book in Lessons 8 and 9, and texts printed in *Rashi* characters in Lessons 2 and 5. After the Latin alphabet was adopted in Turkey, preference for using that alphabet continued to grow. In 1938, for example, the newspaper *La Boz de Oriente* shows articles written with both types of characters. Today, whenever Judeo-Spanish is written, it is in Latin characters and follows the writing styles of *Vidas Largas*, *Aki Yerushalayim* or *Şalom*, all fairly close in spirit (see below).

The graphic style used in this book is basically that of *Aki Yerushalayim*, which appears to be the one most often accepted in the United States, the main difference being that accent marks are used in this book whereas *Aki Yerushalayim* does not generally use them. The graphic systems recommended in Spain for editing texts, while rigorously scientific, are nonetheless based on the Castilian system, which make them complex and not easily legible for those who do not know Spanish; a large number of diacritical marks makes them difficult to reproduce, presenting an obstacle to the circulation of texts. Our approach is therefore less etymological but more practical, and readers throughout a wide variety of locations should be able to read the written texts as given here.

Vidas Largas	Aki Yerushalayim	Şalom
tch	ch	ç
ch	sh	ş
dj	dj	c
gz	x	gz

For a table of Judeo-Spanish writing systems, see page 28.

GOALS AND METHODS OF THIS MANUAL

It is reasonable to assume that not many other Judeo-Spanish grammar books will be appearing soon, in view of the lack of commercial profitability of such an undertaking. This suggests that this manual should be as complete as possible, that it be able to serve learners over widespread geographical areas, of diverse backgrounds and ages, and that it be suitable for classroom instruction as well as for self-teaching purposes.

It should therefore offer, over and beyond the recommended usages, a diversity of other usages (in this respect, we have often consulted the Nehama dictionary, that compendium of Salonikan Judeo-Spanish). This should be the case in matters of writing systems as well as the lexicon, pronunciation, morphology or syntax. In order not to overly burden the length of the lessons, each of them is therefore divided into two parts. Part A follows the recommended writing and linguistic rules. Part B shows the language in its actual usage, which will be more complex than the examples offered in Part A.

This means that each lesson will be long and will present texts at a higher order of difficulty in the second part. Learners who know Spanish will have an easier time than others and so we can offer them texts that are more challenging. Not everything should necessarily be covered by every student; choices should be made depending on each person's abilities. A text that is too hard the first time around can be returned to at the end of the course.

We have not dissociated the language from its culture and civilization. For this reason the dialogues come as close as possible to actual situations that we have truly come across, and they do not attempt to smooth out all the difficulties. Wordplays, exclamations, idiomatic expressions that spontaneously appear in speech in various situations are reproduced here, and may work on the reader through a general understanding even if the details are not understood. For example, if a past tense or the subjunctive is needed for natural expression, we have not eliminated it. The Judeo-Spanish here is given in the natural context in which it is produced. We have not given dialogues about airplane trips or making a hotel reservation because it never serves that purpose. Its domain is that of group activity, the family, the home. It can be heard spontaneously in recollections that people recount, in family disputes, between parents and children, in conversations between older persons, and so on. It is spoken at home, at the club, in a tea garden, on a boat going to the islands off the coast of Istanbul, on a seaside bench, at the corner of a sidewalk café in Paris on the Boulevard Voltaire. It is understood exclusively through such usages.

The situations depicted here are also natural and lead to certain points that can be made about the culture. Ladies making telephone calls to each other to talk about their daily schedules and to invite each other, mothers urging their children to go to Jewish youth clubs, interminable conversations about one's body and health, respect for old people, a grandmother passing on her culinary art to her granddaughter, life in the old Jewish neighborhoods, the separation of families over several continents—these depictions are as true to the objective realities of the Judeo-Spanish world as are exchanges of spiteful feelings or what may appear to be excessively strong language. The distance between people and the barrier between what can be said and not said among people in a relationship of familiarity, are quite different in Judeo-Spanish practices compared with those in French or English-speaking countries.

Outline of lesson contents

In **Part A**, each lesson bears a title indicating the general theme covered. For example, *Kén sos tú?* Who are you? (Lesson 1) introduces terms for introducing people, stating identity, the verb *to be*, etc.

The **objectives** section of the lesson describes the goals for acquiring competence in communicating, materials for acquiring language skills (vocabulary, grammar and conjugation), and the principal points about culture that will be covered.

The **dialogue** reproduces spoken language that is correct, lively and natural, containing elements of communication and language acquisition materials that will be developed in the lesson.

The **glossary** provides a list of new items needed for comprehension. Borrowed words (i.e., not of Spanish origin) are indicated by reference to the linguistic system from which speakers have borrowed them and with which they remain in contact. When dealing with a borrowing from Turkish, we will not be any more concerned with its Persian or Arabic origin than with the French or Italian origin of terms that have entered Turkish.

The **"communication skills"** section explains the elements of communication presented in the dialogue and supplements them with additional expressions classified according to their communicative goals: to greet, to thank, to introduce oneself to another person, etc.

The **vocabulary** section develops the semantic areas covered and supplements the information: kinship, trades, the home, etc. The terms given here are those that constitute the basic language, regardless of any particular dialect. Where relevant, a few regional peculiarities are noted.

The **grammar** section looks at elements given in the dialogues in a logical way by grouping them together. It gives the rules for usage, tables of pronouns and possessive adjectives, the functions of verb tenses, etc. Information is introduced in a progressive manner. This grammar is based on real usage, and presented according to the nomenclature generally utilized to describe the Romance Languages. Where relevant, it makes comparisons with English and highlights points of difference between the two language systems. Certain explanations, however, will come from Spanish grammars, inasmuch as the two languages are related.

The **verb conjugation** section gives the rules for forming tenses for regular verbs and gives the irregular forms while attempting to group certain kinds of irregularities together. It will recommend a certain usage but indicate the other most commonly used forms. It indicates the differences between oral and written styles.

The remarks on **culture** are first given in English and afterwards in Judeo-Spanish, and allow for the dialogue to be placed in the cultural context relevant to it or to introduce social etiquette related to the theme of the lesson: rules for visits, hierarchies of kinship, etc.

The **exercises** allow learners to practice using a particular structure, vocabulary or applying a grammatical rule, to check that points in the lesson have been acquired. A complete list of correct answers is provided at the end of the manual to allow learners to check themselves for accuracy.

Part B will always include a number of proverbs and at least one song, related to the theme of the lesson. Proverbs and lively expressions in fact play a very important role in daily conversation in Judeo-Spanish. As for the body of song material in Judeo-Spanish, it is so extensive and plays such a large role in Judeo-Spanish life, and encompasses so many categories, that this book can only give a brief glimpse of its richness and its diversity. One cannot learn Judeo-Spanish without learning how to sing. A selection of recordings of these songs can be found indicated at the end of the book.

Judeo-Spanish, even when it is set aside in favor of other languages of communication, still serves a role for citing proverbs and singing songs. Proverbs and songs therefore constitute a shared cultural heritage, along with certain religious texts, and are absolutely necessary to fully understand many of the practices of this language, many of its situations of social exchange, and many of its cultural characteristics. They are the privileged props of the language, along with the *konsejas*, those very short stories that are often funny but always edifying.

The **other texts** section presents a variety of pieces: excerpts taken from recorded interviews, children's nursery rhymes, publicity ads, newspaper articles, old or contemporary poems, excerpts from novels and moral treatises, a fragment of the *Agadá*, a handwritten letter, a theatrical sketch, etc.

These texts make it possible to understand the phenomena described and studied in Part A within their authentic context. One can therefore find in them particular characteristics of language usage such as archaisms, dialectal peculiarities, traits reserved for oral speech, etc., that do not appear in Part A. One can also see here the difference announced earlier in this introduction between Ladino and Judeo-Spanish. Readers should not be surprised to find here certain elements that may deviate from the norms taught in A. They do not serve any normative function but show the living language in the diversity of its practices, both oral and written, thereby demonstrating the relativity of the norms taught. As should be apparent, this notion of the relativity of the norms—which can apply differently according to the particular period, style, practice, region, speaking situation and speaker—is an important one.

The texts, particularly those based on a written source or literary piece, are presented with their own specific traits. In Part B can be found comments on the *kopla*, the *romanse*, the *konsejas* of the buffoon figure *Djohá* or the *Me'am Lo'ez*. An **anthology** of supplementary texts will allow the reader to broaden somewhat this admittedly summary approach to Judeo-Spanish literature, and offers several bibliographical listings.

While the writing system of the texts in the earlier lessons has been standardized, we have tended progressively in subsequent lessons to preserve the original spellings, as chosen by the particular writer or publisher, no matter how disconcerting they may seem. We also give examples of writing in *Rashi* and in *Solitreo*, in order to expose students to a variety of practices.

The texts are accompanied by a glossary to allow for their immediate comprehension or to give the most frequent recommended form, along with a few questions (with answers provided at the end of the book) to guide comprehension. When the text lends itself to introducing a new bit of information that will allow the student who so desires to delve deeper, it is accompanied by a comment on the language or the conjugation and, where useful, by practice exercises.

For the student's convenience, and to facilitate the learning process for students working by themselves, the book is supplemented by **verb charts** and a **general vocabulary** of terms used in the lessons and texts.

A detailed **Lesson Summaries** section is provided to facilitate locating specific items.

SIGNS AND ABBREVIATIONS

B. = from Bulgarian
F. = from French
G. = from Greek
H. = from Biblical and Mishnaic Hebrew/Aramaic
I. = from Italian
J.E. = from Judeo-Spanish
L. = from Ladino
S. = from Spanish
Sp.Ar. [or Arab.] = Spanish Arabism
T. = from Turkish
adj. = adjective
A.I.U. = Alliance Israélite Universelle
cf. = compare, refer to
d.o. = direct object
i.o. = indirect object
ed. = edition
ex. = example
fam. = familiar
fem. = feminine

fig. = figurative sense
fut. = future
imp. = imperfect
ind. = indicative
inf. = infinitive
inv. = invariable
lit. = literally
Mr. = Mister
masc. = masculine
Ms. = Mrs., Miss
p. = page, pp. = pages
plu. = plural
plup. = pluperfect tense
pres. = present tense
sing. = singular
subj. = subjunctive
n. = noun
v. = verb
(?). = unknown origin
≠ = opposite
* = see the note below
6 👁 = Listen to CD, track 6

PRONUNCIATION EXERCISES

(Using symbols of the International Phonetic Alphabet)

Symbol	As spelled
[a]	a: el kal, ayá
[b]	b: Shabad, bever, la djumba (cf. English boy)
[d]	d: danyo, dos, ánde, sivdad (cf. dog)
	Between two vowels:
[đ]:	d: el dedo, la boda (cf. those)
[e]	e: este, beve, el
[f]	f: fransé, falso, bafo
	Before the [w] sound the f tends to become h [x]: fui ⇨ hui – esfuenyo ⇨ es-huenyo (Note: a hyphen is inserted to separate the -s and -h; do not pronounce as -sh.)
[g]	g: guay, gayna, godro, gato (cf. gallon)
	Before the [w] the g sounds like a slight guttural h
[ɣ]	g: agua, djugueves
With z:	
[gz]	gz: egzempyo
[x]	h: haham, hazino, Menahem (cf. Hebrew Hanukah)
[i]	i: ija, amariyo
[ž]	j: ijo, kaleja, mojado (cf. azure)
[k]	k: kale, kilo, asukuar
[l]	l: la luna, la leche, loko, kale, la mallé
[m]	m: mamá, mozós, kome
[n]	n: el nono, nada
[o]	o: komo, godro, solo
[p]	p: papú, el pyojo
[r]	r: ratón, bodre, arabá
[r̄]	rr: borracho, perro
[s]	s: savyo, lonso, moso
[t]	t: tadre, todo, pato
[č]	ch: chiko, noche, muncho (cf. child)
[š]	sh: kosho, shashuto, kasha, rashá, Rosh Hodésh
[ǧ]	dj: djente, djénero, adjilé (cf. gender)
[u]	u: uva, papú
[v]	v: bever, vozós, bovo, vuestro, vedre (cf. victory)
[j]	y: yerva, luvya, boyo
[ɲ]	ny: inyervos, Espanya, alkunya
[kj]	ky: kyöshé, kyuprí (cf. thank you)
[z]	z: la meza, la kaza, la koza, el zarzavachí
[w]	u: fuego, fui, agua, es-huegra
[y]	ü: büro (cf. French bureau)
[ø]	ö: mösyö (cf. French monsieur)

WRITING SYSTEMS IN JUDEO-SPANISH				
Latin character	Cursive character (Solitreo)	"Rashi" character	Square character	Examples
a	∫	ƀ	א	אמיגו amigo
b	y	ɜ	ב	בוקה boka
v	y'	ɜ'	ב'	ב'אזו vazo
g	ر	ג	ג	גאייו gayo
dj / ch	ى	ג'	ג'	ג'ינטי djente ג'יקו chiko
d	ל	ד	ד	דולור dolor
a final	J	ה	ה	קאזה caza
o	∕	ו	ו	אומברי ombre מושקה moshka
u	∕	ו	ו	אונו uno מונדו mundo
z	∫	ז	ז	ב'יזינה vizina
j	∫	ז'	ז'	ז'ורנאל jurnal
h	ח	ח	ח	חאב'יר haver
t	ں	ט	ט	טאדרי tadre
e / i	ı	י	י	איג'ו echo איזו ijo
y	ʺ	יי	יי	ייאב'י yave
k/h	[ɔ]	כ (ך)	כ (ך)	חנוכה hanuká ברכה berahá
l	ℓ	ל	ל	ליב'רו livro
m	ʋ	מ (ס)	מ (ם)	מאדרי madre
n	(ل)J	נ (ן)	נ (ן)	נון non
s	ᴘ	ס	ס	סול sol
a	[ν]	ע	ע	עינהרה aynara
p	J,	פ (ף)	פ (ף)	פאדרי padre
f	J'	פ' (ף')	פ' (ף')	פ'רינטי frente
ts	₅	צ (ץ)	צ (ץ)	צדקה tsedaká
k	⸗	ק	ק	קאב'יסה kavesa
r	⸗	ר	ר	רוזה roza
sh	ℒ	ש	ש	שארופי sharope
s	[Ɛ]	ש	ש	שאלוניקו Saloniko
t	[ʒ]	ת	ת	תלמוד talmud

28

Lesson summaries

LESSON 1

Kén sos tú?

OBJECTIVES

Communication skills: How to introduce yourself, explain who you are, what you do, how old you are, where you live, how to ask questions; how to express possession, belonging to a group, greetings, identity, thanks.

Vocabulary: Numbers up to twenty, terms of family kinship, adjectives with opposite meanings, time divisions.

Grammar: Gender and number, articles, possessive adjectives, reflexive verbs, reflexive pronouns, choosing the correct form for *you*, subject pronouns, prepositional pronouns, the two verbs *to be*.

Conjugation: Forming the present indicative; common irregular verbs: *ser*, *estar*, *azer*, *tener*, *kerer*, *saver*, *dar* and *ver*.

Culture: The role played by visits; songs for special occasions (*Pesah* and weddings), proverbs about the family.

---

2 ☉ **Tenemos djente en kaza.**

    (Sona el telefón.)

La boz de Lea:	"Klara, so yo, Lea. Kómo estás, hanum?"
Klara:	"Muy buena, Lea. I tú, kómo estás?"
Lea:	"Muy buena. Mersí muncho. I tú, ké haber?"
Klara:	"Rika, mi ija la grande, está en kaza kon las amigas."
Lea:	"Ké amigas?"
Klara:	"Malka, Grasya i Viktorya."
Lea:	"Grasya kén es?"
Klara:	"Es la ija de madam Dudú, saves? La ke mora en la kaleja del kuaför."
Lea:	"Madam Dudú es aedada, no tyene ija del boy de Rika."
Klara:	"No Madam Dudú la vyeja, madam Dudú la manseva, la mujer de Henry, la ke da lisyones de pyanó."
Lea:	"De ké alkunya es?"
Klara:	"De Pinto."
Lea:	"Ah sí! El marido es komerchero, lavora kon mi primo. Tyene una ija de kinze anyos i un ijo bohor de vente."
Klara:	"Na, la ija es Grasya. Ma kómo se yama el ijo?"
Lea:	"No sé. Alp? Djekí? No m'akodro. Ma la ija no está en la skola de Rika."

35

Klara:	"No, eya está en la skola franseza, ma Rika va a su kaza para ambezar pyanó."
Lea:	"Ya entendí! Ké azésh esta tadre?"
Klara:	"Agora vamos a bever un chay. Los boyikos están kayentes. Keres vinir?"
Lea:	"Mersí muncho, Klara. Ma oy León i su madre vyenen ande mí."
Klara:	"Ké edad tyene León?"
Lea:	"Dizisésh, dizisyete, no so… Ayde, Klara, au revoir, amanyana mos vemos ande Djoya."
Klara:	"Sí."

GLOSSARY

Words of Spanish origin:

la alkunya (Spanish Arabism): family name.

un boyo, un boyiko: (a stuffed pastry).

ya entendí: I understood, I heard you, I got it!

la kaleja: the street.

la kaza: the house.

mansevo, -a: young.

aedado, -a: older, elderly.

vyejo, -a: old.

grande ≠ chiko: big ≠ little.

kayente ≠ friyo: hot ≠ cold.

komerchero: customs clerk.

la amiga: the friend.

la skola: the school.

akodrarse: to remember.

bever: to drink.

ambezar: to learn.

vinir: to come.

vyenen: they come, they're coming.

la tadre: afternoon, evening.

amanyana: tomorrow.

oy: today.

Words from other sources:

ma or *amá* (T.): but.

bohor, -a (H.): eldest sibling (noun or adj.).

un haber (T.): a piece of news.

ayde (T.): OK, come on, let's go.

hanum (T.): term of affection, "sweetie".

el boy (T.): age or size.

kuaför (T., from the French): coiffeur, hairdresser.

el chay (T.): the tea.

lavorar (I.): to work (*el lavoro:* the work).

COMMUNICATION SKILLS

1. Introducing yourself and asking about others

Identifying others:	*Kén sos tú?*	Who are you?
	Kómo te yamas?	What's your name?
	De ké alkunya sos?	What's your family name?
	Kuántos anyos tyenes?	How old are you?
	Ánde moras?	Where do you live?
	Ánde lavoras?	Where do you work?
	Ké echo azes?	What kind of work do you do?
	Ké edad tyenes?	How old are you?
	Kuálo azes?	What do you do?
Greeting, thanking:	*Shalom, bonjur.*	Hello.
	Buenos diyas.	Hello.
	Baruh abá.	Welcome.
	Vinido bueno	Welcome.
	Kómo estás?	How are you?
	Mersí muncho.	Many thanks.
	Al vermos, au revoir.	Goodbye.
	Kedavos en buenora.	So long.
	Te rogo.	Please.
General questions:	*Ké haber?*	What's new? What's up?
	Ké azes/fazes?	What do you do?
	Ké mande?	Pardon?
Introducing yourself:	*Me yamo Faní. De Pinhas. Tengo vente anyos. Moro en Izmir.*	
	Lavoro en una skola. So la ija de Ester i Hayim. So djudiya.	

To give thanks, say hello and goodbye, there are a good many blessings especially adapted to the time of day, the type of visit, the favor performed, the health of the person being addressed, and other particular circumstances.

With the rush of modern life, both Turkish and Judeo-Spanish have borrowed the all-purpose *"merci"* from the French.

2. Asking questions

♦ The most frequently used **interrogative pronouns** are:

ké? what?   *kómo?* how?   *kén?* who?

de ké...? of what...? of which...? *kuálo?* which one? what?

♦ If there is **no interrogative pronoun:** In writing, simply place a question mark at the end of the statement. In spoken speech, the voice takes a rising inflection.

Keres vinir. You want to come. *Keres vinir?* Do you want to come?

VOCABULARY

1. Adjectives with opposite meanings
grande ≠ *chiko:*   big (in size or age), adult ≠ little, child.
aedado, vyejo ≠ *mansevo:* elderly, old ≠ young.
kayente ≠ *yelado, friyo:* hot ≠ cold.
tivyo ≠ *fresko:*   warm, tepid ≠ cool.

2. Time expressions
Oy: today.   *Amanyana:* tomorrow.   *Agora:* now.
Esta[6] tadre: this afternoon, this evening.
Duspués de medyodiya: the afternoon up to about 5 p.m.

3. Terms of family kinship
el primo/la prima:	the cousin (male/female).
el marido/la mujer:	the husband/the wife.
el ijo/la ija:	the son/the daughter.
el ermano/la ermana:	the brother/the sister.
el padre/la madre:	the father/the mother.
el nono/la nona:	the grandfather/the grandmother.
el inyeto/la inyeta:	the grandson/the granddaughter.
el tiyo/la tiya:	the uncle/the aunt.
el sovrino/la sovrina:	the nephew/the niece.

4. Translating "at my house":
ande Djoya: at Joya's house; *ande mí:* at my house (cf. French "chez moi");
en kaza: at home.

GRAMMAR

1. Gender and number
Note that the masculine often ends in -*o* and the feminine in -*a:*
el *ijo,* **la** *ija,* **el** *ermano,* **la** *ermana.*
The plural is indicated by an -*s:* **los** *boyikos kayentes.*
Adjectives always agree with the noun they modify, in gender and in number:
el ijo chiko, los ijos chikos, la ija chika, las ijas chikas.
For adjectives ending in -*e,* there is no difference between masculine and feminine forms: **La** *ija grande,* **el** *ijo grande.*

---

6. *esta* (this), with no accent mark, is pronounced differently from *está* (he/she/it is).

Adjectives of nationality that end in -*es* in the masculine singular *(inglés, fransés* or *fransé)* add -*es* in the plural: *inglezes, fransezes*. For the feminine, the endings are regular: *la skola franseza, las skolas fransezas*.

2. Articles

Observe: *la ija, la mujer, la skola, el marido, las amigas, los boyikos. Lisyones de pyanó, un chay, la kaleja del kuaför. Mi ermano, esta tadre, su madre.*

Articles accompany common nouns when there is no other determining feature. They agree in gender and in number.

		Singular	Plural
Definite articles	feminine	*la*	*las*
	masculine	*el*	*los*
Indefinite articles	feminine	*una*	(n/a)
	masculine	*un*	(n/a)

♦ In the plural, there is no indefinite article.
 Da lisyones de pyanó   She gives piano lessons.

♦ The masc. definite article is joined to the preposition *de: **de** + **el** = **del***
 *Una ija **del** boy de Rika; la kaleja **del** kuaför.*

♦ In Judeo-Spanish, as in Hebrew, the article can be repeated before the adjective: *la ija la grande.*

♦ In oral speech, the initial -*a* of a word is elided into a preceding article; in writing, both forms may be found: *l'amiga* or *la amiga.*

3. Possessive adjectives

Masculine singular	Feminine singular	Masculine plural	Feminine plural
mi pyanó	**mi** kaza	**mis** amigos	**mis** amigas
tu ——	**tu** ——	**tus** ——	**tus** ——
su ——	**su** ——	**sus** ——	**sus** ——
muestro ——	**muestra** ——	**muestros** ——	**muestras** ——
vuestro ——	**vuestra** ——	**vuestros** ——	**vuestras** ——
sus ——	**sus** ——	**sus** ——	**sus** ——

4. Pronouns: Subject, reflexive and prepositional

Subject Pronouns	Reflexive pronouns	Prepositional pronouns
Yo	me	(ande) mí*
tú*	te	ti
él*, eya	se	él, eya
mozós/mozotros**	mos	**mozós**/mozotros
vozós/vozotros	vos	**vozós**/vozotros
eyos, eyas	se	eyos, eyas

* Note the accent mark over *tú* (as opposed to *tu* = your), *él* (*el* = the), and *mí* (*mi* = my).
** Where there are two or more variant forms, the first one, in bold type, is recommended as the more usual form.

♦ The subject pronoun is usually not stated. It is used to avoid an ambiguity or for insistence:
> *bevo:* I drink.   *yo bevo: I* drink.

For further insistence it can be placed after the verb:
> *bevo yo:* I'm the one who is drinking

♦ The reflexive pronoun is placed before the verb:
> *Me yamo Marko:* My name is Marko.

If the subject pronoun is stated, the reflexive pronoun comes immediately after it: *Yo me yamo Marko: My* name is Marko.
♦ A negative word comes between the two:
> *Yo no me yamo Marko: My* name is not Marko.

♦ The reflexive pronoun *se* is used for both masculine and feminine, and both singular and plural:
> *Se yama Danon:* His/her name is Danon.
> *Se yaman Danon:* Their name is Danon.

5. Interrogative pronouns

Observe the following: *Kén sos tú? Ké azes? Ké haber? Kómo stas?*

When writing Judeo-Spanish, it is useful to place an accent mark over interrogative pronouns, to indicate the strong stress and also to distinguish them from other words. For example, interrogative pronoun *ké* is distinguished from relative pronoun *ke*.
Ké azesh?: What are you doing? But: *la **ke** da lisyones de pyanó:* the woman who gives piano lessons.

Kén? Who?   *Ánde?* Where
Kómo? How?   *Ké?* What?
Kuálo? What? Which?
Kuánto(s)? How many, how much?
Ké karar? What quantity, how much?

VERB CONJUGATIONS

1. Forming the present tense

♦ There are three principal verb groups: verbs where the infinitive ends in
-ar, *-er*, or *-ir*. The three verbs for to reside (*morar*), to drink (*bever*) and
to live (*bivir*), below, provide models for the three regular conjugations. It
is particularly important to learn the endings for each group: *yo moro, tu
beves, eya bive*, etc.

Subject	*-ar* verbs	*-er* verbs	*-ir* verbs
	morar	**bever**	**bivir**
yo	mor**o**	bev**o**	biv**o**
tú	mor**as**	bev**es**	biv**es**
él, eya	mor**a**	bev**e**	biv**e**
mozós	mor**amos**	bev**emos**	biv**imos**
vozós	mor**ásh**	bev**ésh**	biv**ísh**
eyos, eyas	mor**an**	bev**en**	biv**en**

Many verbs are irregular. Some of the most common include:

ser (to be)	estar (to be)	azer (to do)	tener (to have)
so	estó	ago	tengo
sos	estás	azes	tyenes
es	está	aze	tyene
semos	estamos	azemos	tenemos
sosh	estásh	azésh	tenésh
son	están	azen	tyenen

♦ **Variants:**
There are variants in Judeo-Spanish conjugation forms due to regional differences. The main ones here are: *so* in Istanbul is *se* in Izmir; *azer* is written
and pronounced *fazer* in Salonika.

41

♦ Elision:

The initial *e-* in *estar* is often dropped, giving the pronunciation *yo sto, tú stas, él sta*, etc. In writing, the complete form should be used.

♦ Accentuation:

The accent mark is added to indicate an irregularity in the general rules for accentuation (see the Introduction). For example, *estó* is pronounced with the stress on the *-o*. When the *e-* is elided, there is no further need to keep the accent mark: *sto, stas*, etc.

♦ Use of the present tense:

The present is used to state general facts, information that has no explicit time duration: *me yamo, moro*, etc. To state actions that are going on, the progressive form is commonly used (to be studied in Lesson 4):

Ké azes? What do you do? (How do you spend your days, what is your job, etc.); but

Ké estás azyendo? What are you doing? (right now)

♦ Reflexive verbs:

Note the following: *Kómo **se** yama el ijo?*
*No **m'**akodro.*

The verb *yamarse* consists of *yamar* + *se*.
The same is true for *akodrarse: akodrar* + *se*.

Yamarse	Akodrarse
(yo) me yamo	me akodro
(tú) te yamas	te akodras
(él, eya) se yama	se akodra
(mozós) mos yamamos	mos akodramos
(vozós) vos yamásh	vos akodrásh
(eyos, eyas) se yaman	se akodran

When the verb begins with a vowel, the tendency in oral speech is to elide the vowel *-e* of *me* and *te: m'akodro, t'akodras*, etc.

The verbs *ser* and *estar*

There are two verbs for *to be* in Judeo-Spanish; choosing which one depends upon the particular circumstances.

ser	estar
—serves to identify, to define by name, age, profession, nationality, etc. *De ké alkunya es?* *El marido es komerchero.* —relates to defining qualities that are considered essential to being.	—situates someone in a location. *Mi ija está en la skola de Rika.* —asks about how one is. —relates to qualities that are considered accessory, non-defining.

CULTURE

Visits are very important and highly appreciated. They should be announced ahead of time and should not last too long. Guests are received in the living room, which is always kept in good order for this purpose and serves as the showcase of the home.

Guests are first offered a spoon filled with sweet preserves, *dulse*, with a glass of ice water, *agua yelada*, so that the words exchanged will be sweet. Beautiful containers in crystal or silver can be found, with a set of silver spoons hanging around the exterior. Next, tea is served which should be replenished when the glass is empty, or Turkish coffee in demitasse cups, accompanied by *unturyo*, or *kozas de orno*, salt or sweet pastries for dipping; *boyikos* or dry pastries with anis, pepper or sugar; *borrekitas*, turnovers stuffed with cheese or with cinnamon and raisins; *reshikas* in Rhodes, *roskitas* in Salonika, etc.

Dos chayes i boyikos.

People chat or play cards. They take leave of each other well before the evening meal. People do not leave as long as their glass has not gone cold; this would be impolite. Coffee is not served too rapidly to the guests, who might think that they are being hurried out.

When there is an unwanted visit by a neighbor, a mother may discreetly tell her daughter: *Dales un amargo ke se vayan,* make it a bitter one (referring to the coffee, but totally meaningless to anyone not understanding Judeo-Spanish) so that they'll leave. This expression is also used jokingly.

A *vijita de Ermení* (visit from an Armenian) refers to a visit that goes on forever or that becomes prolonged at the doorway. When guests dig in, the recommended cure is to place an upside-down broom behind the door, with a little needle on top, which is supposed to make people get up. If, after an evening meal, guests stay on much longer than they should have, the hosts say jokingly: *Mos echaremos ke se keren ir* (let's go to bed because they want to leave).

La eskova detrás de la puerta.

Exercises

Exercise 1. Here is the answer; what is the question?
1. "Sevim Behar." ....?
2. "Dizimueve anyos." ....?
3. "De Behar." ....?
4. "Lavoro en una skola." ....?

Exercise 2. Introduce yourself to someone.

Exercise 3. Translate into Judeo-Spanish:
1. The tea is warm. 2. The house is old.
3. My friend is small. 4. The hairdresser is elderly.
5. The pastry is cold. 6. His wife is young.

Exercise 4. State the family kinship:

Roza-Salvo

↙ ↓ ↘

Blanka Sará David

Exercise 5. Make the adjective in parentheses agree with the noun:
1. Su ija es (grande).   2. Sus ermanos son (aedado).
3. El chay está (kayente).   4. Albert es (aedado).
5. Rika es (mansevo).   6. Sus amigas son (vyejo).
7. La skula es (fransé).   8. Los boyikos están (yelado).
9. Sus ijas están (bueno).   10. Los pyanós son (fransé).

Exercise 6. Add the appropriate article, as needed:
1. Estó kon ____ amigas de ____ skola.   2. Es ____ ija ____ kuaför.
3. Da ____ lisyones.   4. Komemos ____ boyikos i bevemos ____ chay.
5. Tyenen ____ ijos.   6. Es ____ marido de ____ ermana de Rika.
7. Son ____ ermanos de Albert.

Exercise 7. Transform these sentences, following the model:
*Model: Tenésh un ermano: es **vuestro** ermano.*
1.   Tenemos amigas: son _____ amigas.
2.   Tyenen un pyanó: es _____ pyanó.
3.   Tengo una madre: es _____ madre.
4.   Tyene una mujer: es _____ mujer.
5.   Tenésh boyikos: son _____ boyikos.
6.   Tyenes ermanas: son _____ ermanas.
7.   Tyenes chay: es _____ chay.
8.   Tyene kaza: es _____ kaza.
9.   Tenemos ijos: son _____ ijos.
10. Tenésh un pyanó: es _____ pyanó.
11. Tengo ijas: son _____ ijas.

Exercise 8. Place the appropriate interrogative pronoun:
1. _____ es tu primo?   2. _____ aze tu primo?
3. _____ está tu kuaför?   4. _____ tyene Alp, tu ijo el bohor?
5. _____ alkunya sos?   6. _____ se yama tu ermana?
7. _____ haber?   8. _____ da lisyones de pyanó?
9. _____ anyos tyene tu marido? 10. _____ keres?

45

Exercise 9. The verb **lavorar** *in the dialogue is regular; conjugate it in the present tense.*

Exercise 10. Conjugate the verb **ambezarse** *in the present tense.*

Exercise 11. In the following, give the appropriate form of ser *or* estar*:*

1. Los ijos de Luna _____ aedados.
2. El chay _____ kayente.
3. Los ijikos _____ buenos.
4. El padre _____ en kaza.
5. La skola _____ franseza.
6. Vozós _____ en una skola.
7. Ánde _____ vozós.
8. Madam Dudú i su ija _____ en el kuaför.
9. Los amigos de Henry _____ komercheros.
10. Tú _____ el marido de Lea.
11. Yo _____ muy grande.
12. Mozós _____ mansevos.
13. Henry _____ mi ermano.
14. Kén _____ vozós?
15. Mozós _____ ande Djoya.

Exercise 12. What are the verb endings common to all verbs:

1. for the 1st person plural (*mozós*).
2. for the 2nd person singular (*tú*).
3. for the 2nd person plural (*vozós*).
4. for the 3rd person plural (*eyos*).

Vijita ande Indjí i madam Algranti (Hertzliya, Israel).

Readings

Proverbos i dichas

Agua al chiko, palavra al grande (Water for the child, words for the adult). At the table, the woman of the house first serves her children water, then food to the man; she only speaks to the adults, thus marking the priority status of adults over children. This is a rule of etiquette.

Ijo, dukado vyejo (Son, an old ducat). A son is a sure value, like an old ducat (gold coin).

Ija, para la vejéz (Daughter, for old age), A daughter will take care of her old parents more than a son, who goes off to start a family. And yet, in Judeo-Spanish society, it is the son who takes his old parents into his house.

Ermano, para el diya malo/negro. (Brother, for a bad day). A brother is still a brother, you realize this in bad times. Note that *negro* (black) has tended to replace *malo* in the sense of bad, evil.

3 ◎ *Konsejika del sodro*

"Ké haber, Hayimachi?"
"En Kulaksiz moro."
"Kómo está vuestra mujer?"
"Ayí mos echó el Dyo."
"Es ke sosh sodro?"
"Si so godro, de vuestro pan no komo!"

Glossary

Hayimachi: popular diminutive for *Hayim.*	*la mujer:* the wife.
ayí mos echó el Dyo: God put us there.	*echar:* to throw, put, lay.
sodro: deaf. *godro:* fat. *el pan:* the bread.	*komer:* to eat.

Kulaksız is a neighborhood in Istanbul (the Turkish letter *ı*, which sounds somewhat like the American pronunciation of *oo* in *look, book*, comes into Judeo-Spanish as an *i*). In Turkish the name literally means *"earless."* The first two rejoinders are often used as ironic expressions by themselves. The first *(En Kulaksiz...)* means: He doesn't understand anything you ask him; the second *(Ayí...):* Don't waste your time asking him questions.

Questions: *1. Kómo se yama el sodro? 2. Ánde mora? 3. Es godro?*

47

This song is sung at the end of the Passover seder *meal that commemorates the flight from Egypt under the leadership of Moses (*Moshé Rabenu *in Judeo-Spanish). This is one of two "cumulative" songs sung on this occasion, the other being "El kavretiko" (Lesson 6B).*

The refrain goes as follows:

Ken supye(n)se i entendye(n)se
Alavar al Dyo kerye(n)se.

[1 – Refrain]
Kuálo es el uno?
Uno es el Kriyador.
Baruhú baruh Shemó.

[2 – Refrain]
Kuálos son los dos?
Dos son Moshé i Arón.
Uno es el Kriyador.
Baruhú baruh Shemó.

[3 – Refrain]
Kuálos son los tres?
Tres muestros padres son.
Dos son Moshé i Arón.
Uno es el Kriyador.
Baruhú baruh Shemó.

[4 – Refrain]
Kuálos son los kuatro?
Kuatro madres de Israel.
Tres…

[5 – Refrain]
Kuálos son los sinko?
Sinko livros de la Ley.
Kuatro…

[6 – Refrain]
Kuálos son los sesh?
Sesh diyas de la semana.
Sinko…

[7 – Refrain]
Kuálos son los syete?
Syete diyas kon Shabad.
Sesh…

[8 – Refrain]
Kuálos son los ocho?
Ocho diyas de la hupá.
[or de la milá]. Syete…

[9 – Refrain]
Kuálos son los mueve?
Mueve mezes de la prenyada.
Ocho…

[10 – Refrain]
Kuálos son los dyez?
Dyez mandamyentos son.
Mueve…

[11 – Refrain]
Kuálos son los onze?
Onze ermanos sin Yosef.
Dyez…

[12 – Refrain]
Kuálos son los dodje?
Dodje ermanos kon Yosef.
Onze…

[13 – Refrain]
Kuálos son los tredje?
Tredje anyos de la mizvá.
Dodje…

Glossary

alavar: to praise.

el Kriyador: the Creator.

Baruhú baruh Shemó (H.): Blessed be He, blessed be His Name.

sinko livros de la Ley: five books of the Law (reference to the Torah).

la hupá (H.): wedding.

la milá, or *el berit* (H. *brit mila*): the circumcision.

la prenyada: means pregnancy here; normally means the pregnant woman.
  The usual word for pregnancy is *el prenyado*.

el mandamyento: the commandment.

la mizvá (H.): here refers to the *Bar Mitsva* ceremony marking a boy's coming
  of age; normally means a good deed.

Note: *supyese, entendyese* and *keryese* (and *supyense,* etc.) are forms of the
imperfect subjunctive, now disappeared from usage, of the verbs *saver* (to
know), *entender* (to understand), and *kerer* (to want).

Vocabulary

1. Time divisions

el diya: the day.   *el mez:* the month.

la semana: the week.   *el anyo:* the year.

Una semana tyene syete diyas. Un mez tyene kuatro semanas.
Un anyo tyene dodje mezes.

2. Numbers

1 uno	6 sesh	11 onze	16 dizisésh (dyez i sesh)
2 dos	7 syete	12 dodje	17 dizisyete (dyez i syete)
3 tres	8 ocho	13 tredje	18 diziocho (dyez i ocho)
4 kuatro	9 mueve	14 katorze	19 dizimueve (dyez i mueve)
5 sinko	10 dyez	15 kinze	20 vente

Expressing arithmetical operations:

2 + 4 = 6: *dos i kuatro son sesh.*

5 − 2 = 3: *dos de sinko son tres.*

3 − 2 = 1: *dos de tres es uno.*

Exercise: Write out these operations:

a) 16 − 5 = 11;   b) 14 + 3 = 17;   c) 9 + 3 = 12;   d) 20 − 7 = 13;

e) 18 − 15 = 3;   f) 10 − 9 = 1;   g) 11 + 4 = 15.

5 🎵 Kantika de novya

Of a very different sort is the song of the bride, the kantika de boda, *a wedding song that women traditionally sing at wedding festivals which in olden days would last eight days,* ocho diyas de la hupá, *as stated in the preceding song. It is only to be sung in the context of a wedding, and it would be unlucky to sing it in the presence of an unmarried woman (although exceptions may be made by announcing something like "*Amá tenemos demuazel akí … De novya ke la veamos i eya…*"). In this version sung in Istanbul by Mrs. Gentille Behar, only a short portion is given. The song is very long and introduces the fiancé who speaks to his bride, praises her beauty and extols the path of light that has brought her to him. In this part the mother-in-law is asking her to come to her home gladly, asks her to be a good wife and to love her. A daughter-in-law who cries under her mother-in-law's roof is considered inauspicious.*

Todo le ke vos kero dainda no savésh
Dizíme bulisa si byen me kerésh
kon todo vos rogo ke seyásh mazaloza
ke por todo el mundo seyásh alavada
Ay sinyora novya ke sosh namoroza
anke non se topa otra mas ermoza
byen save la roza en ké kara poza
di a tal amor ke el novyo es para vos

Eya es alta komo el pino
arelumbra el oro fino
el amor le yeva el tino
gran savor le da, gran amor
 le da

Eya es blanka komo el djaspe
arelumbra el diyamante
el amor la yeva en parte
gran savor le da, gran amor
le da.

Glossary

dainda: still.
bulisa: lady (also, *sinyora*).
rogar: to beg.
mazalozo, a: lucky.
ke seyásh: may you be.
alavado, a: praised.
namorozo, a: in love.
ermozo, a: handsome, pretty.
apozar: to land on, rest on.
la roza: the flower (in general), the rose (sometimes).
Byen save la roza en ké kara poza is a proverb that is still found in Spain.

alto,a: tall.
el pino: the pine or cypress.
arelumbrar: to shine, light up.
el tino: the mind.
blanko, a: white
el oro: the gold.
el djaspe: jasper.

COMMUNICATION SKILLS

Using *You* in Judeo-Spanish

The word *tú* is generally used for "you" (singular) among friends and relatives, and certainly when an older sibling speaks to a younger one (remember that the plural of *tú* is *vozós/vozotros*).

- When addressing an older person or when desiring to show respect for the other, the third person singular is used (known as *avlar kon mersé*, to speak respectfully): *Kén es eya, Sinyora?* Who are you, ma'am? (See Lesson 6). Formerly, children used this respectful form when addressing their parents: *sinyor padre, sinyora madre*. It is used systematically when addressing one's parents-in-law (remember that the plural of *eyo/eya* is *eyos/eyas*).
- A second type of respectful form is the use of *vozós*, similar to *vous* in French. It can be found in old *romansas* and in certain stories and anecdotes. In the song of the bride, for example, the mother-in-law says to her daughter-in-law: *Ay sinyora novya, ke **sosh** namoroza...* Oh, lady bride, you who're in love... And in the *konsejika del sodro: Es ke **sosh** sodro? Kómo está **vuestra** mujer?*
- **Note:** Now that it has fallen into disuse, the respectful form with *vos* can take on a familiar tone: *Bovo sosh vos?!* Are you being foolish or something?

CONJUGATION

Note these verb forms:
Vos kero. Me kerésh. Le da. No savésh. From Part A.: *No sé. La ke da lisyones de pyanó. Keres vinir? Es la ija de madam Dudú, saves? Todo lo ke vos kero dainda no savésh.*

Dar (to give) and *kerer* (to like, to want) are regular in the present tense. The verb *saver* (to know) is irregular:

Dar	Kerer	Saver
do	kero	se
das	keres	saves
da	kere	save
damos	keremos	savemos
dash	kerésh	savésh
dan	keren	saven

6 💿 *La ija del rey i el ijo del haham*

En una kamaretika ay un manseviko ke s'ambeza la Ley. Lo ve la ija del rey i batea la puerta. Avre el manseviko i ve una ermoza donzeya.

Disho él: "Kén sos tú?"

Disho eya: "Yo so [se] la ija del rey." Demandó: "Kén sos tú?"

Disho él: "Yo so [se] ijo de un rav, amá no sé d'onde [de ande] vini [vine][7] yo akí, en ké sivdad morí. No sé nada!" (Porke no saviya).

Pensó eya: "El sta ermozo!" Disho: "Kuálo azes? Ké livros estás meldando?"

Disho él: "La Ley muestra."

"Ké Ley?"

"Na, esta Ley."

Kada noche eya abashava ande él i él empesó a ambezarle la Torá, el Tanah. Estuvo mezes kon él. Un anyo entero. El le mityó el nombre de Sará, porke se izo djudiya kom'an [komo] él. I eya lo yamó Avram.

From *Tehiat ametim* by Matilda Koen-Sarano, *Konsejas i konsejikas del mundo djudeo-espanyol*, Jerusalem: Kana, 1994, p. 281.

Glossary:

una kamaretika: a little bedroom.

ambezarse: to learn.

la Ley: the Law (Torah, Pentateuch).

lo ve: he/she sees him.

batear la puerta: knock at the door.

porke: because.   *se izo djudiya:* she became a Jew (she converted).

un rav (H.): a rabbi.

meldar (H.): to read.

la noche: the night.

abashar: to go/to come down.

avrir: to open.

CONJUGATION

1. **Reminder:** In Izmir, *se* is used instead of *so* for "I Am."

2. **The verb *ver*,** to see, is irregular and possesses a number of different forms depending on the region or the particular speaker.

veyo	*or* veo	*or* veygo
ves	vees	ves
ve	vee	ve
vemos	veemos	vemos
vesh	veésh	vesh
ven	veen	ven

---

7. Several verbs here are in the past tense: *disho (dizir), vini (vinir), morí (morar), pensó (pensar), empesó (empesar), estuvo (estar), mityó (meter), se izo (azerse), yamó (yamar). Saviya* and *abashava* are in the imperfect tense. See Verb Charts at end of book.

Ánde moras?

OBJECTIVES

Communication skills: Expressing "there is/there isn't," identifying oneself, "kada uno i uno," poking fun with the *-dero* construction.

Vocabulary: Terms of family kinship (continued), here/there, the days of the week, the months and seasons, words for professions and trades, teachers and students, religious offices, marital status, the Turkish suffix *-djí*.

Grammar: Diminutives, possessives (continued), the immediate future with *ir*, the relative pronoun *ke*, direct objects.

Conjugation: Irregular verbs: in *-er* and *-ir*.

Culture: Calendars, engagements, family kinship through marriage, old trades.

---

7 🎙 **Charlina en la guerta**

Primera vizina: "Bonjour, Madam Sará. Kómo estásh?"

Sigunda vizina: "Muy buena, i vos?"

Primera vizina: "Estó un pokitiko desrepozada, ma no ay nada."

Sigunda vizina: "Ay djente ande Madam Ester. A esta sinyora alta kon una fusta preta, la ke avla kon eya, la konosésh?"

Primera vizina: "Demanyana matrana vos vino piskuzadero Madam Sará?!"

Sigunda vizina: "Esto no es piskuzadero, es vezindadero!"

Primera vizina: "Tenésh razón, del Dyo i del vezino no se puede eskonder! Es su ermana, la ke mora en Israel. Kada anyo i anyo vyene a vijitar akí. Tyene dos kriyaturas chikitikas. La ijika tyene tres anyos i el bohor kuatro. Son muy luzyos. Están akí para pasar una semana. Para alhad van a tornar a sus kaza."

Sigunda vizina: "Una semana es muy poko."

Primera vizina: "Sí. Ma eya lavora. Es maestra de skola. Está kazada kon un Lehlí de ayá. El es mimar, arshitekto."

Sigunda vizina: "Ah, el marido no es de akí? No es turkino?"

Primera vizina: "No! No save avlar ni en fransé, ni en turko, ni en djudyó. Solo ivrit e inglés."

Sigunda vizina: "Kómo se dan a entender kon la es-huegra i la kunyada?"

Primera vizina: "A las mudeskas!"

GLOSSARY

Words of Spanish origin:

la charlina: chitchat.

la kriyatura: infant, child.

vezina/vizina: neighbor.

luzyo, -a: handsome, beautiful.

desrepozada: tired.

tornar: come back, return.

nada: nothing.

djudyó: Jew, Jewish, Judeo-Span. lang.

preto: black.

darse a entender: to make oneself understood.

avlar: to speak.

kunyado, kunyada: brother-in-law, sister-in-law.

piskuzar: snoop around.

demanyana matrana: at the break of day.

vezindar: to be neighborly.

a las mudeskas: using gestures like the deaf-mute

eskonder: to hide.

(in Salonika, *a las mudayas*).

Words from other sources:

alhad (Spanish Arabism): Sunday.

Lehlí, Lehliya (T. for "Polish"): Ashkenazi Jew.

ivrit (H.): Hebrew.

mimar (T.): architect.

una fusta (T.): a skirt.

COMMUNICATION SKILLS

2. There is/there isn't/there are/there aren't

Observe: *ma no ay nada, ay djente.*

ay: there is, there are; *no ay:* there isn't, there aren't. There is no article in this construction. For example: *ay djente:* there are people; *no ay pan*, there isn't any bread.

Special usage: *no ay nada* (literally, there is nothing) means "don't worry, no problem." When a child knocks over his glass or does something wrong, the hostess is quick to say: *"No ay nada."*

2. Defining and identifying

De ánde sos? So de Turkiya.
Ánde moras? Moro en Paris.
Ké echo azes? Lavoro en una butika, so empyegada.
Estás kazada? No, so espozada.
Tyenes ermanos? Sí, tengo dos ermanos.

3. Use of the suffix *-dero*

Observe: *Esto no es piskuzadero, es vezindadero.*

To poke fun at some little mania, the suffix *-dero* (invariable) is added to the infinitive of the verb after dropping the *-r*.

Vezindar (to pay neighborly visits) ⇨ *(el) vezinda****dero***
    (the mania for visiting neighbors).
Komer (to eat) ⇨ *(el) kome****dero*** (the mania for eating).
Durmir (to sleep) ⇨ *(el) durmi****dero****/durme****dero*** (the mania for sleeping).

At the Paris subway stop Trocadéro, two young Spanish-Jewish cousins have a good laugh: *trokar* means to change something, *trokarse* means to be changed. Since they often have to transfer (change directions), they find the *manya de trokadero* (craze for constantly changing directions) an entirely appropriate name for this subway station.

4. *Kada uno i uno*

Observe: *kada anyo i anyo* (every year). Another way to say this is *todos los anyos* (every year).

This turn of expression is modeled on the Hebrew; it appears systematically in translations of the Bible in a linguistic calque, or transfer, called *Ladino*. The most frequent of such word-for-word transfers is *kada uno i uno* (lit., each one and one), a calque of the Hebrew *kol ehad ve ehad*. Since this expression is felt as literary it offers a frequently used model for other expressions.

kada...i... = *todos los/todas las...* (*cf.* "each and every")
kada *persona **i** persona* = *todas las personas*
kada *ombre **i** ombre* = *todos los ombres*

Vocabulary

5. Terms of family kinship

El es-huegro i la es-huegra: the father-in-law, mother-in-law. (The hyphen here is to indicate two separate sounds, *-s* and *-h;* do not pronounce as an *-sh* sound).
El kunyado, la kunyada: the brother-in-law, sister-in-law.
La ermuera, el yerno: the daughter-in-law, son-in-law.
Los kosuegros: el kosuegro i la kosuegra: This term designates the relationship to each other that unites the parents of children who have married. The verb *konsograr/kosuegrar* means to become related to another family through the marriage of a son or daughter.

A family member through marriage is considered as an adjunct but not really a part of the family. Such a person will abstain from taking part in the affairs of the in-laws or might permit him- or herself to make a remark by beginning: *Yo so gueso ajeno, amá…:* I am a foreign bone, but… This reference to a bone to denote one's natural state is from the Bible.

6. Here and there

Observe: *Vyenen a vijitar akí. Está kazada kon un Lehlí de ayá.*
      El marido no es de akí.
akí means "here" and is the opposite of *ayá,* "there."
*Estar mas de **ayá** ke de **akí**:* literally, "to be more from there than from here," means "to have one foot in the grave."

7. Time expressions

The days of the week are: *alhad, lunes, martes, myérkoles, djueves (djugueves), vyernes, shabad.*

To express a full duration in time, the suffix *-ada* is added:
    La semana ⇨ *la semanada.*
    El mez ⇨ *la mezada* (originally: a month; now: monthly salary).
    El anyo ⇨ *la anyada.* (For *Roshashaná,* greetings for an
    anyada buena are exchanged for the new year).
    La noche ⇨ *la nochada (nochada buena!).*
    La tadre ⇨ *la tadrada.*

Un anyo tyene dodje mezes.
Tres mezes de primavera: avril, mayo, djunyo.
Tres mezes de enverano: djulyo, agosto, septembre.
Tres mezes de otonyo: oktobre, novembre, desembre.
Tres mezes de invyerno: enero/janvyé/djenayo, febrero, marso.

Ex.   *Mos vamos **para** alhad.* We're leaving on Sunday.
        Ké diya es oy? What day is today?
        Oy es djueves dos de febrero. Today is Thursday, February 2.

 la **primavera**    el **enverano**

el **otonyo**   el **invyerno**

Note: A day lasts from one sundown to the next. *Noche de shabad* is Friday evening, *noche de alhad* is Saturday evening. The days of the week have Spanish names with the exception of *shabad*, the Hebrew word for the holy day, and *alhad*, "the first," an Arabic word that was already being used in Spain to avoid *domingo*, "the day of the lord."

The month follows the phases of the moon for everything involving religious matters. The months bear their Hebrew name but one also finds French and Turkish names through multilingualism.

The religious year is counted from the month of *Tishrí* (in September or October), beginning with the holiday of *Roshashaná*. The full set of names for the months are: *Tishrí, Heshván, Kislev, Tevet, Shevat, Adar* (an extra month is periodically added to catch up with the solar year: *Veadar*), *Nisán, Iyar, Siván, Tamuz, Av, Illul* (late August or September). The years are counted from the date of "the creation of the world." To convert the Western year to the Hebrew year (before Rosh Hashanah), add 760, disregarding the thousands column. The year 2002, for example, gives the Hebrew equivalent (5)762; after Rosh Hashanah, of course, add one. To convert the Hebrew year to the Western year (again, disregarding the thousands column), add 239 from Rosh Hashanah to December 31, or 240 from January 1 onwards; hence, 5763 may be 2002 or 2003.

People will therefore say, for example, *stamos en djulyo de mil novesyentos noventa i syete* (July 1997) or the Hebrew equivalent, *Tamuz de sinko mil setesyentos sikuenta i syete* (5757) These are the dates that show up on the houses of Jewish quarters.

8. Professions and trades

korredor de kazas: real-estate agent.
sarraf (T.): gold exchanger.
merkader: merchant.
komerchante: businessman.
empyegado: employee.
kashero, a: cashier.
banker (T.): banker.
médiko, doktor: doctor.
dantist(o) (F.): dentist.
avokato (F., T.): lawyer.
manifaturadjí (T.): hosier, fabric dealer.

fabrikatör (T.): industrialist.
moso: waiter, *mosa:* maid.
sekreter (T. from F.): secretary.
terdjumán,tradjumán: interpreter.
gazetero/jurnalisto: journalist.
eskritor/eskrivano: writer.
lavorante: worker.
patrón: boss.
hammal (T.): loader, porter.
indjenyero: engineer.
vendedor: salesman.

Observe: *Es mimur, arshitekto. Es maestra de eskola.* As can be seen from the above, French terms are widespread for modern trades and often compete with a Spanish or Turkish equivalent.

GRAMMAR

1. Diminutives

Observe: *la ija/la ij**ika***. *es muy poko/un pokit**iko***. *kriyaturas chikit**ikas***.

♦ *-iko, -ika, -ikos, -ikas* and *-itiko, -a, -os, -as* are the most commonly used diminutives. They are widely used and can transform a noun, adjective or adverb.
Examples: *poko* ⇨ *pokitiko, chikas* ⇨ *chikitikas, buena* ⇨ *buenika, ija* ⇨ *ijika.*

♦ If the last syllable contains a *k* sound, *-itiko* is added rather than *-iko*.

♦ In certain cases the suffix *-iziko* is found: *una florizika* (a little flower), *un paniziko* (a little breadroll), *la manizika* (the little hand).

Note: These diminutives add a variety of nuances to the basic meaning of the word. The main one, besides that of simply marking a diminutive aspect, is one of affection, of tender feeling. When one speaks of children and of food, diminutives become very abundant.

2. The immediate future

Reminder from Lesson 1: *Agora vamos a bever un chay.*
Observe: *Para alhad van a tornar a sus kaza.*
The idea of a future event is often rendered by a construction consisting of the verb *ir* (to go) + *a* + verb infinitive. For example, *Agora vo a komer. Manyana vas a eskrivir. Oy va a kozinar. Vamos a durmir. Vash a tornar esta tadre. Van a vinir amanyana.* (English has the same type of construction; for example: I am (I'm) going to eat now, tomorrow you are (you're) going to write, etc.).
Note: In oral speech and sometimes in writing, *vo* and *va* tend to absorb the preposition *a*, giving: *yo va (vo a) ir a ver, va ir (vo a ir or va a ir).*

3. The relative pronoun

Observe: *La sinyora alta ke avla kon eya. Su ermana, la ke mora en Israel.*
      Ke aga lo ke kere (Lesson 2B).
◆ The relative pronoun *ke* may be the subject or the direct object; that is, it translates English "who," "that," "which," as well as "whom." Unlike English, it can never be omitted.
*La ijika **ke** ves es mi ermana*: The little girl (**whom**) you see is my sister. *La ijika **ke** está en la kaleja es mi ermana*: The little girl **who** is in the street is my sister.
Reminder: The relative pronoun *ke* does not take the written accent mark, whereas the interrogative pronoun *ké?* does.

4. Direct objects (for persons or things)

◆ In Judeo-Spanish, a direct object referring to a person is preceded by *a*: *Konosésh **a** esta sinyora ke avla kon la vizina?* (Do you know the lady who is talking with the neighbor?). *Konoses **a** este perro?* (Do you know that dirty guy?). [Note that the word for dog can be a strong insult for a person].
Even though such a noun is preceded by *a*, when it is replaced by a pronoun, the direct object is used (*not* the indirect object): *A esta sinyora alta, **la** konoses?* (That tall lady, do you know her?) *Ves **a** este sinyor? Sí, **lo** veo.* (Do you see that man? Yes, I see him).
As we are dealing with an animate and conscious being here, the preposition *a* shows that the action is addressed towards him.
◆ A direct object referring to a thing or an animal is not preceded by *a*: *Konoses la kaleja del kuaför?* (Do you know the street where the hairdresser is). *Konoses este perro.* (You know this dog).

CONJUGATION

Entender	Ir	Venir/vinir
entyendo	vo	vengo
entyendes	vas	vyenes
entyende	va	vyene
entendemos/entyendemos	vamos	**venimos**/vinimos
entendésh/entyendésh	vash	**venísh**/vinísh
entyenden	van	vyenen

Note: Because of differences in regional dialects, *vinir* has two forms. *Venimos* and *venísh* are the more commonly used forms. Vowel closure is even stronger in the Sarajevo dialect, where *vinimus* is found, the *-u* tending to replace unaccented *-o*.

♦ The verb *konoser* (to know)[8] is irregular in the first person singular, as are all verbs in *-ser, -oser, -eser*: **Konosko** *(irr.)*, then the regular forms: *konoses, konose, konosemos, konosésh, konosen.*

EXERCISES

Exercise 1. Give a noun expressing the type of mania suggested.
Ex.: A teacher, tired of seeing a student chew *(mashkar)* gum tells her, laughing: *Tyenes mashkadero, parese!* You must be on a chewing craze!
1. Irritated because his wife is always falling asleep *(durmir)*, her husband says to her:
2. Irritated that her husband is constantly reading *(meldar)*, his wife tells him:
3. A mother tells her son who keeps getting up *(alevantar)* at the table:
4. She tells her daughter who doesn't stop singing *(kantar)*:
5. A lady tells her friend who constantly runs around *(korrer)*:
6. A daughter tells her mother who shops *(emplear)* a lot:

Exercise 2. Sketch out this family's genealogical tree:
—Ida, ija de Perla i Shelomó Barokas, se kaza kon Edí, ijo de Mazaltó i Sabetay Vidas.
—Perla i Shelomó son la es-huegra i el es-huegro de Edí. Edí es su yerno.
—Mazaltó i Sabetay son los es-huegros de Ida. Ida es su ermuera.
—Mazaltó i Perla son kosuegras. Shelomó i Sabetay son kosuegros.
—El ermano de Ida es el kunyado de Edí. Las ermanas de Edí son las kunyadas de Ida.

---

8. **konoser** means to know in the sense of being familiar with; **saver** means to know in the sense of a fact, a truth. For example, *Konoses a esta sinyora?* but *Saves ánde mora?*

Exercise 3. Do the same with the names of your parents and grandparents.

Exercise 4. Give the date for today, tomorrow, yesterday.

Exercise 5. What is my job?

Ex.: *Yevo karga en una kufa: so hammal.*

1. Yevo karga en una kufa. 2. Lavoro en la kaza kon la sinyora. 3.Vendo oro i merko oro. 4. Lavoro en una fabriká. 5. Lavoro en una banka. 6. Lavoro en la kasha de un magazén. 7. Me do a entender en inglés, en fransé, en espanyol i en turko. 8. Eskrivo en una gazeta. 9. Fabriko motores. 10. Fraguo kazas. 11. Vendo kazas i butikas. 12. So patrón de un magazén. 13. So patrón de una fabriká. 14. Lavoro en la duana. 15. Lavoro en una butika.

Exercise 6. With the aid of the Glossary below, identify the job that corresponds to each description:

1. Ago pan. 2. Vendo pishkado. 3. Vendo karne. 4. Ayudo al balabay (sinyor) en kaza. 5. Vendo gaynas i poyos para Shabad. 6. Vendo salatas i legumbres. 7. Todos beven rakí en mi butika. 8. Yo do a komer. 9. Yo baylo. 10. Kon mi barka la djente pasa al otro bodre de la mar. 11. Aferro pishkados kon mi barka i los vende el balukchí. 12. Vendo aniyos de oro i bonbonyeras de plata. 13. Ago mobilya para la kaza. 14. En mi guerta kresen salatas, domates, pereshil… 15. Kuando aze friyo todos merkan mis samarras. 16. Lavo i lavo kada diya i diya. 17. Yo tengo un vapor kon munchos marineros. 18. En mi butika chikitika se topa todo lo ke kere la balabaya (sinyora) de kaza para komer, bever, i lavar.

Glossary:

bakal (T.): grocer.
balukchí (T.): fish dealer.
bayladera/bayladora: dancer (fem.)
guertelano/bahchevän (T.): gardener.
kapitán: captain.
kasap (T.)/*karnesero:* butcher.
kayikchí/barkero: boatman, ferryman.
kuyumdjí (T.)/*djoyero:* jeweler.
lavandera: washerwoman.

lokantadjí: restaurant owner.
marangoz (T.): woodworker.
meyanadjí (T.): tavern keeper.
moso: waiter/valet.
panadero: baker.
pishkador: fisherman.
samarrero: furrier.
taukchí (T.): poultry dealer.
zarzavachí (T.): greengrocer.

Exercise 7. Put these sentences into the immediate future:

1. Komo pan. 2. Bevemos kavé. 3. Veních. 4. Entyendes. 5. Me da un livro. 6. Vemos a la vizina. 7. Torno a kaza. 8. Lavorásh. 9. Avlan. 10. Saves.

Exercise 8. Translate into Judeo-Spanish:

1. Do you know my neighbor (fem.)? 2. I visit the museums *(muzeos)*. 3. I know that skirt. 4. We know the rabbi. 5. I visit my mother-in-law every week. 6. Do you see Mrs. Lucie's house? 7. We see your cousin (fem.) who is coming here. 8. I see a little cat *(un gatiko)*. 9. She sees Suzi's school, but she doesn't know it. 10. I'm going to school to see the teacher. 11. Do you see that man? [That man, do you see him?]

El merkader de teshidos Yusuf Reyna (Istanbul).

Marsel Gülçiçek, patrón de fabriká (Istanbul).

El estampador i su haver, Sami Vitas (Istanbul, 1950).

READINGS

Proverbos i dichas

Proverbs are used all the time in conversations. There are thousands of them; one could hold a whole conversation just using proverbs. New ones are created using existing models, and anyone can draw a proverb out of some personal anecdote. For example, a lady speaking about her children leaving home might say: *Penas para verlos vinir, penas kuando se van.* Another, seeing homely parents with a beautiful child, might exclaim: *Mira feor de padres, mira luzyor de ijos* (See the homeliness of parents, see the beauty of their children—meaning, you can't be sure about anything).

2●

Proverbs about months and days

Ken kozina vyernes kome Shabad (He who cooks on Friday will eat on Saturday). Meaning: You have to look ahead, prepare beforehand.

Largo komo la aftará de Tisha be Av (As long as the Haftarah portion on Tisha Be'Av). The ninth day of Av is the day of mourning to commemorate the destruction of the Temple in Jerusalem. Meaning: It goes on forever, you could die of boredom.

Adar amostró su kavo, no deshó ni arado ni sembrado (The month of Adar has shown its end, it has left neither a plowed field nor a sown one). Meaning: (By the end of winter) there are no provisions left, everything has been used up.

En martes ni te kazes ni t'embarkes (On Tuesday, don't get married and don't embark, set sail, start something new). Meaning: Tuesday is considered an unlucky day.

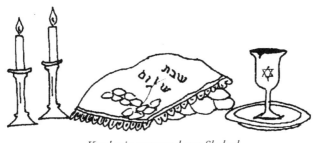

Ken kozina vyernes kome Shabad

Many proverbs concern in-laws

Topadura de kosuegras! (Mothers-in-law happening to run into each other). Meaning: Running into someone with false enthusiasm.

Es-huegra ni de barro buena (Mother-in-law not even good when made of earth). This proverb, which can also be found in Spain, relates to a Medieval tale where an earthen statue of a mother-in-law falls and wounds her daughter-in-law. Refers to a bad relationship between these two in-laws.

Amor de yerno komo sol de invyerno (A son-in-law's love like the winter's sun). Meaning: The love of a son-in-law is not as warm as the love of a son but it's still some consolation.

Amor de es-huegras i ermueras, de los dyentes para ahuera (Love between mothers-in-law and daughters-in-law, teeth outside). Meaning: The demonstrations of friendship between a mother-in-law and her daughter-in-law are only just words, "with teeth bared").

Para kén es esta paparrona? Para vos, sinyora es-huegra. Para mi esta paparrika? (Who is that big pot of porridge for? For you, mother-in-law ma'am. That little pot of porridge is for me?) Meaning: A mother-in-law thinks that a thing offered to her daughter-in-law is a generous gift, but when the daughter-in-law offers her that same thing, the mother-in-law thinks the daughter-in-law is stingy.

Ken no kere konsograr demanda muncho ashuguar (He/she who does not want to become related by marriage asks for a very large trousseau). This is said of people who set excessively high conditions because they are not really interested in pursuing a particular venture.

Proverbs relating to trades

Saká en botika, shastre en pyés, tanyedores en bedahayim (A water-carrier in a shop, a tailor standing, musicians in a cemetery). This funny proverb depicts a world gone topsy-turvy: a water-carrier can be found walking the streets, not inside a shop; tailors sit down to do their work, they don't stand up; and musicians do not play in a cemetery.

El sapatero yeva sapato roto (The shoe repairman wears a torn shoe). Tradespeople and professionals are the ones most in need of their own services.

No s'eskrive en ketubá ma byen se ve ande está: La boz i la koka (It may not be written in the *ketubá* but one can see where he's at: A voice and a ponytail). Even if the marriage contract does not say anything about a bride's seductive features, the husband is not indifferent to them.

Culture

Trades

El shastre sews men's suits, *la kuzindera* sews women's clothes. Certain seamstresses used to run sewing schools for young girls.

El sapatero is the shoe repairman, the cobbler. Terms from the Turkish are also used: *kunduryero* or *kunduryadjí*.

Tanyer means to play a musical intrument in general. *Un tanyedor* is therefore a musician. They are called upon for weddings and banquets, to escort the bride to the ritual bath, etc. Women singers, *kantaderas* or more rarely *kantadores* were hired separately for certain occasions, notably weddings and circumcisions. *La endechadera*, a hired mourner, would compose funeral elegies for the defunct.

The term *saká*, sometimes *sakadjí* (T.), is more widespread than the term *aguador* (fem. *aguadera*) found in Salonika. A job for men, it consisted of delivering drinking water to homes by means of goatskin bags, sometimes loaded on donkeyback. This water was kept in *la tinaja*, a large earthen jar covered with a lid, a *tapón*. Water was drawn out by means of the *djarro*, a cup with a handle. Running water and bottled mineral water, of course, brought this trade to an end.

La tinaja i el djarro

Other trades have also disappeared. *El arenadjí*, from the Spanish *arena* (sand) with the Turkish ending *-dji* (doer, maker, seller, etc.) sold sand for scrubbing copper pots and sinks. *El ateshdjí* , or "fire starter" for *Shabad,* was a job created by Jews obviously to be performed by non-Jews.

In former times the trade of rag dealer was also practiced by Jews. The term *ropavejero*, of Spanish origin, alternated with *paryaruhadjí* based on the Greek for "old rags" (the rag dealer's cry) and the Turkish suffix seen previously.

Merchandise was sorted out and old pieces and objects of value were sold by antique dealers, *antikadjís* (plural), who ran their own stores on the street. They were *butikaryos*—that is, they had real shops. Spanish Jewish dynasties became illustrious through this trade; their names are still well known among experts in Oriental antiques.

GRAMMAR

The suffix *-djí* borrowed from Turkish

The names of trades ending in *-djí,* borrowed from the Turkish, also have a feminine form ending in *-djiya*:

 el ateshdjí/atedjí becomes *la ateshdjiya/atedjiya.*
 el arenadjí becomes *la arenadjiya.*
 el kapudjí (concierge) becomes *la kapudjiya.*
However, not all the trades listed above necessarily take the feminine form.

KANTIKAS

1. Si me dizes ke no

 Si me dizes ke sí
 Kon repozo vo a bivir
 Si me dizes ke no
 De pena vo murir

(Note here that the *a* of *vo a murir* has been elided).

Glossary
dizes: you (*tú*) say. *la pena*: the pain. *murir*: to die.

66

Hayim Bedjerano, Grand Rabbi
of Edirne, Turkey, 1910.

Jewish vegetable peddler,
Salonika, late 19th century.

The silk mill of Bay Feres, Bursa (Turkey), early 20th century.

The School of the Alliance Israélite Universelle in Edirne, Turkey, in 1910.

Jewish child going to school accompanied by a Turkish *kavás* (Salonika, 1915).

Pupil taking a Hebrew class at summer school of the *Mazet ha Torah* Society (Istanbul).

8 🎵 **2. Kantikas de ijikos**

Kayikchí, Balata
Pishkadikos de la mar

Oy es vyernes
Pitikas kayentes
Mamá kon la pala
Papá kon los dyentes.

chup chup
a la mar, a la mar, a la mar.

Kon los dedos de la mano:
Este dize: dame pan
Este dize: no ay mas
Este dize: vamos a arrovar
Este dize: no, ke mos mata el rubí
Este dize: por akí, por akí, por akí

Ande vas ijo del Dyo?
A meldar la Ley del Dyo
Kon el pan i el kezo
I el livriko al pecho
El Dyo ke te guadre
A ti i a tu madre
I a tu sinyor padre
Ke es un buen djudyó
I la komadre
Ke te aresivyó.

2b

Glossary

la pala: the shovel.
un(a) dyente: a tooth.
arrovar: to rob.
matar: to kill.
un pishkado: a fish.
pecho: chest, breast.

aresivir: to receive.
el kezo: the cheese.
guadrar: to keep.
ke te guadre: may he keep you (subjunctive).
la komadre: the midwife.

GRAMMAR

Demonstrative pronouns and adjectives

Demonstrative pronouns

	masculine	feminine	neuter
singular	éste	ésta	ésto
plural	éstos	éstas	

The demonstrative adjectives are: *este, esta, estos* and *estas,* without accent.

Vocabulary

1. Teachers and students

Teachers and students have different names according to the type of school frequented.

El rubí is *un haham,* a rabbi, who teaches the rudiments of Hebrew to students—*talmides* or *talmidim*—at the *meldar* or *talmud torá.*

La maestra, or *mestra,* used to take care of little children at nursery schools and kindergartens—*mestrikas* or more recently *ganes* (H.)—that existed in neighborhoods from early times on.

In schools of the Alliance Israélite Universelle, French was the language of instruction and the terms used were *profesora de la skola, profesor* or *profesör* (F. *professeur*), *direktor* or *direktör* (F. *directeur*), feminine *direktora* or *direktrisa* (F. *directrice*), *los elevos i las elevas* (F. *élèves*).

En la universitá, at the university, these terms are used: *profesor, -a* and *estudyantes, elevos,* or *talmidim* (influence of modern Hebrew).

2. Religious offices

It is hardly surprising to find here a large number of terms from the Hebrew. We have seen *haham* and *rubí.* The "shamash" of the synagogue is the *sanmás* (sometimes *shamash*), the ritual slaughterer is the *shohet,* the circumsizer is the *moel,* the synagogue cantor is the *hazán,* the judge of the rabbinical court is the *dayán de Bet Din* and the washer of the dead (*ken mal te kere!*[9]) is the *rohets.* The rabbi is also called *el rabino.* The community head is *el gran rabino,* or the *hahambashí* (T.).

Exercise 1. *What is my job?*

Ex.: *Kanto kantikas, so kantadera* (or *kantador*).

1. Vendo agua. 2. Ambezo la Torá a los ijikos. 3. Tanyo la gitarra. 4. Kuzgo kostümes. 5. Ago kalsados. 6. Degoyo los kodredos asigún la Ley. 7. Estó en todos los berites. 8. Guadro la puerta del kal. 9. Vendo kozas vyejas en una butika. 10. Meldo fransé en la skola. 11. Ambezo el djudyó a los estudyantes de la universitá. 12. Ago vistidos para las mujeres. 13. Lavo a los muertos (leshos!). 14. Meldo en la tevá i kanto los piyutimes. 15. Djuzgo en el Bet Din. 16. So el grande de la komunitá djudiya. 17. Ago fuego i toko lumbre diyas de Shabad en kaza de Djudyós. 18. Kuando nase una kriyatura, la aresivo yo. 19. Kaminando de kaza en kaza, espozo i kazo a las mansevikas i a los mansevikos (see page 72 for *el kazamentero*). 20. Kamino por las kalejas i merko kozas vyejas.

---

9. Literally: he who wishes you evil, a formula used to ward off the outcome of an allusion to an ill-fated event.

CONJUGATION

Dizir (to say) and **Pueder** (to be able) are irregular verbs:

digo (I say, etc.)	puedo (I can, etc.)
dizes	puedes
dize	puede
dizimos	**puedemos**/podemos
dizísh/dizésh	**puedésh**/podésh
dizen	pueden

The verb **pueder**/*pod̄er* tends to take a regular form for most of its conjugation.

9 🔊 *Arvolés*

Arvolés yoran por luvyas
i montanyas por ayres.
Ansí yoran los mis ojos
por ti, kerida amante.

Blanka sos, blanko vistes,
blanka es la tu figura,
blankas flores kayen de ti,
de la tu ermozura.

Enfrente de mi ay un andjeló,
kon sus ojos me mira.
Avlar kero i non puedo,
mi korasón suspira.

Ven verás i ven verás
ven verás i veremos:
amor ke tenemos los dos
los dos mos aunaremos [lo gozaremos.]

*This love song is very popular among Judeo-Spanish communities. The
following refrain is sometimes added, giving it a rather tragic tone:*

Torno i digo, ké va a ser de mi?
En tyerras ajenas yo me vo a murir.

Glossary

el arvolé: the tree.
la luvya: the rain.
la montanya: the mountain.
el ayre: the wind.
yorar: to cry.
un andjeló: an angel.
los ojos: the eyes.
mirar: look at
kerer: to want, to love.

suspirar: to sigh.
vestir/vistir: to wear (clothing).
kayer: to fall.
ermozura: the beauty.
ven verás: come, you'll see.
aunarse: to join together.
gozar: to enjoy.
ké va ser de mi: what will become of me?
el korasón: the heart.

GRAMMAR

Use of the possessive

Observe: *Los mis ojos. La tu ermozura.*
         La tu figura. Kon sus ojos…

In addition to the simple expression of the possessive that precedes the term possessed (Lesson 1A, *kon sus ojos*), one can also find the article preceding the possessive (*los mis ojos*). This is a literary or emphatic turn of expression.

10 ⊙ *El ayudador del kazamentero*

El kazamentero tyene un ayudador ke lo ayuda. Kada vez ke el kazamentero dize ke la novya sta ermoza, él dize: "muy ermoza". Syempre puja un poko.

 Un diya el kazamentero vyene kon el ayudador ande una famiya a dizir ke tyene una novya para el ijo. Dize: "*Tengo una novya muy ermoza! Muy rika! Todo bueno!* I el ayudador dize: "*Sí, sí, sí! Muy muy ermoza, muy muy rika! Todo muy bueno!*" "*Amá,*" dize el kazamentero "*solo un defekto tyene: tyene una korkova.*" Dize el ayudador: "*Kuálo! Una korkova? Dos korkovas!!!*"

From Matilda Koen-Sarano, *Konsejas i konsejikas del mundo djudeo-espanyol*, Jerusalem: Kana, 1994, p. 251.

Glossary

ayudar: to help.	*pujar*: to increase.
ayudador: helper, assistant.	*un defekto*: a defect.
la novya: the fiancée, bride.	*una korkova*: a hump (of a hunchback).

Questions: 1. *Ké echo aze el kazamentero?* 2. *I el ayudador?* 3. *Kómo es la novya?* 4. *Ké defekto tyene?*

Note: *el kazamentero (la kazamentera)* was a known and respected figure in the community. The sign of his profession was an umbrella, *un chadir*. When someone would introduce a man to a woman, people would jokingly ask: *Te merkaremos un chadir?* Shall we buy you an umbrella?

72

Communication skills

Marital status

♦ **Apalavrado, a:** la ijika promete kazarse kon el mansevo.
♦ **Espozado, a:** vyene el haham a kaza de la ijika kon los paryentes del mansevo. Aregalan konfites en una bonbonyera de plata. Se mete una data para el kazamyento.
♦ **Kazado, a:** el novyo i la novya se kazan en el kal, se meten los aniyos de kidushim, i se eskrive la ketubá. Se azen fyestas ke turan ocho diyas: ocho diyas de la hupá.
♦ **Kito, a:** (leshos!) duspués de estar kazados, no se avyenen marido i mujer, se esparten i se kitan. El haham les da el get.
♦ **Bivdo, a:** (El Dyo ke no mos dé!) kuando se muere el marido o la mujer.

2b

Glossary

la palavra: the word.[10]
prometer: to promise.
aregalar (dar regalo): to give a gift.
un konfite: a candy.
una bonbonyera: a candy dish.
la plata: the silver.
el kal (H.): the synagogue.
el aniyo: the ring.
el aniyo de kidushim: wedding ring.

la ketubá (H.)*:* the marriage contract.
turar: to last.
avenirse: to get along.
espartirse: to separate.
kitarse: to get divorced.
dar el get (H.): to grant a divorce.
duspués de: after.
se muere: he/she dies.

Las bonbonyeras de plata kon konfites.

---

10. *palavra* means "word" in the sense of "to give one's word" (cf. *apalavrada, "promised."*) "Word" as an element of speech is *byervo*.

II ⊙ Entre madre i ijo en el telefón

(la madre en Istanbul, el ijo en Israel)

"Mamá, tú sos?"

"Sí, ijo de la madre, kómo estás?"

"Byen mamá, kero irme este enverano, un meziziko a Istanbul."

"Siguramente presyado, te aspero a ojos a ojos."

"Va vinir kon mi mujer. Ánde mos vas a echar?"

"Vos va dar mi kamareta, tú perye kudyado!"

"Tú, ánde te vas a echar i el papá?"

"Ya mos echamos en el salón, no te merekiyes."

"Keremos ir kon los ijos, ánde los vas a echar?"

"Ya los echamos en el salón."

"Tú i el papá ánde vos vash a echar?"

"Ya mos echamos en la kamareta chika."

"Amá a mi es-huegra, ánde desharla?"

"Bueno ijo, tráyela."

"Ánde la vas a echar?"

"Le daremos la kamareta chika."

"I vozotros, ánde vos vash a echar?"

"Yo ya me echo de la ventana, tu padre ke aga lo ke kere."

Eli Shaul in *Akí Yerushalayim* (1986) anyo 8, reprinted in *Folklor de los Judios de Turkiya*, Istanbul: Isis, 1994, p. 21.

Glossary

asperar: to wait.

a ojos a ojos: impatiently.

echar: to throw, put to bed.

echarse: throw oneself, go to bed.

la kamareta: the room, the bedroom.

no te merekiyes, perye kudyado: don't worry.

deshar: to let, leave.

tráyela: bring her.

le daremos (future): we will give him/her.

la ventana: the window.

ke aga lo ke kere: let him do what he wants.

Questions: 1. *Kén son las personas ke avlan?* 2. *Ánde mora el ijo?* 3. *Ánde mora la madre?* 4. *Kuálo kere azer el ijo?* 5. *De ké se kere la madre echar por la ventana?*

Grammar

1. Use of the possessive (continued)

Observe: *van a tornar a sus kaza.*

       sus is in the plural, *kaza* is in the singular.

When there are several possessors of the same thing, Judeo-Spanish often uses the plural possessive form to agree with a singular noun.

2b

2. Direct object pronouns*
*(Indirect object pronouns will be studied in Lesson 7A.)

Reminder: Certain direct object pronouns are the same as reflexive pronouns seen in Lesson 1A (*yamarse*).

Here: *ánde **mos** vas a echar?*

Observe: *a mi es-huegra... ánde **la** vas a echar?*

*los ijos... ánde **los** vas a echar? **lo** ke kere*: what he wants.

	Singular	Plural
Masculine	**lo**	**los**
Feminine	**la**	**las**
Neuter	**lo**	n/a

Placement: The object pronoun comes before the conjugated verb. However, it is directly joined to the infinitive and imperative forms of the verb, just as we saw in the case of reflexive verbs such as *ambezarse, yamarse,* etc.

Observe (referring to la *es-huegra*): *deshar**la**, tráye**la**.*

Exercise: Replace the words in bold by the appropriate pronoun.

Ex.: *Komen **los bizkochos** en el salón* ⇨ ***Los** komen en el salón.*

1. Beven **la agua del bokal**. 2. Dize a su madre **ke los vizinos están en kaza** (the neuter form replaces a whole clause). 3. Mi ermano traye **sus ijos** a kaza. 4. Bevo **mi kavé**. 5. La madre melda **las gazetas**. 6. Keremos muncho a **muestros ijos**. 7. Mi padre mira **la televizyón**. 8. La nona echa **las ijikas** en la kamareta. 9. El rubí me da **sus livros**. 10. Yo sé **mis lisyones** (fem.).

מואיסטרו קומפאנ"ירו

אברהם שם טוב ששׁון

קון מאדמואזיל

ריקיטה די יצחק אנג'יל

איספוזאדוס

מואיסטרו קומפאנ"ירו

יצחק שם טוב ששׁון

קון מאדמואזיל

ביינב'ינידה ארון ב'יאיסי

איספוזאדוס

Announcements from *La Solidaridad Ovradera*, of March 31, 1911[11]

Muestro kompanyero
Abraham Shem Tov Shason
kon madmuazel
Rikita de Its-hak Andjel
espozados.

Muestro kompanyero
Its-hak Shem Tov Shason
kon madmuazel
Byenvenida Aron Viesi
espozados.

La Solidaridad Ovradera was a socialist journal in Salonika that appeared every Friday.

11. These announcements were the subject of a doctoral dissertation by Nicole Cohen-Rak: *"La Solidaridad Ovradera," a publication with 7 issues; with translations, various indices, and linguistic analyses*, University of Paris III, 1986, vol. 2, annexes, 013 [in French].

Rabbi Eli and his wife,
la rubisa, Istanbul, ca. 1920

Ketubá of Mrs. Anavi,
Plovdiv (Bulgaria), 1944.

*El novyo i la
novya debasho
del taled.*

77

Pranso en la kamareta de komer de Ida i Rubén (Istanbul).

Ida aze kavé en su mupak.

Vijita en el salón de madam Moussafir i su tant Vikí, Neuilly (Paris).

LESSON 3

En kaza

OBJECTIVES

Communication skills: Expressing where you are, where things are, what you do, your situation and location; asking questions, expressing obligation.

Vocabulary: From hot to cold, the house, prepositions of place, ordinal numbers, colors, the various meanings of *echar*.

Grammar: The uses of *estar* and *kaler*, uses of the present subjunctive.

Conjugation: The present subjunctive, the verbs *tener* and *azer*.

Culture: The arrangement of the house, more customs, the character of Djohá.

---

12 ⊙ *A la haragana tadre le vyene la gana.*

Etí:	"Mamá está desrepozada, kale ke espajemos las dos. Yo vo a fregar."
Selén:	"Mamá, myentras estás echada en la sofá, vamos a enderecharte todo."
La madre:	"Mersí muncho, ijikas. Vo a tomar una kura i vo a mirar de durmir un poko."
(En el mupak)	
Etí:	"Yo vo a enshavonar i enshaguar, i tú, vas a sekar kon este handrajo i guadrar. En primero las kupas… (shrak!) Guay de mí! Se va a aspertar la mamá!"
La madre:	"Kuálo sta afitando?!"
Selén:	"No ay nada mamá, solo ke se kayó una kupa en basho. Está pedasos."
La madre:	"Ké kupa es?"
Selén:	"La ke metes enriva del armaryo en el kantoniko."
La madre:	"Na! El vazo de la bula. Vazo malo no kaye de la mano."
Etí:	"Kapará por ti! Ande está el fregón?"
Selén:	"Nalo, en la pila, al lado del shavón."
Etí:	"Agua kayente no ay. Está yelada. Uuy, yelada buz."
Selén:	"Kale avrir el gaz del shofbén i deshar la agua ke korra un puntiko. Ya sta kemando las manos."
Etí:	"Mamá, ánde está la payla?"

79

La madre:	"Debasho de la pila ande se guadran la leshiya i el chöp. Ajenas sosh! Mijor me alevanto yo i lo ago."
Selén:	"No mamá, kale ke te arepozes! (*a Etí*) Ande meto los pirones i kuchiyos?"
Etí:	"Aryentro el sigundo kashón, al lado de las kucharikas."
Selén:	"Las kasherolas kale ke se eskurran. La eskova está detrás de la puerta. Yo vo a barrer…"
Etí:	"Lo ke ve la es-huegra!"

GLOSSARY

Words of Spanish origin:

espajar: to clean, tidy up.

enshaguar: to rinse, wipe.

el handrajo: the rag, dishcloth.

guadrar: to put in order.

enderechar: to straighten out.

la kupa: drinking glass.

guay de mí! Oh my! ("Woe is me").

ago (from *azer*): I do.

el kashón: the drawer.

la eskova: the broom.

barrer: to sweep.

está pedasos: It's in pieces, it's all broken.

el fregón: washing brush, scouring pad.

la pila: the sink.

el shavón: the soap.

la payla: the wash-basin, pail.

la leshiya: the bleach.

el armaryo: cupboard, closet.

afitar: to happen.

el kuchiyo: the knife.

la kuchara: the spoon.

eskurrir: to drip.

Words from other sources:

el mupak (T.): the kitchen.

kapará por ti! (H.): let that count as a sacrifice for you.

el shofbén (F.): the water heater.

buz (T): ice.

el chöp (T.): the garbage, trash can.

el pirón (G.): the fork.

el chiní: the chinaware, dishes.

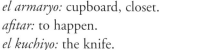

el pirón

el chiní

las eskovas

las kupas

el shofbén

el kuchiyo

el armaryo/dolap.

el chöp

la kuchara

el kashón

COMMUNICATION SKILLS

1. Situation, location

Observe:

Estó desrepozada, kale ke me eche i ke durma.
Estó kansada, kale ke me arepoze.
Para arepozarse kale echarse i durmir.
Estó hazina, kale ke tome una kura.
Estó en la kama, estó echada.
Estó asentada en la siya, en el sofá, en el koltuk.

Note that the verb *estar* + adjective serve to express the following:

a state or attitude in which one finds oneself.	*Mamá está desrepozada, está hazina, está kansada.*
a position one has taken or in which one finds oneself.	*Está asentado, a. Está echado, a.*
a characteristic that is not permanent.	*La agua está friya, está kayente, está yelada.*
the result of a transformation.	*La kupa está pedasos.* The glass is (reduced to a state of) pieces [note how highly condensed this expression is].

2. Location

nalo, nala, nalos, nalas: here it is (masc. and fem.), here they are.
akí: here. *ayá:* there (Lesson 2).
enbasho: below, down, on the floor.
   Ex.: *echar en basho,* to knock down, knock over.
enriva de…: on top of, above.
   Ex .: *meter las kupas enriva de la meza,* to put the glasses on the table.
debasho de…: below, under. Ex.: *estar debasho de…* to be under…
adyentro/aryentro (de)…: in, inside.
afuera/ahuera (de)…: outside.
al lado de…: next to…
detrás de…: behind…
delantre de…: in front of…
enderedor de…: around, about…

3. *Mirar de* + infinitive

Mirar de azer una koza: to try to do something.
Ex.: *Miro de durmir.* I'm trying to sleep.

4. *Afitar*

Afitar is a regular verb meaning: to happen.
Ex.: *Kuálo afitó?* What happened?
     Kuálo te afitó? What happened to you?

5. Obligation

Observe: *Kale deshar la agua ke korra.*   *Kale ke espajemos.*
         Kale ke te arepozes.   *Kale avrir el gaz.*

♦ The verb *kaler* in the 3rd person singular + infinitive means: It is necessary to, one has to (do something).
Ex.: *Kale lavorar muncho.* One has to work a lot.

♦ *Kale ke* + subjunctive means: one has to, it is necessary that.
Ex.: *Kale ke lavores muncho.* You have to (you've got to) work a lot.
    Kale ke te kazes, Kalina. You've got to get married, Kalina (this is said of
    people who always go about saying *kale.*)

VOCABULARY

1. Adjectives

♦ **From cold to hot**
Yelado buz: The association of *yelado* (frozen) with the Turkish term *buz* (icc)
to mean "as cold as ice" is another example of a highly synthesized way of
associating an adjective and a noun, frequent in Judeo-Spanish.

yelado/friyo (cold) ⇨ *fresko* (cool) ⇨ *tivyo* (lukewarm, tepid) ⇨ *kayente* (hot)
⇨ *buyendo* (boiling).

♦ **More adjectives with contrary meanings:** *muevo* ≠ *vyejo* (new/old),
    limpyo ≠ *suzyo* (clean/dirty), *seko* ≠ *mojado* (dry/wet).

2. House work

♦ *La kolada:* The wash used to be a formidable enterprise for which help was garnered from friends, relatives or a hired woman, *la djudiya de la kolada,* the Jewish washerwoman. There was no public washhouse; women did the wash at home. Dirty laundry was prepared for soaking, *remojar,* then for washing, *lavar,* with soap or washing powder. *Duspués kale enshaguar* (to rinse), *esprimir* (to wring dry), *espander* (hang on a line), *enkolgar* (hang up), *arekojer* (gather), *dublar* (fold), *dar utí* (to iron), *guadrar* (put away in the closet).

♦ *La limpyeza* (lit., cleanliness): Housekeeping. The housecleaning that precedes *Pesah*—that great Spring cleaning project—is the most stringent of all. *Barrer* (to sweep), *espondjar* (to mop the floor), *fregar* (to scrub), *eskurrir* (drain, let drip), *enshuguar* (to dry), *alimpyar* (to clean) or *azer limpyeza* (do the house cleaning), *adovar* (to repair), *espajar* (to put in order).

3. *La mobilya* (The furniture)

la siya

el (la) sofá / la kanapé   el minder

el koltuk/la poltrona

la mesa

la buzyera

el espejo

el frijider

la lampa

el tapet

la kama

el banyo

el orno/forno

la pila

83

4. *Las kamaretas de la kaza* (The rooms of the house)

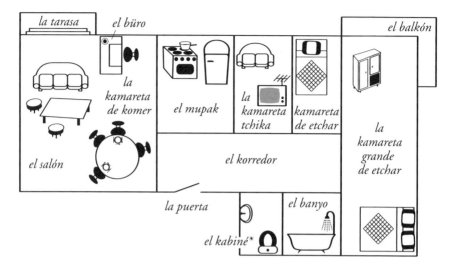

Also called: la kozina (in Istanbul)/*el nümeró/la privada/la tualet.*

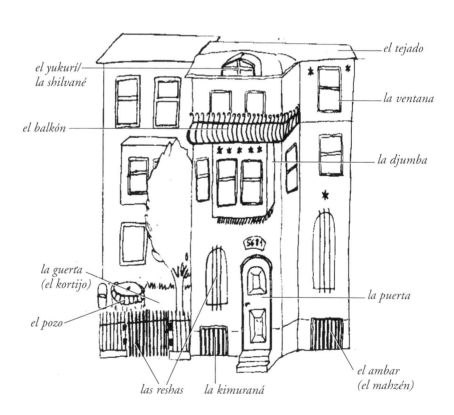

84

CONJUGATION

The present subjunctive

Until now we have been using the **indicative** mood of the present tense but there is also a **subjunctive** mood, used to express a sense of emotion, doubt, hesitation, obligation and a variety of other attitudes regarding a particular action or situation. As we saw above, the verb *kaler* requires that the conjugated verb in the next clause be in the subjunctive. We will be considering additional uses of the subjunctive as we go along.

The following chart summarizes the formation of **regular verbs** in the present tense, showing the Indicative (Ind.) and Subjunctive (Subj.):

(3a

Verbs in *-ar*		Verbs in *-er*		Verbs in *-ir*	
Ind.	Subj.	Ind.	Subj.	Ind.	Subj.
kant**o**	kant**e**	kom**o**	kom**a**	biv**o**	biv**a**
kant**as**	kant**es**	kom**es**	kom**as**	biv**es**	biv**as**
kant**a**	kant**e**	kom**e**	kom**a**	biv**e**	biv**a**
kant**amos**	kant**emos**	kom**emos**	kom**amos**	biv**imos**	biv**amos**
kant**ásh**	kant**ésh**	kom**ésh**	kom**ásh**	biv**ísh**	biv**ásh**
kant**an**	kant**en**	kom**en**	kom**an**	biv**en**	biv**an**

Verbs in *-ar*, in the subjunctive, take endings with the vowel *-e-*. Verbs in *-er* and *-ir*, in the subjunctive, take endings with the vowel *-a-*. Note that, because the subjunctive is generally used in dependent clauses introduced by *ke*, they are often indicated with this word: *ke kante, ke komamos, ke bivan*.

Formation of **irregular verbs:** To find the subjunctive of irregular verbs, use the first person singular of the indicative as the base and add the subjunctive endings. For example, in the verb *tener, yo tengo* provides the base, drop the ending *-o* and add the subjunctive endings.

Tener		**Azer**	
Present		Present	
Indicative	Subjunctive	Indicative	Subjunctive
tengo ⇨	ke **tenga**	**ago** ⇨	ke **aga**
tyenes	ke teng**as**	azes	ke ag**as**
tyene	ke teng**a**	aze	ke ag**a**
tenemos	ke teng**amos**	azemos	ke ag**amos**
tenésh	ke teng**ásh**	azésh	ke ag**ásh**
tyenen	ke teng**an**	azen	ke ag**an**

konoser: konosko ⇨ ke konoska, konoskas, etc.

The *e* of *ke* is frequently elided before a vowel: *k'arepoze, k'avra, k'espaje,* etc. The subjunctive, used without *ke,* is often used in blessings. For example, when someone sneezes, you say: *Bivas, kreskas i engrandeskas!* May you live, grow, and become older! This expression is sometimes jokingly condensed into: *Freskas!* Fresh!

Culture

The Home

In the houses of Bulgaria and Greece, there was often a *kortijo,* a closed courtyard that contained different structures where other members of the family were housed. This is described by Elias Canetti in the story of his childhood in Ruschuk (also called Ruse) in Bulgaria.

In Istanbul a number of houses were built of wood and had a garden in front where there were fruit trees and a well. Other houses were large structures where numerous members of the family lived. Finally, because of the scarcity of space and the number of poor people that had to be housed, tenement buildings were rented out room by room to Jewish families. They were called *yahudhane* (see p. 244).

La Kaye Ancha in Rhodes at the beginning of the 20th century.

EXERCISES

Exercise 1. Answer these questions by referring to the picture.

Ánde están: 1. La televizyón? 2. El telefón? 3. La menorá? 4. La chanta? 5. El djarro? 6. El tapet? 7. La meza? 8. La siya? 9. El livro? 10. La gazeta? 11. La lampa? 12. Las kortinas? 13. El espejo? 14. El minder?

(3(

Exercise 2: Complete the drawing by following the directions given.

Tyenes el plano de la kaza. Mete agora los koltukes delantre de la ventana; el espejo enfrente de la ventana; la lampa en el kantoniko a la derecha de la puerta; el armaryo kontra la pared kon el sofá delantre; el djarro enriva del armaryo; la televizyón enfrente de la puerta.

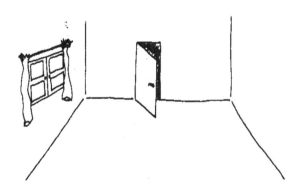

Exercise 3: Give advice to a friend based on the following statements.

Ex.: *kale durmir ⇨ kale ke durmas.*

1. kale lavar. 2. kale meldar. 3. kale eskrivir. 4. kale komer. 5. kale fregar. 6. kale aspertarse. 7. kale bever agua. 8. kale azerlo.

Exercise 4: Use complete sentences to answer the following questions, referring to the vocabulary below.

a) Ánde se mete(n): 1. La mezuzá? 2. El tapet? 3. El saksí de rozas? 4. La kama? 5. El chöp? 6. Ánde se guadran los chinís? 7. Ánde se meten las kortinas? 8. I la menorá? 9. Ánde se mete la leshiya?

b) Ké azemos: 1. En el mupak? 2. En el banyo? 3. En la kamareta de echar? 4. En la kama? 5. En el koltuk? 6. En el salón? 7. En el sofá? 8. En el büro? 9. En el balkón?

Vocabulary:

durmir	arepozar	meldar	gizar	fregar	lavarse	komer
tomar aver		bever	echarse	lavorar	eskrivir	aspertarse
mirar ahuera		mirar la televizyón			avlar kon la djente…	

Elmaz mundando bamyas en la tarasa (Istanbul).

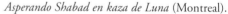

Asperando Shabad en kaza de Luna (Montreal).

READINGS

Proverbos i dichas

A la haragana tadre le vyene la gana (To the lazy woman, late comes the appetite).
Meaning: The lazy woman's desire to do something will always come too late.

La vida de la mujer, lavar, kriyar i barrer (The life of woman is to wash, raise children and sweep).
Woman's lot is to do all the tasks relating to the house and the children—a lot of work.

Limpyeza es medya rikeza (Cleanliness is half wealth).
When you are poor, the cleanliness that marks your house makes you proud, as though you were rich.

Meza i siya i almenara (Table and chair and chandelier).
This is enough for a frugal happiness: a table for eating, a chair for resting, and light, the source of life. Also said is: *pan i kezo i dos kandelas* (bread and cheese and two candles).

Vazo malo no kaye de la mano (A bad glass does not fall from the hand). It's not the bad glass that will fall and break. Instead of *vazo* the word *kupa* is more often substituted, and instead of *malo* the word *negro/negra* is used.

Para eskansar, el papú en brasos (To rest, grandpa in your arms).
This is an ironic way of saying that after you have worked hard and are ready to rest, some other task comes along; on top of everything else, this too.

Kandelika de la kaye, a eskuredá de la kaza (The little light in the street, to darkness at home).
This is said of someone who seems joyful when in a social group but ill-tempered and unpleasant once at home.

La primera eskova, la sigunda sinyora (The first broom, the second lady).
When there is a second marriage, the second wife is treated better than the first.

No tomes kaza, toma vizino (Don't take a house, take a neighbor).
It is not the house that is important but rather neighbors with whom one can live in good harmony.

Kantikas

1. Mansanikas koroladas

Elias Canetti quotes this Judeo-Spanish song that he knew in his childhood.

Mansanikas koroladas
son las ke vyenen d'Estanbol,
aryentro tyenen un guzano
ke les buraka el korasón.

Glossary
mansana: apple.
korolado/kolorado/korelado: red.
guzano: worm, insect.
burakar: to make a hole.
el korasón: the heart.

2. Kantika

Here is the first stanza of a risqué little song, with verbs in the imperfect tense (*aviya*, for example, the imperfect of *aver*, means "there used to be").

En Estanbol aviya
una djudiya
lavava kon leshiya
i espandiya…

13 🎵 *Tres klavinas (kantika)*

Tres klavinas en un sesto*
una blanka i una roz
la d'en medyo korolada
empesijo del amor

Amán minúsh, minúsh
djanim minúsh, minúsh

A los syelos vo a suvir
A las syete tabakás
flechas de oro vo a echar
Ande kaye es mi mazal

Amán minúsh, minúsh
djanim minúsh, minúsh

A la mar me vo a echar
un pishkado vo a aferrar
Syete novyas vo a kitar
yo a ti te vo a tomar

Amán minúsh, minúsh
djanim minúsh, minúsh

*An older version gives *tyesto*, a flowerpot.

Glossary

la klavina: the carnation.
el sesto: the basket.
roza (poetic: *roz*): rose-colored.
el empesijo: the beginning.
Amán! (T.): My, oh my!
minúsh (T.): kitty.
djanim (T.): my little sweetie.
la tabaká (T.): the level.
echar: (here) to shoot.
el mazal (H.): luck, fortune
  (here: my loved one).
aferrar: to catch.
tomar: to take.

las rozas

la klavina

el sesto

Notes:

1. *Las syete tabakás:* the seven layers of heaven (*cf.* "to be in seventh heaven" in English). *Los syelos* (biblical plural): heaven, the heavens.
2. The various meanings of the verb *echar:*
echar (en basho): to throw away, throw down on the ground.
echarse: to lie down, go to bed.
echar flechas: to shoot arrows.
echar gritos, vardas: to cry out, to shout.
echar lágrimas: to cry, shed tears.
echar agua en la kupa: to pour water into the glass.
echar boy (T.): to grow taller (literally, to throw size).

Vocabulary

Colors

vedre: green.   *amariyo, a:* yellow.   *maví* (T.): blue.
blu (?): blue.   *korolado/kolorado, a:* red.   *blanko, a:* white.
preto, a: black.

Zurzuví, an undefinable color, is used ironically. *Tyene los ojos zurzuvís* provokes a laugh. Originally this term designated navy blue (with the same etymology as Spanish *azul,* "azure," both terms deriving from a Persian word as found in lapis lazuli).

14 ◦⁰ *Konsejika del ashuguar*

(Ken no kere kosuegrar demanda muncho ashuguar).

El sanmás del kal es muy muy prove. Ma tyene de kazar a su ija i kale aparejar ashuguar. I los del novyo keren dota. El no está topando remedyo. Se va ande el haham.
"Sinyor haham…"
"Kuálo tyenes, Simantov?"
"Yo so prove i la famiya del novyo me demanda muncho ashuguar! Kuálo ke aga?"
"Ké t'están demandando?"
"Koltukes moltukes, savanás mavanás, kasherolas masherolas, kolchas molchas…"
"Agora te lo enderecho yo. Las savanás se las das, las mavanás no las des; los koltukes se los das, los moltukes no los des."

Story told by Lucienne Barouh, Paris

Notes

1. This story relies on the fact that in Judeo-Spanish (as in Turkish) one can repeat a term by substituting an *m-* for the first consonant or by adding an *m-* when the term begins by a vowel. This means "and that kind of thing," "and such and such." *Livro mivro* can mean "books and such" or "books, you bet!"
2. The word for "bedsheet" is *sávana.* In telling this story, the narrator, a woman from Turkey, has shifted the accent: *savaná.*

92

Glossary

el ashuguar: the trousseau.
el sanmás (H.): the synagogue "shamash."
la sávana: the bedsheet.
la kolcha: the bed cover, comforter.
aparejar: to prepare.
la dota: the dowry.
topar remedyo: to find a solution.
enderechar: to straighten out.

Questions: *1. Ké echo aze el sanmás? 2. De ké no kaza a su ija? 3. Ké aze el haham?*

3b

15 🔊 *Konsejika del hammal*

Ay un vyejiziko ke mora en una kazika chikitika. No tyene echo. Es hammal amá no lavora porke es muy vyejo i no le dan echo. Ay un riko ke kere trokar kaza, ma es eskaso, eskaso pinya, i no kere dar muncha pará. Dize: "*Vo a tashidear la kaza kon los ijos* (tyene dos ijos barraganes), *i lo ke keda, la vidreriya de kaza, vo a topar un hammal barato.*"

Los ijos tashidean la mobilya i él bushka ver si topa un hammal barato. Le demanda a uno, kere muncha pará. Le demanda a otro, kere i mas. Peshín ke ve al vyejiziko de la kazika, se dize entre sí: "*Na, este provetiko me va a tashidear la vidreriya.*" Le demanda al vyejiziko: "*Me keres tashidear la vidreriya de kaza?*" Salta el vyejiziko i dize: "*Buyrún, pashá, kuántas parás me vas a dar?*" "*Yo, parás no do.*" "*Tú, parás no das?!*" "*No, parás yo no do, ma te vo dar tres konsejos.*" Agora el vyejiziko pensa un poko; dize: "*Fin'agora no me ize benadam, puede ser ke kon estos konsejos m'enderecho yo. I bueno, 'sin parás ke sea'.*"

Suve el vyejiziko la kufa kon la vidreriya, i al primer etaj demanda el primer konsejo. Le arresponde el otro: "*Si te dizen ke kaminar a pye es mijor de kaminar kon arabá, no te kreas.*" "*Esto konsejo es?! Aspera veremos.*" Al sigundo etaj, sigundo konsejo: "*Si te dizen ke no komer es mijor de artar, no te kreas.*" "*Pekí, i esto es konsejo? Veremos el treser!*" "*Si te dizen ke ir desmudo es mijor de vistir samur, no te kreas.*" Esta vez se inyervó muy muncho el vyejiziko. Toma la kufa yena i la echa abasho la eskalera i le dize al patrón: "*Kuatrén konsejo: si te dizen ke kedó un chiní sano sin romper, no te kreas!*"

As told by Izak Arditi.

93

Glossary

trokar kaza: to move, change houses.

eskaso: stingy.

pará (T.): coin.

tashidear (T.): to carry, transport.

la vidreriya: the glassware.

buyrún pashá (T.): yes indeed, sir.

un konsejo: a bit of advice.

sano: healthy, in good condition.

azerse benadam (H.): to become a person of import.

arabá (T.): a car.

no te kreas!: don't believe it!

aspera veremos: Let's wait and see.

artar: to satisfy hunger.

pekí (T.): very well.

desmudo: naked.

samur (T.): sable.

inyervarse: become irritated.

kufa (T.): basket.

Vocabulary

Ordinal numbers (adjectives)

1st	primer.	6th	sején.
2nd	sigundo.	7th	setén/syétimo.
3rd	treser.	8th	ochén.
4th	kuatrén.	9th	muevén.
5th	sinkén.	10th	dyezén.

16 💿 *La mujer sorretera*

This is a story about Djohá. This fictitious character comes from the Mediterranean basin and appears very frequently in Judeo-Spanish literature and folklore. He is sometimes confused with the Turkish character of Nasreddin Hodja. But the characteristics of the Jewish Djohá—a parasite, simpleton, chiseler—make him out to be more of a social misfit and unconventional person than a philosophical moralist.

Dizen la djente a Djohá:

"Djohá, tu mujer es muy sorretera. No se está un punto en kaza. Apenas sales, ke eya sale detrás de ti. Se va ande la vizina. Pishín salyó, entra ande la otra. I ansina de kaza en kaza diya entero."

"Si es ansina komo dizísh," responde Djohá, "i a mi kaza va a vinir."

Glossary:

sorretera: gadabout, a woman who goes out often.

salyó: she went out.　　　　*apenas:* barely, hardly.

un punto: a moment.　　　　*diya entero:* the whole day.

salir: to go out.　　　　*el otro, la otra:* the other one.

pishín (T.): immediately.　　*i a mi kaza:* to my house too.

Questions: *1. Ké es una sorretera? 2. Ánde va la mujer de Djohá? 3. Djohá se aravya* (gets angry) *kon eya?*

Note: For a woman not to stay at home is frowned upon, yet Spanish Jewish women like to go out for walks, go shopping or visit friends. They all accuse the women from other communities of being more *sortukas* or *sorreteras* than they. This word, which comes from the Turkish, has also undergone the influence of *korretear,* to run about here and there—no longer used—and of the French *sortir,* to go out.

SCENES OF LIFE

17 🔘 *1. Memories of a street vendor*

"En Balat aviya zarzavachís ke vendiyan vedrura, kon kufas. Para burlarsen de las balabayas les gritavan ansina: 'Madam k'avra!'¹² para ke avran la puerta de kaza. La kavra es una hayá!"

As told by Mr. Azuz.

Glossary

vedrura: greenery, vegetables.

la kufa (T.): the basket.

para burlarsen: to poke fun at.

la balabaya (H.): the lady of the house.

les gritavan ansina: cried out to them thusly.

avrir: to open.

la kavra: the goat (fem.).

una hayá (H.): an animal.

Questions: *1. Kuálo venden los zarzavachís? 2. Tyenen butika? 3. A kén venden? 4. Ké modo se burlan?*

---

12. There is a pun here: *kavra* (goat) and *k'avra* (open up).

2. La kaza de Madam Lucie

Madam Lucie es una vyeja moradera de Balat. Kuando su madre kazó, su padre izo fraguar una kaza. Eya mos konta komo era:

"Komo kijo eya [su madre] de su repozo. En la kamareta de asentar teníyamos mozós un *armoire* para enkolgar las vestimyentas de kada noche de las kriyaturas [...]. En el mupak por la parte de por akí al lado teníyamos una grande kaldera de kovre para buyir la ropa de lavar [...] i debasho era komo orno. Kon la lenya se kalentava la agua. El mupak teniya dos ventanas: la una dava para la pila, el levyé, la otra ventana dava para un sofá onde s'alevantava el kapak i saliya aryentro la pastera. La pastera para lavar la ropa [...]. Para meter las komidas un armaryo grande de tres tabakás, para meter las kalderas, la makina de moler, el mortero, todo, i un dolap otro aviya para todo modo de kuras, akeles, *boîte de petite pharmacie*."

From an interview recorded with Mrs. Lucie Tarí, née Babani.

Glossary

fraguar: to build.

asentar: to sit.

armoire (F.) = *armaryo*.

la kaldera: the kettle.

el kovre: copper.

buyir: to boil.

la lenya: wood for burning.

el levyé (F. *l'évier*): the sink.

el kapak (T.): the cover, lid.

la pastera: the washtub.

el mortero: the mortar.

el dolap (T.): the closet.

moler: to grind, chop.

Note: The demonstrative *akel,* "that," "that one," can be used as a noun. *El akel* thus means "the thing," "the thingamajig." *Los akeles* = the kitchen utensils. It can also be used as a verb, *akear,* "to put something together," "fool around with things."

La kaye del Kal d'Ahrida (Balat, Istanbul).

La kaza de madam Lucie (Balat).

Customs

1. El tenemaká i el alikobení

Los diyas de kolada viniya a ayudar la djudiya de la kolada porke no aviya makinás. La madre lavava en una pastera ke teniya lumbre por debasho i los ijos, los mandavan ande la vizina: *"Disho mamá ke kale ke me de un poko de alikobení."* Alikobení es una dicha en turko para dizir: *"guádrame en tu kaza,"* lo mezmo ke *tenemaká (tenme aká)*. La vizina entendiya i dava una ves dulse, otra vez un boyiko, otra vez un bomboniko, i los ijikos demandavan: *"Ma kuálo es alikobení? Dulse? Bombón? Kada vez es una koza mueva!"*

As told by Mr. and Mrs. Izak Arditi.

Notes:
1. *aká,* hither, here (moving in this direction).
2. In Rhodes, people would say *el turburdá* (T.), "stay here."

2. La mueva kaza

Kale entrar en una kaza mueva kuando la luna krese o para Rosh Hodésh. En la mueva kaza trayen un pokitiko de polvo de la kaza vyeja i lo meten en un burakito detrás de la puerta. Kale trayer un guevo (vida), un poko de levadura (para ke puje), asukuar (vida dulse), i un espejo (vida klara).

As told by Mrs. Sará Elmaz.

Glossary

la makiná/mákina: the machine.
la lumbre: the fire.
mandar: to send.
una dicha: an expression.
dava: dar in the imperfect.
una vez: once.
el dulse: sweet preserves.
muevo, a: new.
kreser: to grow.
rosh hodésh (H.): New moon, beginning of the month.

el polvo: the dust, powder.
un burako: a hole.
trayer: to bring.
un guevo: an egg.
la levadura: the yeast.
pujar: to increase.
la asukuar: the sugar.
dulse (adj.): sweet, sugary.

Engleneándosen en kaza (Istanbul).

Damas djuguando kartas (Princes' Islands, Istanbul).

LESSON 4
Kaminando i avlando

OBJECTIVES

Communication skills: Negatives, making comparisons, expressing likes and dislikes, desires and wishes, need and obligation.

Vocabulary: Games, pastimes, occupations, amusements; the effect of the -ozo and -dero suffixes.

Grammar: Progressive form of the verb, present and past participles; translating impersonal expressions, using the conjunction i.

Conjugation: The verbs kerer and trayer; the subjunctive of irregular verbs; forming the present and past participles.

Culture: Children's games, the gazino, the festival of Purim, emigration to Israel.

(4a

---

18 🎧 *Izak no aze nada.*

La madre: Izak! Ké estás azyendo?

Izak: Estó meldando la gazeta, mamá, kuálo keres?

La madre: Los ijos de la vizina están índosen al klub muestro de akí. De ké no vas kon eyos?

Izak: I para kuálo se kere ido ayá?

La madre: Atyó! Lo ke azen todos no puedes azer i tú?!? Englenearte kon la mansevés djudiya de la mallé, sintir muzika, azer tiyatro, djuguar djuguos, kantar kantikas, ambezarte en ivrit… Mas kuálo keres?!

Izak: Ayá m'estó enfasyando. Los vizinos son mas grandes de mí… No mos avenimos. A mí no me plazen los bayles ni akeyas bavajadas ke se azen ayá.

La madre: Mira mursá! Nunkua no tyenes ido ayá! Se azen nochadas ande se kontan konsejas, se avla de vyajes, de istorya, este modo de kozas… Dizen ke es muy enteresante… Puede ser ke topas amigos kon ken avlar.

Izak: Nochadas mochadas… No vo a topar a dinguno, mamá. Yo no tengo menester de amigos. Kon la eskola i el tenis, ya m'abasta.

La madre: Esta noche se van a ir ayá tu ermana kon tu prima, kero ke las akompanyes. Mijor ke de estar mirando televizyón noche entera.

Izak: Uuf! Lo ke mos mankava!

Glossary

Words of Spanish origin:

atyó!: Dear Lord!

sintir: to listen.

enfasyarse: to be bored.

avenirse: to get along well.

las bavajadas: nonsense

la konseja: the story.

la istorya: History.

topar: to find.

m'abasta: that's enough for me.

mijor ke de: that's better than…

lo ke mos mankava!: just what we needed!

Words from other sources:

englenearse (T.): to have fun.

la mallé (T.): the quarter, part of town.

mursá (H.): unpleasant person.

enteresante (F.): interesting.

mochadas: nochadas + m (T., see p. 92).

Communication skills

1. Negation

♦ Observe: *No aze nada. No vo a topar a dingunos. No me plazen los bayles ni akeyas bavajadas. Nunkua no tyenes ido.*

no… nada: not anything, nothing.

no (or *non*) + verb: do not, does not + verb.

no … ni… : neither… nor

no… nunkua/nunka: never.

no… dinguno, dinguna, dingunos, dingunas; or *dinguno no,* etc.: nobody, no one. There is grammatical agreement with the person understood. The neuter is: *dinguno(s).* One can also find *ninguno, a, os, as.*

dinguno no avla: no one speaks, none of them speaks.

dinguna no avla: no one speaks (referring to a woman).

dingunos no avlan: none of them speaks.

dingunas no avlan: none of them speaks (referring to women).

2. Comparisons

♦ Observe: *Los vizinos son mas grandes de mí.*
           Mijor ke de estar mirando televizyón.

To express a comparison: *Hayim es mas grande de* (or *ke*) *Selén.*
For "better than" use *mijor de/ke.* For "worse than" use *peor de/ke.*

The construction with *de* or *ke* is equally common. *Mi prima es mas aedada*
de *mí* or *Es mas aedada* ***ke*** *mí.*

♦ *Mas muncho* (literally, "more much") is a very common formula in Judeo-
Spanish to mean "more" or "much better." *Esto me plaze mas muncho:* I like
this much more *or* I much prefer this one...

4a

3. Expressing likes and dislikes

Observe the construction for "I don't like": *a mi no me plazen los bayles*
(literally: to me, dances are not pleasing to me). Both *a mí* and *me* are expressed.

a mí no me plaze tenis.
a ti no te plaze ir al sinemá.
a él, a eya no le plaze durmir.
a mozós (mozotros) no mos plaze meldar.
a vozós (vozotros) no vos plaze sintir muzika.
a eyos, a eyas no les plaze lavorar.

If the subject is in the plural, the verb *plazer* must agree. Note that the subject
often comes after the verb:

   *a mí me plaz**en los livros**.*   *a mí me plaz**e tu livro**.*

Verbs in the infinitive do not take agreement: *a mí me plaz**e ir i vinir**.*

4. Expressing desires and wishes

Observe: *Kero ke las akompanyes.* In Judeo-Spanish, there is no construction
such as the English "I want for you to accompany them." This idea must be
expressed by the verb *kerer* + *ke* + verb in the subjunctive (literally, "I want
that you accompany them"). If there is no change of subject, simply use the
infinitive:

   No change of subject: *Kero vinir:* I want to come.
   But: *Kero ke vengas:* I want you to come.

5. Expressing need and obligation

"to need" = *tener menester de;* "not to need" = *nȯ tener menester de.*

No tengo menester de amigos: I don't need friends.
Estó kansada, tengo menester de durmir: I am tired, I need to sleep.

Se kere + past participle
Para kuálo se kere ido ayá? Why does he need to go there?
No se kere avlado: There is no need to talk.
No se kere durmido: There is no point in sleeping.

♦ Reminder: *kale:* it is necessary, one must; *no kale:* one must not... (see Lesson 3A). Also note:
Kale plus a noun: *kale agua* (water is needed).
Kale plus a past participle: *kale dicho* (it needs to be said that...).

GRAMMAR

1. The progressive form of the verb

Observe: *Ké estás azyendo? Estó meldando. M'estó enfasyando.*
Mijor ke de estar mirando televizyón.

As in English, the progressive form consists of *to be (estar)* + present participle (the *-ing* form of the verb). This form is used extensively in Judeo-Spanish and is the normal expression for the immediate present. *Estó meldando:* I am reading. *Ayá m'estó enfasyando:* literally "I am getting bored over there," I spend my time getting bored over there.

Forming the present participle:
verbs in *-ar* ⇨ *-ando:*   *meldar* ⇨ *meldando*
verbs in *-er* ⇨ *-yendo:*   *bever* ⇨ *bevyendo*
verbs in *-ir* ⇨ *-yendo:*   *sintir* ⇨ *sintyendo*

Note that the present participle of the verb *ir* is *indo* or sometimes *yendo*.

The present participle is invariable:
Está komyendo. Estamos kantando. Estás bevyendo. Vos estásh arepozando. Está durmyendo. Están avlando.

The negative form: *No estó lavorando.* I'm not working (right now).

2. The past participle

Observe: *echarse* ⇨ *echado, asentarse* ⇨ *asentado, ir* ⇨ *ido.*
Para kuálo se kere ido. No tyenes ido.

The past participle of the verb is invariable, always ending in *o,* no matter what the helping verb may be. Ex.: *Perla aviya komido la mansana:* Perla had eaten the apple (pluperfect tense).

If, however, a form derived from a verb is used as an adjective, it must agree in gender and number with the noun it qualifies. For ex.: *Eya está echada, nozotros estamos asentados.*

verbs in *-ar* ⇨ *-ado:*   *kantar* ⇨ *kantado*
verbs in *-er* ⇨ *-ido:*   *komer* ⇨ *komido*
verbs in *-ir* ⇨ *-ido:*   *bivir* ⇨ *bivido.*

(4a

Some past participles are irregular; for ex: *romper* ⇨ *roto* (sometimes *rompido*); *dizir* ⇨ *dicho* (sometimes *dizido*); *azer* ⇨ *echo.*

Note: There are only two compound tenses in Judeo-Spanish, the pluperfect (*yo aviya ido*) and a particular usage of the past tense (*tengo ido*) that will be studied in Lesson 5.

3. Impersonal expressions

Observe: *Se kontan konsejas:* They tell stories *or* Stories are told.
           Se azen nochadas ayá. Se avla de vyajes.
Note that these forms are the equivalent in English to "They + verb" or to a construction in the passive voice.

♦ This impersonal use of *se* + verb is formed in the 3rd person, singular or plural. It agrees with the subject of the verb (note in the first example that the subject may come *after* the verb).
Se aze un tiyatro: They are putting on a play (literally, a play is doing itself).
Se azen nochadas: They hold evening parties (lit., evening parties do themselves).

♦ There are other impersonal expressions in the 3rd person.
Dizen ke es muy interesante: They say (people say) that it is very interesting.
Note that when there is a subject such as *la djente,* the verb is more often in

the plural (the word can be thought of as a collective plural), *la djente dizen,* although the singular is also possible: *la djente dize.*

Vyenen: "They" are coming (without knowing who or what). This form is often used to speak of something feared—the Turks, ghosts *(los shedimes),* etc.

Van a vinir de noche, with no subject expressed, means "the Turks are coming," or "ghosts are coming," depending on the context.

CONJUGATION

1. The verb kerer

Present Ind.	Present Subj.
kero/kyero	**ke kera**/kyera
keres/kyeres	**ke keras**/kyeras
kere/kyere	**kc kcra**/kycra
keremos/kyeremos	**ke keramos**/kyeramos
kerésh/kyerésh	**ke kerásh**/kyerásh
keren/kyeren	**ke keran**/kyeran

El ke kere no puede, el ke puede no kere: He who wants cannot, he who can does not want.

Ke kera o no kera…: Whether he likes it or not…

2. Irregular verbs in the present tense: *sintir, pueder, ir, venir*

Sintir		Pueder	
Indicative	*Subjunctive*	*Indicative*	*Subjunctive*
syento	ke syenta	puedo	ke pueda
syentes	ke syentas	puedes	ke puedas
syente	ke syenta	puede	ke pueda
sintimos/sentimos	ke sintamos*	puedemos*	ke puedamos*
sintísh/sentísh	ke sintásh*	pucdésh*	ke puedásh*
syenten	ke syentan	pueden	ke puedan

ke syentamos and *ke syentásh, podemos* and *ke podamos, podésh* and *ke podásh* are also forms that are used.

Ir	**Venir**/vinir
Present subjunctive	*Present subjunctive*
ke vaya	ke venga
ke vayas	ke vengas
ke vaya	ke venga
ke vayamos	ke vengamos
ke vayásh	ke vengásh
ke vayan	ke vengan

avenirse: to get along, to become reconciled, is conjugated like *venir*.
Me avengo, te avyenes… ⇨ *Ke m'avenga, ke t'avengas…*

EXERCISES

Exercise 1: Rewrite the following sentences using **plazer.**
Ex.: a ti *(no)* los livros ⇨ a ti no te plazen los livros.
1. A él tus amigos. 2. A mozós *(no)* el tiyatro. 3. A ti la televizyón. 4. A vozós avlar kon las vizinas. 5. A mí las kantikas. 6. A mi madre *(no)* las kamaretas chikas. 7. A tu es-huegro tu kaza.

Exercise 2: Answer the following questions by beginning **a mí (no) me plaze…** Ex.: Kómo te plaze meldar? A mí me plaze meldar asentada en la sofá, al lado de la ventana/echada en la kama…
1. Kómo te plaze englenearte? 2. Kómo te plaze arepozarte? 3. Kómo te plaze el banyo? 4. Ké modo de amigos te plazen? 5. Ké lavoros de kaza no te plazen? 6. Ánde te plaze ir? 7. Ánde no te plaze ir? 8. Kuálo te plaze meldar?

Exercise 3: Put in the progressive form.
1. Djuguamos. 2. Tanyen mandolino. 3. Komésh. 4. Se enfasyan. 5. Avlásh muncho. 6. Meldamos los haberes. 7. Miro ahuera. 8. Se arepoza. 9. Te lavas. 10. Durmen. 11. Sintísh la kantika? 12. No lavoro. 13. No se ambezan. 14. Se englenea. 15. Ké azésh?

Exercise 4: **K'estás azyendo?** *(Give complete answers using the verbs below):*
ambezarse – meldar – sintir – bever – komer.

Exercise 5: Translate.
1. My sister is smaller than I. 2. To read a book is better than going to the movies. 3. The water in the kitchen is colder than that of the bathroom. 4. His mother is older than his father.

Exercise 6: Guess what these people are doing.

Ex.: El padre en el mupak: El padre está bushkando una kupa en el mupak.
1. El padre en el mupak. 2. La madre en el salón. 3. La ermanika en su kamareta. 4. La tiya ande la vizina. 5. El tiyo en su magazén. 6. Tu nona kon tu madre. 7. Tu primo en el klub.

Exercise 7: Kuálo keres ke aga? *Answer by using the verbs given or other verbs you know.*

Ex.: vinir ⇨ kero ke vengas.
komer – bivir – durmir – lavorar – meldar la gazeta – barrer la kaza – lavarse – fregar los chinís – djuguar – ambezarse en inglés.

Exercise 8: Translate the following sentences using an impersonal expression.
1. The ghosts are going to come. 2. Turks go to the Turkish bath. 3. They say that you are foolish *(bovo)*. 4. They say a lot of things. 5. At their place, they sing all night long. 6. For *(para)* Roshashaná we write letters *(letras)*. 7. At the club they sing songs. 8. "Good night" is said when one goes to bed. 9. They say that schools are going to open in the summer. 10. Turks drink rakí. 11. At home we watch a lot of television.

Asperando el vapor (Princes' Islands, Istanbul).

Readings

Proverbos i dichas

Kaminando i avlando (Walking and talking).
Meaning: You have to solve your problems as you go along; one day at a time.

Azno batal (batlán), provecho para el vezindado (A lazy donkey, a profit for the neighborhood).
Everyone will take advantage of somebody who is not on his guard.

Desha de komer i no de azer (Stop eating, not doing).
Action, above all else.

En ké se le va al tiyo Moshé el diya? En kitar i sakudir la barva! (How does the day go by for uncle Moshé? In pulling on his beard and shaking it!).
What a waste of time doing useless things!

Ken no tyene de azer, kita los ojos de la mujer (He who has nothing to do takes his wife's eyes out).
He who has nothing to do gets easily into fights with his wife; this is said about people who become picky because they have nothing else to do.

Apanya moshkas (He's catching flies). *Estás paryendo uevos?* (Are you laying eggs?).
This is said of people who have nothing to do, who are taking it easy.

Mijor es poko i bueno ke muncho i negro (Better little and good than a lot and bad).

I no no mas muncho me keda. (And no no, there will be much more left for me).
This is said jokingly to someone who says no to a second helping.

Ay ay ay, ke muncho ay i nada no mos dan. (Ay ay ay, there is so much and they don't give us a thing).
This complaint (said jokingly or seriously) contains a pun with *ay* (there is).

Mas vale prátika ke gramátika! (Practice is worth more than grammar).
It is better to do than to talk.

19 🎵 *En el gazino del Fener*

This song uses as its backdrop the gazino del Fener, *the outdoor café in the Greek quarter neighboring the Jewish quarter of Balat, on the Golden Horn. Jewish families would go there to listen to Turkish-style music. On* noche de alhad, *people would stroll over on foot, planning out prospective marriages or engagements. For the future fiancés, it was a chance to get a look at the other party and to give their approval by a sign to the marriage arrangers.*

En el gazino del Fener
ay luzes de kolores
ansí está mi korasón
kemado de amores

Tres de la noche vo a pasar
kon todos mis amigos
en tu ventana vo a pozar
tanyendo mandolino

Yazidjí me vo azer
yazidjí de la banka
i yo a ti te vo tomar
komo la roza blanka

Por la tu puerta yo pasí
i la topí serrada
la yavedura yo bezí
komo bezar tu kara

Ermoza sos en kantidá
onestedad no tyenes
milyones si me vas a dar
mi djente no te kere.

Glossary

el gazino: outdoor café with music.
Fener (T. lighthouse): a Greek quarter of Istanbul.
las luzes: the lights.   *la banka:* the bank.
yazidjí (T.): clerk, secretary.   *la yavedura:* the doorlock.

Marido i mujer en una guerta (Salonika, 1890).

Merkader djudyó fumando nargilé en un gazino (Istanbul, 19th century).

Tanyedores i bayladoras
(Salonika, 1912)

The wedding dress,
Perlin Ojalvo (Istanbul).

This is one of the most frequently sung wedding songs, especially in Izmir. It is accompanied to the heavy beat of a tambourine and the clapping of hands. The women call to the bride to finish getting herself ready and come down, for a husband does not like to wait.

Ay sinyora novya abashésh abasho *(repeat)*
no puedo no puedo ke m'estó peynando
peynado de novya para el manseviko

Ay sinyora novya, abashéslı abasho *(repeat)*
no puedo no puedo ke m'estó vistyendo
vistido de novya para el manseviko

Ay sinyora novya, abashésh abasho *(repeat)*
no puedo no puedo ke m'estó afeytando
afeytado de novya para el manseviko

Ay sinyora novya abashésh abasho *(repeat)*
k'el ijo del ombre servido kere *(repeat)*.

Glossary

peynarse: to comb one's hair. *el peynado:* the coiffure.
vistirse: to get dressed. *el vistido:* the clothes, dress.
afeytarse: to put on makeup, put on ornaments.
el afeytado: the makeup, ornaments.
servir: to serve.

Notes:

1. We find again the use of the formal "you" with *vos,* in *abashésh,* 2nd person plural of the subjunctive of the verb *abashar,* to go down.
2. The redundancy of *abashar abasho* is a frequently sought after form in Judeo-Spanish, where pleonasms are appreciated for their sonority and their closeness to calques based on the Hebrew of biblical translations.
3. *Servido kere:* must be served. The verb *kerer* used with a past participle (see Lesson 4A) implies obligation. The order here is reversed (we would normally expect *kere servido*) for poetic effect.

Questions: *1. Kuálo está azyendo la novya? 2. Kén la está yamando? 3. Ké está azyendo el novyo? 4. Kuálo kale ke aga la novya?*

The kopla *(generally referred to in the plural,* koplas*) is a literary poetic genre composed by authors whose names are known. The term* las koplas *may be translated as "couplets." These* koplas de Purim, *with 34 stanzas of 9 verses, celebrate the story of Queen Esther, wife of King Ahashverosh, who saved the Jews from the threats of Haman,* Aman arashá, *the traitor, or* el mamzer, *the bastard, enemy of Mordohay (Mordecai), Esther's uncle. This* kopla—*somewhat modified through transmission—is the work of Abraham de Toledo and dates from the first half of the 18th century.*

These koplas *are always sung at Purim, when people drink wine, play dice (los dados de Purim) and lotto, and hold costume parties. Whenever the name of Haman is pronounced, during the reading of the* Megilá de Esther *at the synagogue, people stamp their feet loudly or shake rattles (*takatukas). *People eat* folarikos *(boiled eggs wrapped in strips of dough) and* orejas de Amán, *a kind of fritter. Because the texts have a great deal of dialogue, such* koplas de Purim *are thought to be at the origin of Judeo-Spanish theater.*

Empesar kero a kontar	Bendicho sea el Dyo
echas del Dyo alto	de el alto syelo
De lo ke kero enmentar	porke tan sensya mos dyo
nada yo no falto	para konoserlo,
kon grito i kon salto	en verano e invyerno
i kon gran plazer	lo alavaré
porke Amán el mamzer	tambyén lo bindiziré
mos kijo matarmos	tadre i manyana
tambyén atemarmos, ay.	kon toda mi alma.

Glossary

empesar: to begin.
kontar: to tell, recount.
las echas: the great deeds.
alto: tall, high, great.
enmentar: to mention.
faltar: to fail, omit.
un grito: a cry.
un salto: a leap.
e: and (rather than *i* when the next word begins with an *i*-).

un mamzer (H.): a bastard.
kijo: he wanted (past tense of *kerer*).
matar: to kill.
atemar: to exterminate.
bendicho: blessed (past participle).
la sensya: the knowledge, intelligence.
konoser: to know, be acquainted with.
bindizir: to bless.
el plazer: the pleasure.

Bat-mitsvá (Princes' Islands, Istanbul).

Zaki Matalón in Purim costume
(Syria, 1919).

La barmizvá de Izzet.

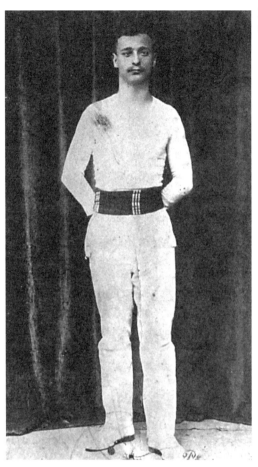

Marko Danon in Maccabee
uniform (Istanbul, 1913).

An old center of *la Makabí*
in Balat (recent photograph).

This marching song is one of the Zionist songs urging the youth of various communities to move to Palestine. This one was sung by the Young Zionists. Zionist organizations were particularly numerous in Bulgaria, but Maccabee clubs existed in all the large cities. This version is sung by Mrs. Gentille Behar of Istanbul.

Adyó mamá yo kale ke te deshe	Vate en buena ora mi kerido
Mi korasón se rompe por partir	El Dyo ke giye sovre ti
Una koza me forsa ke yo me aleshe	Tus ijikos sin pekados
La Palestina liberá	Syempre rogarán por ti
Mira los drohim k'están pasando	Ven rogaremos endjuntos
I no kale mas tadrar	A el Dyo la salvasyón
Las trompetas me están yamando	A ti mi ijo mi kerido
Adiyó keridá mamá	I a toda la nasyón
Ay una memorya en los syelos	Non yores ni penses tú keridá
Ande mos puedemos aunar	El Dyo está kon mozotros keridá
I non puedo mas tadrar	Non yores ni penses tú
Keridá mamá	Keridá mamá

Glossary
deshar: to leave.
partir: to depart.
forsar (F.): to force.
tadrar: to be late.
aunarse: to join, unite.
alesharse: to move at a distance, be separated from.
los drohim (H.): the Young Zionists.
los syelos: the heavens.
giyar sovre: to guide, look after (someone).
pensar: to think, worry.
sin pekados: without sins.
rogar: to pray, ask.
endjuntos (adj.): together.
yorar: to cry (shed tears).

Questions: *1. En la kantika kén avla kon kén? 2. Ánde kere irse el ijo? 3. De ké? 4. A kén yaman los drohim? 5. A kén kale ke deshe el mansevo? 6. Kómo se van a aunar? 7. De ké yora la madre?*

Aliyá (H.) literally means "going up." The contemporary expression *azer su aliyá* means "to go up" to Israel, to emigrate to Israel.

♦ In 1949, Turkey recognized the State of Israel and a significant number of the Jewish community of Turkey emigrated there. This immigration, which had started at the beginning of the century, continued on a sporadic basis. Given the geographic proximity of the two countries and their good relations, trips are taken back and forth between the two very frequently.

Un artíkulo sovre la lingua

In an article in Judeo-Spanish published by the Istanbul newspaper *Şalom*, dated January 15, 1992, Rachel Bortnick called for the creation of a foundation for Judeo-Spanish, as follows. (We have respected the original capitalizations and punctuation and adapted the spelling).

[…] Esto mos traye al sujeto del "vakif" (fondasyón) para el Judeo-Espanyol. Para poder deskutir kon todos los enteresados […], azer estudyos i tomar desizyones ansi ke para dar ayudo materyal i moral a los investigadores, los eskrivanos, poetas i kompozitores en JudeoEspanyol, tenemos menester de una fondasyón sentral […].

Yo kreyo ke este vakif tyene ke ser una organizasyón ENTERNASYONAL, ande los membros de la komité van a ser Sefaradim ke la konosen i tyenen amor por la lingua, i tambyén tyenen la kapachitá i eksperyensya menesteroza. Esta manera de personas ya están lavorando i azyendo lo ke pueden para avansar i enrejistrar la lingua i la kultura judeo-espanyola (adelantre de todos Sr Moshe Shaul de Israel i el profesor Haim Vidal Sephiha en Fransya) ma kada uno i uno está izolado en su lavoro, deve de publikar kon las posibilitades ke tyene personalamente i en el lokal ande bive.

La djente de una parte del mundo puede ser ke no tyenen haber de lo ke se está eskrivyendo o publikando en otras partes. Una fondasyón mondyal va tener la fuersa menesteroza para pueder fomentar la kultura sefaradí i la lingua judeo-espanyola i asuguraremos ke esta erensya ermoza i presyoza va kedar biva, i va enrikeser la vida de las jenerasyones venideras.

Glossary

trayer: to bring.

vakif (T): foundation.

deskutir: to discuss.

ansí ke para …: as well as.

ayudo: help, aid.

sentral: central.

los Sefaradim (H): the Sephardim.

kedar: to stay, remain.

bivo, a: alive, living.

la kapachitá (I.): the ability.

tener haber de: to have news of.

la fuersa: the strength.

asugurar/asegurar: to assure.

la erensya: the heritage.

ermoza: beautiful.

presyoza: precious.

konoser: to know.

enrikeser: to enrich.

Notes:

1. One finds fluctuating forms for a number of verbs; *poder,* for example, alternates with *pueder.* As a result of the increased circulation of texts and movement of people, regional variations can be found in the same speech by the same person.

2. There has been a great deal of French influence, especially for abstract terms and modern concepts. They have been phonetically integrated into Judeo-Spanish: *mondyal, organizasyón, fondasyón, los membros, la komité* (feminine because of the final *e*), *la kultura, enrejistrar, izolado, lokal, enternasyonal,* etc.

3. In 1997 the *Otoridad Nasyonala para el Ladino* (national authority for Judeo-Spanish) was created in Israel with the goal of preserving Judeo-Spanish culture and language, under the presidency of Itzhak Navon (former President of the State of Israel) and Moshe Shaul (Director of the journal *Aki Yerushalayim*). Rachel Bortnick subsequently founded an internet web site for exchanges in Judeo-Spanish, Ladinokomunitá (see *Bibliography* for address).

Questions: *1. Porké kale ke ayga una fondasyón para el djudeo-espanyol? 2. A kén kale ke ayude? 3. Kómo? 4. Ké están azyendo los investigadores? 5. De ké todos no tyenen haber de lo ke se aze para la lingua? 6. Ánde biven los Sefaradim ke avlan djudeo-espanyol?*

GRAMMAR

1. The conjunction "*i*"

Note the abundance of times the conjunction *i* is used in this text (with the simple sense of "and"). As in Hebrew, the conjunction is always expressed.

117

2. *Puede ser ke…*

Puede ser ke + indicative = maybe, perhaps…
Puede ser ke no tyenen haber: maybe they don't have any news.
An imagined idea that is considered a possibility is expressed with the indicative form of the verb. *Puede ser ke topas kon ken avlar:* Maybe you will find somebody with whom to talk.

3. Suffixes

♦ Note that *presyo* (price) becomes the basis for *presyozo, presyoza* (*precious,* but also *pretty*). The suffix *-ozo, -oza* can thus tranform a noun or verb into an adjective. The meaning of such words can have an active or passive value (sometimes both), as in these examples:

—*Temer:* to be afraid, serves as the basis for *temerozo* which has the sense of "frightening," as in *el Dyo el grande el temerozo… Espantar:* to frighten, gives *espantozo* which has the meaning of "frightened, afraid." (However, one also finds rare cases where *espantozo* means "frightening").

—*Menester* (need) gives *menesterozo, -oza,* an adjective meaning "necessary" or a noun meaning "a needy person."

♦ Note the expression: *Los diyas venideros:* days to come, days that will come. The verbal suffix *-dero, -dera,* transforms the verb into a verbal adjective with the sense of "to + infinitive" or "that will" + verb).
*Palavra dize**dera,*** when you are explaining something or want to correct yourself, means "I mean…"
Caution, however: This suffix cannot be applied to all verbs. For other meanings of the *-dero* suffix see Lesson 2A.

4. Expressing obligation (continuation)

Observe: *este vakif tyene ke ser una organizasyón…*
          (kada uno i uno) deve de publikar.
Tener ke + infinitive = to have to, must + infinitive.
Dever de + infinitive = ought to, should + infinitive.

The first expresses a general sense of obligation while the second is less categorical and expresses a wish rather than a law.

Conjugation

Trayer and *kreyer*

The verb *trayer/traer* (to bring, carry) is irregular. The verb *kreyer* (to believe) has two forms. One is regular: *kreyo, kreyes…* which gives the subjunctive *ke kreya, ke kreyas…* The other is irregular, as shown below:

Trayer		Kreyer	
Pres. Ind.	*Pres. Subj.*	*Pres. Ind.*	*Pres. Subj.*
traygo	**ke trayga**	**kreygo**/kreyo	**ke kreyga**/kreya
trayes	ke traygas	kreyes	ke kreygas
traye	ke trayga	kreye	ke kreyga
trayemos	ke traygamos	kreyemos	ke kreygamos
trayésh	ke traygásh	kreyésh	ke kreygásh
trayen	ke traygan	kreyen	ke kreygan

Vocabulary

Here are a few more names for professions:
un eskrivano: a writer.
un investigador: a researcher.
un poeta (masc.): a poet.
un kompozitor: a composer.

Kómo mos engleneávamos en chika

Madam Sará: "Djuguávamos en la kaye, bilyas, futbol, koches, diávolo… kuedra saltávamos… djuguávamos al kosheziko kon pyedrizika, ke es *la marelle* [F. hopscotch]. En kaza noche de alhades se arekojiyan todos en kaza de uno i djuguavan tombolá, findjanes… Se tomavan findjanes i los aboltavan, debasho de uno metiyan un kimuriko. Aboltavan los findjanes, unos duspués de otros. Si topávamos el kimuriko ganávamos dyez groshes, sinko groshes, lo ke era…"

Madam Bekí: "Ande mozós se metiya un *gage* [F. wager], por egzempyo ken lo topó, va gritar komo azno o komo perro… Koza de riyir."

Mrs. Sará Elmaz and Mrs. Bekí Bardavid.

Glossary

las bilyas: marbles.

los koches (T.): jacks (game)

el diávolo (I.): diabolo (game).

la kuedra: the cord, jump-rope.

saltar: to jump, leap.

kosho: lame, crippled.

el kosheziko: hopscotch.

la pyedra: the stone, pebble

el findján (T.): the cup.

aboltar: to turn around.

topar: to find.

un kimuriko (T.): a little piece of coal.

arekojerse: to gather.

ganar: to earn, win.

un grosh (T.): a penny, a coin.

gritar: to shout, cry.

Questions: *1. Kómo se djugua a los findjanes? 2. Porké se djugua noche de alhad? 3. Kómo se djugua al kosheziko?*

Notes:

—This text is recounted in the imperfect tense, to be studied in Lesson 6.

—The game of *tombolá* is a Bingo type of game (see Lesson 5B).

COMMUNICATION SKILLS

♦ *Djuguar* is often expressed with no article before the noun; *djuguar kartas:* to play cards; *djuguar koches, djuguar tombolá:* to play at jacks, lotto.

♦ *Lo ke es:* what there is, whatever is there. This is an expression of an uncertainty in the context.

♦ *Koza de* + infinitive means "something to …" *Koza de riyir:* something to make you laugh. *Koza de tresalir:* something that makes you laugh, makes you happy and enthusiastic.

Ires i vinires

OBJECTIVES

Communication skills: Expressing time, telling time, figuring prices, selling and buying, measuring quantities, finding one's way, need and obligation (continued).

Vocabulary: Numbers (continued), means of transportation, verbs of motion, expressing location (continued).

Conjugation: The present subjunctive of the verbs *aver, ser;* the verb *kuzir.*

Culture: Customs relating to birth, amusements for *noche de Alhad.*

---

23 🎧 *Echos buenos!*

Etí:	Babá, amanyana de la demanyana kale ke vaygamos a merkar hasé. Se keren kamizikas para la fashadura de Rozi, ke ya entró en el setén[13] mez. Fin a Roshashaná va a parir parese.
David:	Kale alevantar tempran, a las syete, syete i medya si kerésh estar en la kaza de Rozi a la una de la tadre. Es muncho kamino.
El padre:	Kale merkar en el charshí, ande mösyö Brudo.
Etí:	Ay hasé ande mösyö Brudo?
El padre:	Sí, kómo no?! Kale ke ayga, siguro! Vo lo va a dar a buen presyo. Ma kale tratar un poko para ke lo abashe. A syen i sesenta el piko kale ke vo lo deshe. A la meatá!
Selén:	Agora no kedó pikos, babá, se merka kon metro!
El padre:	Sí, hanum, pikos en ginnam!
Efí:	Ánde se topa su butika?
El padre:	A la salida de la kaleja grande, a la derecha duspués de los djoyeros. Butika grande de manifatura i teshidos. Tyene muncha ropa.
Eti:	Kómo vamos a ir fin ayá?
David:	Kale abashar fin al kyuprí kon el otobüs dodje, duspués pasar enfrente en kaminando i tomar el dolmush o el tranvay. Ma kon arabá se va mas presto.

---

13. The speaker on the accompanying CD says *treser* but the celebration does not actually take place until the seventh month.

El padre:	Siguro! Del kyuprí al charshí kon arabá es dyez puntos lo ke surea. Ma el dodje kale asperarlo muncho, pasa kada ora, a las ocho manko un kuarto, a las mueve manko un kuarto … ansina.
Etí:	Oh, oh! Ich no tenemos suvido al dodje. Por ánde pasa?
David:	A la punta de la kaleja, en la kyöshé, vash a tomar a la isyedra i asuvir un pokitiko.
Etí:	Atyó! Mos vamos a pyedrer por las kayes!
El padre:	Bovas sosh?! Si estásh pyedridas, me avrísh el telefón en el magazén de Menahem, tengo de ir ayá a la medyodiya, tenemos kuentos de mirar. Puedemos komer endjuntos si eskapásh de merkar antes de midí.
David (a Selén):	Kon dolmúsh es karo ma es mas kolay, kon otobüs es mas barato… Muncho muncho mil liras…
Selén:	… I kaminando es de baldes! A mí me plaze kon vapor…
David:	Kon vapor es a las adás!

GLOSSARY

Words of Spanish origin

la fashadura: the layette, baby's trousseau.

entrar en el setén mez: to go into the 7th month of pregnancy.

tratar: to bargain.

el teshido: the cloth, textile goods.

la ropa: the merchandise.

avrir el telefón: to telephone, pick up the receiver (T. syntax).

Other origins

babá (T.): papa, dad.

el hasé (T.): cotton goods.

Roshashaná (H.): New Year.

el charshí (T.): the bazaar, covered market.

el dolmúsh (T.): the group taxi, "jitney."

mösyö/musyú (F.): monsieur, mister.

hanum: dear, sweetie (in T. Madam).

la kyöshé/la kyushé (T.): street corner.

la manifatura (I.): clothing shop.

kolay (T.): easy.

midí (F.): noon.

la arabá (T.): the car.

surear (T.): to last.

ich (T.): not at all.

el magazén (F.): general store.

el kyuprí (T.) the bridge.

las adás (T.): the islands.

el vapor (T.): the steamship.

Note: *vos lo* becomes *vo lo,* with the -*s* dropped. Similarly, *mos lo* ⇨ *mo lo* (see Lesson 7A).

Communication skills

1. Expressing time, telling time

Various time expressions

Reminder: *oy, amanyana, ayer, agora, la manyana, la tadre, la noche, los mezes del anyo, los diyas de la semana.*

Observe: *Amanyana de la demanyana. Se va mas presto.*
Tadra muncho. Fin a Roshashaná.

—*tadre:* late ≠ *temprano/demprano:* early.
—*en de diya:* by day ≠ *en de noche:* by night.
—*amanyana de la demanyana:* tomorrow morning.
—*demanyana matrana:* bright and early in the morning (Lesson 2A).

—*para midí; antes de midí; duspués de midí.*
—*a(l) medyodiya/a (la) midí:* at noon.
—*a (la) medyanoche:* at midnight.
—*martes a la tadre:* on Tuesday evening.
—*fin a las sesh de la tadre:* until six o'clock in the evening.
—*martes a la noche: duspués de las sesh.*

—*ya:* already.
—*endagora:* now, just now, a minute ago.
—*desde … fin a… :* from … until… (in Salonika, *fasta* is used rather than *fin a*).

—*de agora adelantre:* from now on.
—*tadrar:* to be late (in doing something).
—*kedar tadre:* to be late (for an appointment).
—*se va mas presto:* one can go faster.

Telling time

	1:00 p.m.	*(la) una duspués de medyodiya.*
	2:00 p.m.	*(las) dos duspués de medyodiya.*
	6:00 p.m.	*(las) sesh de la tadre.*
	7:00 p.m.	*(las) syete de la tadre.*
	1:00 a.m.	*(la) una de la noche/manyana.*
	2:00 a.m.	*(las) dos de la noche/manyana.*

una ora: an hour (also: a watch, clock).

un punto: a minute.

la ora djusta: the exact hour, the exact time.

sesh i medya (de la tadre): half past six (in the evening).

una i un kuarto: a quarter past one.

dos manko un kuarto: a quarter to two.

tres manko un punto: a minute before three.

dos i sinko: two-O-five (2:05).

—*ké oras son?/ké ora está?/ké ora tyenes?*

—*(las) dos i medya/está dos i medya.*

—*ya se izo dos:* it's already two o'clock.

—*a las dos:* at two o'clock.

—*va por las dos:* it's going on (almost) two o'clock.

Note: *un punto* (a minute) is frequently used in time expressions. *Aspera un puntiko:* wait a bit, wait a minute. Precision time-telling rarely goes as far as the seconds *(un segondo).*

2. Figuring prices, selling and buying

Vender i merkar: to sell and buy.

Pagar (in general), *pechar* (for a tax): to pay.

Tratar: to bargain.

Kuánto kosta? (from the verb *kostar*): how much does it cost?

A kuánto está? How much does it go for?

♦ Prices are figured in *liras* (Turkish pounds), *frankos* (francs), *markas* (marks), *euros* (Euros), *dolares* (dollars)—in short, in local or foreign money with His-panicized names. *El grosh* (the kouroush or the piastre), a division of the Turkish pound which is no longer current, means "a penny"—that is, something not worth very much. *Mirar el grosh* (watch the penny) means to be prudent in spending.

Es muncha pará: that's a lot of money.   *Es karo:* it's expensive.

Es barato: it's cheap.   *Es de baldes:* it's free, it's a steal.

Es un buen presyo: it's a good price. *Dar a buen presyo:* to offer at a good price.

Abashar el presyo: lower the price.   *Pujar:* to increase.

La vida puja muncho: the cost of living is going up a lot.

♦ *Estar a…* (+ the price): to be worth, to be at (such and such) a price.

Agora el dolar está a syen i sikuenta: the dollar's at a hundred fifty now.

♦ *Tener poder* does not mean "to have power" but "to have money."
El marido no puede: Her husband does not have enough money.

♦ *Muncho muncho (mil liras),* literally "much much (a thousand liras)":
at the most (a thousand liras).

la pará: money (in the abstract sense). Other words are also used for money:
el dinero, la plata, la moneda, las parás.
tyene muncha pará: es riko, rikinyón.
no tyene muncha pará: es prove.
ich no tyene pará: es prove aní (here is a case of repeating the same term but
in a non-Spanish language source, to intensify the meaning: *prove* (S.) + *aní*
(H.): poor poor = very poor.

♦ *Echos buenos!:* Have a good business day! This is a blessing one gives to the
merchant upon leaving his shop.
Rikos i dovletlís!: Rich and well-to-do/powerful! This is to wish someone
prosperity.

3. Measuring quantities

el pezo

Observe: *La **meatá.***
        *No es kon **pikos,** es kon **metros.***

manko: minus, less.
tres kuartos: three quarters.
muncho: a lot, a great deal.
poko: a small amount.
pezar: to weigh.
el pezo: the weight, scale.

mas: plus, more.
la meatá: half.
muy muncho: a very great deal.
un pokitiko: just a little bit.
mezurar: to measure.
kaji/kaje: almost

Note: *el piko* is an old measure for length and *la oka* an old measure for weight.
Like *el dukado,* which was an old gold coin, these words can only be found in
older texts, songs, proverbs and expressions.

Examples:
(Echar) pikos en ginnam (to measure Hell) means to work for no good reason,
something that makes no sense doing.
Ijo dukado vyejo: A son (is an) old gold ducat—that is, a very precious thing
to have.

These old measures have been replaced by:

El metro: the meter.

El kilo/los gramos (infrequently used). People mainly use *kilo* and *medyo kilo* (half a kilo—that is, 1.1 U.S. pounds).

El litro: the liter.

♦ For eggs, thirteen to the dozen *(una dozena)* is expressed as *una duzenika franka:* a European dozen.

♦ Often the container serves as a measuring device (in recipes).

una redoma de vino: a bottle of wine.

una kupa de agua: a glass of water.

una kucharada de…: a spoonful of…

un findján de…: a cup of…

4. Finding one's way, asking for directions, getting around town

Observe: *En la kyöshé. Asuvir un poko. A la isyedra. A la punta de la kaleja. Por ánde pasa? Abashar. Del kyuprí fin al charshí. Es muncho kamino. Pasar (de) enfrente. Pyedrerse/peryerse. Ánde está…? Ánde se topa…?*

mi	el	la
kaza	kuaför	kavané

La kaleja de los barkeros

el	la	la kaza
kal	skola	de Matí

la guerta

*Mi kaza está **enfrente del** kal i **al lado del** kuaför.*

*Mi kaza está **en** la kaleja de los barkeros.*

*La guerta está **detrás del** kal.*

*El kal está **delantre de** la guerta.*

*El kuaför está **entre** mi kaza i la kavané.*

*La kavané está **al lado del** kuaför, **enfrente de** la kaza de Matí i **en la sirá*** (the row) *de mi kaza.*

*Mi kaza i el kal están **en la kyushé de*** (at the corner of) *la kaleja.*

*Mi kaza i el kal están **a la punta de*** (at the end of) *la kaleja.*

*Kuando estás **delantre del** kuaför, mi kaza está **a la syedra del** kuaför i la kavané **a la derecha** (del kuaför). El kuaför está **en medyo*** (in the middle).

♦ Means of locomotion.

En la sivdad se puede kaminar a pye/ir kaminando. Se puede ir kon arabá/otomobil (kon dolmúsh o kon taksí o kon otobüs). Se puede ir kon vapor o kon barka/kayik para pasar la mar o el riyo.

Conjugation
1. Irregular subjunctives

Ser
ke sea/seya
ke seas/seyas
ke sea/seya
ke seamos/seyamos
ke seásh/seyásh
ke sean/seyan

Aver
ke ayga, ke aya (3rd person sing.)
ke aygan, ke ayan (3rd person plur.)

Note: "to have" in the sense of "to possess" is expressed by *tener* in Judeo-Spanish. *Aver* is used to express "there is, there are."

2. Kuzir (to sew), Pezar (to weigh)

Pres. Ind.		*Pres. Subj.*	*Pres. Ind.*		*Pres. Subj.*
kuzgo	⇨	**ke kuzga***	**pezgo**	⇨	**ke pezge***
kuzes		ke kuzgas	pezas		ke pezges
kuze		ke kuzga	peza		ke pezge
kuzimos		ke kuzgamos	pezamos		ke pezgemos
kuzísh		ke kuzgásh	pezásh		ke pezgésh
kuzen		ke kuzgan	pezan		ke pezgen

*The first person singular *(kuzgo, pezgo)*, after dropping the final -o, gives the root for the subjunctive forms.

Present participle:	kuzyendo	pezando
Past participle:	kuzido	pezado

Note: Do not confuse *pezar* (to weigh) with *pezgar* (to be "heavy" in the sense of being a nuisance), used for both people and events.

Vocabulary
Numbers (final section):

30 – trenta.	200 – dosyentos(as).
40 – kuarenta.	300 – trezyentos(as).
50 – sikuenta.	400 – kuatrosyentos(as).
60 – sesenta.	500 – kinyentos(as).
70 – setenta.	600 – sheshentos(as).
80 – ochenta.	700 – setesyentos(as).
90 – noventa.	800 – ochosyentos(as).
100 – syen (invariable).	900 – muevesyentos(as) at beginning of number.
1,000 – mil (invariable).	900 – novesyentos(as) in middle of number.

2,000 – dos mil.	100, 000 – syen mil.
3,000 – tres mil.	200,000 – dozyentos(as) mil.
10,000 – dyez mil.	300,000 – trezyentos(as) mil.
20,000 – vente mil.	400,000 – kuatroshentos(as) mil.
	500,000 – kinyentos(as) mil.
1,000,000 – un milyón.	600,000 – sheshentos(as) mil.

Note: For dates, the masculine form is used.
1998: *mil novesyentos noventa i ocho.*

For an indefinite quantity, people jokingly say *haloshento, a, os, as.*
Bivyó haloshentos anyos: He lived for a bunch of years.

Culture

1. La fashadura

Kuando una mujer está prenyada, unos mezes antes de parir, konbida a sus amigas i a las mujeres de su famiya para kortar fashadura, kijo dizir aprontar las kamizikas, las fashas, los kuleros (esetra …), ke va a vistir el chikitiko.

Por esto se merka hasé. Kale tener padre i madre en vida para merkar i para "echar tijera": kijo dizir empesar a kortar la primera kamizika. En la ropa se echa asukuar i konfites para ke la vida de la kriyatura seya dulse.

Se kuze la kamizika muy larga para ke seya su vida larga. Esta primera kamizika se viste en el primer diya, o en la vijola para las ijas o el berit para los ijos.

Agora se topa todo pronto en las butikas ma se yama dainda a fashadura i se kuze la primera kamiza kon las bendisyones.

Glossary

la prenyada: the pregnant woman.
aprontar: to prepare.
la kamizika: the baby shirt.
la fasha: the newborn's blanket.
el kulero: the diaper.
la vijola: ceremony where the rabbi bestows a name on a baby girl.
el berit or *la brit milá:* the circumcision ceremony.

kijo dizir: that is to say…
los konfites: the candy.
se kuze: they sew.
pronto: ready.
la tijera: the scissors.

Many customs relate to pregnancies and births. If a woman loses a child at birth, she will borrow little clothes from her neighbors who have children in good health. This is probably the origin of the proverb: *ken se viste de sedaká bive munchos anyos* (he who is dressed through charity lives for many years).

If there has been a death in the family before the birth, parents sell the child symbolically to a female relative or friend. The child will then not be called by its name but by Merkado (bought), or its substitute Marko, or in the case of a girl, Merkada. Every year the "godmother" will take care to give the child a present, and when he or she gets married, she will stand in place of the mother.

A child traditionally bears the first name of the paternal grandfather or grandmother; later children take the name of the maternal grandparents. For this reason cousins often have the same name.

2. La tombolá

5a

On *noche de alhad,* Saturday evenings, after Shabbat, families, friends and neighbors used to get together in lively fashion for social activities, the most popular of which were *los findjanikos* (Lesson 4B) and *la tombolá. La tombolá* is a bingo-type game where the main attraction is the person who is the most *sangrudo* (full-blooded, lively, funny) shouting out the numbers, along with jokes and humorous comments of all sorts.

♦ Some of the numbers might be announced in Italian, so for example number one would be:
1 *"Primo... Primo ladrón de Konstantinópoli!"*

♦ Certain of the calls relate to the shape of the written number:
8 – *Ocho, dos biskochikos* (two little round pastries).
22 – *Vintidós, dos palazikas chikas* (two little ducks).
71 – *Setenta i uno, la baltá i el klavo* (the axe and the nail).
88 – *Ochenta i ocho, dos tinajikas de bonbón sin kulo ni tapón* (two little candy jars with no bottom or top).

♦ Others are based on puns involving another language:
14 – *Katorze* could be pronounced like the Greek word *katúrise* ("he peed on himself").

♦ Still others on alliterations:

44 – *Kuarenta i kuatro, karakaká buraká, el pyojo en la yaká, si lo ves al saká burakalde la kirbá.* This does not make much sense; word by word it translates as: *karakaká,* make a hole, a flea in his collar, if you see the water carrier, make a hole in his animal-skin water-jar. In fact, the only significant thing here is the special sound effect of repeating the *k* sound.

♦ Some of the calls refer to the use of certain numbers in particular trades or in the religious sphere:

10 – *Minyán,* Hebrew for the assembly of the ten devout men necessary to hold a service.

♦ Others, finally, consist on verbal revenge against the "Other," particularly the Orthodox Greeks who were considered as the principal parties responsible for the ritual murder slander against the Jews.

33 – *Trenta i tres, isa isa le disheron lo forkaron en Purim.* Thirty-three, Jesus, Jesus, they told him, they hanged him on Purim. *Isa* is Jesus in Turkish, thirty-three is the age of his death and he is here assimilated to Haman the traitor, enemy of the Jews, who was hanged on Purim.

Hebrew, Turkish, Greek, French and Italian all come into play for double-entendre jokes, often very coarse beneath their apparently innocent surface.

Exercises

Exercise 1: Answer the following questions.

1. Ké ora está 2. Kuánto tyempo toma para ir a tu kaza? 3. Kuándo vas a lavorar? 4. A ké ora te alevantas? 5. Kómo vas a lavorar? 6. Kuánto kosta un pan? 7. A kuánto está una arabá mueva? 8. Kuánto peza un litro de agua?

Exercise 2: Read the times aloud, and then write them out using letters. Specify the time of day.

Ex: 6:15 p.m. *Las sesh i un kuarto de la tadre.*

a) 8:45 a.m.   b) 12:15 p.m.   c) 12:45 a.m.   d) 1:35 p.m.

e) 10:00 p.m.   f) 8:08 p.m.   g) 12:00 a.m.   h) 10:30 a.m.

i) 12:00 p.m.   j) 7:25 p.m.

Exercise 3: Here is the answer; what is the question?

1. Kuarenta mil liras. 2. Kuatro pikos i medyo. 3. Una i un kuarto. 4. A sinko mil liras el gramo. 5. Tres kilos. 6. Ay dos kilos. 7. Una kucharada. 8. Kon vapor. 9. A las sesh manko un kuarto. 10. Se keren syete de eyas.

Exercise 4: Describe the relationship between each of the objects in the drawing below.

Erercise 5: Write the following numbers using letters and say them aloud:

Ex: 1,356 liras = Mil (i) trezyentas (i) sikuenta i sesh liras.

a) 200,000 frankos.   b) 7,548 markas. c) 2,350,674 liras.

d) 6,389 dolares. e) 537,925 pesetas.   f) 365,293 dukados.

Exercise 6: Translate into Judeo-Spanish.

1. I'm going to the bazaar to buy two meters of cloth to make a skirt.
2. He has to [use the impersonal construction] find a watch shop.
3. "How much does that cost?"
"Two hundred francs a meter."
" That's expensive!"
4. "How much does that weigh?"
"Two and a half kilos."
"I want half of it."
5. This meat is cheap but it's not good.
6. This one is better but it costs twenty pounds more.
7. Two thousand five hundred marks? It's a steal!

Exercise 7: Look at the drawing, then answer the questions below by describing the relationships between the places mentioned.

A. Dízeme kómo vo a ir.

1. del kal al banyo.
2. del banyo a la meshkita.
3. de la kaza de Hamdi Bey a la guerta del gazino.
4. de ande Madam Sará al orno.
5. de la skala del vapor a la guerta del gazino.

B. Ánde está…

1. el banyo?
2. el Bet Din?
3. el balukchí?
4. el orno?
5. la kaza del Rav Shimón?
6. la kavané?

An old city map of Balat.

5a

Pidyón, the purchase of the first-born (Istanbul).

Fyesta de fashadura
de E. Mizrahi
(Istanbul).

133

El balukchí djudyó de Kuledibí (Istanbul) *vende masá para Pesah.*

M. Asaz, merkader, delantre de su butika (Çanakkale, Turkiya).

Place de la République (Salonika, ca. 1910), the Matarasso-Saragoussi-Rousso store.

Bushkando pará para merkar guevos (Istanbul).

READINGS

PROVERBOS I DICHAS

Relating to births:

Desde la fasha fin a la mortaja
(From baby blanket to the shroud).
Meaning: People always stay the same, they never change.

El padre (or *la madre*) *en fashas*
(Father or mother in baby wrap).
This is said of a child who looks a lot like its father (or mother).

La ija en la fasha, el ashuguar en la kasha
(Daughter in a baby wrap, her trousseau in the chest).
As soon as a daughter is born, parents have to start thinking of her marriage and the dowry.

Relating to business:

Abasha un eskalón toma mujer, asuve un eskalón toma haver
(You go down a step to take a wife, you go up a step to take a partner).
Men should take a wife a step below them (respect of the wife for the husband) and take a business partner a step above (for his business experience).

There are a thousand different expressions relating to poverty. We have already seen *prove aní. Aniyero ugursuz* (H.+S.+T.), literally poverty-ridden and unlucky. *Aniyut kon kola* (H.+S.): "poverty with a tail."

El Dyo ke te lo dé kon su demaziya
(May God give it to you with his surplus).
A blessing: may heaven grant you excessive gifts.

Si el emprestar era bueno, emprestava el rey a su mujer
(If lending were a good thing, the king would lend to his wife).

Djohá ke merka a dos i vende a uno
(Djohá who buys at two and sells for one)—said of someone who does not know how to do business.

Tadró tadró, arekavdó
(He waited, waited, reaped).
He who waits will win the deal.

Ken fuye de un komercho paga dos
(He who runs away from paying a tax will pay two).
Trying to avoid paying an expense may prove to be more costly than the expense itself.

Kén te emprovesyó? Lo barato
(What made you poor? The cheap things).
The same idea can be found in *Lo barato es karo i lo karo es barato* (What is cheap is expensive and what is expensive is cheap). What is cheap is generally of poor quality; it is cheaper in the long run to invest in good quality.

(El) ijo ande el rubí i (el) marido en el charshí
(The son at the teacher's and the husband at the bazaar).
The son studies the Law and the husband tends to the store. This is an expression relating to social success; a mother's happiness consists of having a devout and learned son and a husband whose business prospers.

El mal entra a kintales i sale a metikales.
Evil arrives by the ton and departs by the ounce.

Relating to passing time:

Pasar por el kyuprí de los anyos
(To pass over the bridge of the years): to grow old.

Pasó tyempo vino tyempo
(Time came and went): time went by. This expression appears frequently in stories (see *Delgadiya,* Lesson 6B).

El tyempo no tyene ni empesijo ni fin
(Time has neither beginning nor end).

A la ora orada.
(At the last possible hour): *in extremis.*

Todas las oras no son unas
(All hours are not alike). Sometimes we laugh, sometimes we cry.

24 🔊 *Konsejika del merkader de teshidos*

Una eshenika de tiyatro. Ambézatela i djúguala kon un(a) amigo(a).

Aviya un merkader en el charshí. Vino una balabaya kon su ijiko al lado. Le demandó el merkader:
"Kuálo dezeya?"
Disho: "Sikuenta pikos de hasé."
"Bashustuné madam!"
Tomó la mezura en la mano i empesó a kontar: "Uno, dos…" *i a demandar:*
"Pardon, madam, ke me ekskuze, amá ijos tyene?"
"Sí, tengo sinko, sinko ijos."
"Sinko! Mashallá, ke le bivan!… sesh, syete, i, éste? Kuántos anyos tyene este chikitiko?"
"Ya tyene mueve anyos, kaji dyez… "
"Dyez! Mashallá, ke le biva!… onze, dodje, tredje, eee… i ke sinko ijos tyene, i el mas grande, ya deve de ser…"
"Es manseviko, tyene dizisyete anyos…"
"Mashallá!… diziocho, dizimueve… Ma eya es manseva, ké edad se kazó?"
"Yo me kazí de ventitrés anyos."
"Muy bueno! Ventitrés!… ventikuatro, ventisinko… I su marido, ké edad tyene?"
"Mi marido tyene ya kuarenta i un anyo."
"Ke no le manke nunkua! Kuarentiún anyo, ké famiya! … kuarentidos, kuarentitrés…
Eya ke se va a kaza, en luguar de sikuenta pikos topa ventidós!

From a *konseja* of Mr. Izak Arditi.

5b

Note: *un, ventiún, kuarentiún any**o*** (singular).

Glossary
la balabaya (H.): the lady of the house.
bashustuné (T. "on my head"): right away, at your orders.
mashallá (T.): thank God.
ke no le manke nunkua: cf. "bless his soul!" (a blessing said after a husband is mentioned by his wife).

Questions: *1. Kuálo vende el merkader? 2. De ké le demanda munchas demandas? 3. En lo ke le responde kuálo es emportante? 4. La mujer entendyó kuálo afitó?*

This passage is an excerpt from the book by Marcel Cohen, written in the form of an open letter addressed to the Spanish painter Antonio Saura. Marcel Cohen evokes here the Judeo-Spanish world of his childhood. (Note that the spelling is somewhat different from the one adopted for this book.)

Y ahora te avlare de Stambol ke, de memorya, konosko yo. [...]

Momentos: un jamal, kon un almaryo en las espaldas, kamina agile agile en una kalegika cerka de Yeni djami,[14] gritando: "Dour, dour." Una madam s'espanta de traversar la kaye tanto grande es el embatako. En Pera, dos vieji-zikas ke se van a pasear miran al cyelo para saver si se van a tomar el chadir. Un empiegado, o un merkader, arrapado de fresko, se aravyo kontra el chofeur del dolmouch porke no le kyere pagar tanto paras.

Marcel Cohen, *Lettre à Antonio Saura*, bilingual edition.
Paris: L'Echoppe, 1997, p. 60.

Glossary

ahora [agora]: now.
avlare [avlaré]: I will speak
jamal [hammal] (T.): porter.
agile [adjile] (T.): quickly.
dour [dur] (T.): stop.
el chadir [tchadir] (T.): the umbrella.
el embatako (T.): the mud, rut.
Pera: a European quarter of Istanbul.
ar(r)apado: shaven.

El kyuprí de Galatá, de antes, kon la Kulá, en Stambol.

---

14. *Yeni Djami* (the "New Mosque") is in the old city, at the end of the Galata Bridge.

Kantika de las oras

Here is another example of koplas (see Lesson 4B), a "song of the hours" that begins with an introductory couplet and ends with the announcement that the assembled rabbis have reached a judgment. The contents of these koplas differ from one version to another but they all follow the twelve hours of the day.

En la mar baten las olas
las muchachas durmen solas
si kerésh saver mi dama
la kantika de las oras

alta alta va la luna
kuando durme la kriyatura
si kerésh saver mi dama
la ora ya va por una

de kantar no me kedó boz
el tyempo va por lodós
si kerésh saver mi dama
la ora ya va por las dos

de kantar no me kedó ses
el tyempo aboltó karayel
si kerésh saver mi dama
la ora ya va por las tres

a mí me agrada garato
kuando está el vino barato
si kerésh saver mi dama
la ora va por las kuatro

en Balat ya venden sisko
ya lo pezan kon peziko
si kerésh saver mi dama
la ora ya va por sinko […]

Glossary

la ola: the wave.
la boz and *ses* [T.]: the voice.
lodós and *karayel* are the names of winds that blow over Istanbul.
aboltar: to turn.
me agrada: I like.
el garato: a salted, sliced Mediterranean fish, highly prized.
a mí me agrada garato = a mí me plaze garato (see Lesson 4A).
Balat was one of the main Jewish quarters of Istanbul.
el sisko: the coal dust.
pezar: to weigh.
pezo: weight, scale.

Reminder: *la ora va por las kuatro,* it's going on (almost) four o'clock.

Una demanda de matematika

Aldina Quintana has studied the vocabulary of arithmetic manuals used in Judeo-Spanish schools (before the founding of schools by the Alliance Israélite Universelle) where religion was taught but also mathematics, such as this paragraph on the "rule of three reversed." (The original texts are in Rashi characters and have been transcribed here using our spelling norms.)

Regla de tres arevés

Para apartar i konoser dela regla de tres derecha a la regla de tres arevés kale saver ke si las kuentas ke tenemos para azer kuento sean de un modo ke si se muchigua la kuantitá de la kuenta primera se muchigua mas la kuantitá de la kuenta sigunda, esta es regla de tres derecha. Ma si las kuentas ke tenemos son en un modo ke kuando se muchigua la kuantitá de la kuenta primera se enchikese mas la kuantitá de la kuenta sigunda, akeya es regla de tres a revés.

Por enshemplo ke la demanda es 12 (dodje) maestros ke fraguaron una kaza en 25 (ventisinko) diyas, si son 30 (trenta) maestros en kuántos diyas la akavan? Akí, en esta demanda, kuanto mas se muchigua la kuenta primera ke son los maestros, mas se enchikese la kuantitá dela kuenta sigunda ke es el tyempo.

Kon esto kale azer este kuento kon la regla de tres arevés. De este modo azemos las kuentas a la regla, i matropikamos la kuenta de en medyo 25 kon la primera 12 ke está a la estyedra: se azen 300. I después lo espartimos kon 30 sarlá 10. Ke esto mostra ke si son 30 travajadores, lo azen en 10 diyas.

Aldina Quintana, "Una informasion de la aritmetika y una muestra de los kuentos" in *Hommage à Haim-Vidal Sephiha*, Bern: Peter Lang, 1997, pp. 295–314.

Glossary

a revés: reversed, backwards.
derecha: straight, simple.
la kuenta: the number.
el kuento: the addition, sum.
muchiguar: to increase.
la kuantitá: the quantity, size.
enchikeser: to decrease.

el enshemplo: the example.
fraguar: to build.
demanda: question, problem.
matropikar: to multiply.
estyedra: isyedra/syedra.
espartir: to divide.
el travajador: the worker.

Questions: *1. Ké reglas egzisten? 2. Ké es la diferensya entre el kuento i la kuenta? 3. Ké es lo ke enchikese kuando se muchigua la kuantitá de travajadores?*

VOCABULARY

The four arithmetical operations

♦ *la adisyón*
adjuntar: to add.
3 + 2 = 5: *tres i dos son* (or *azen*) *sinko.*

♦ *la supstraksyón*
kitar: to remove, subtract.
3 − 2 = 1: *dos de tres keda uno.*

♦ *la matropikasyón*
matropikar: to multiply.
3 x 2 = 6: *tres por dos aze sesh* or *tres vezes dos azen sesh.*

♦ *la divizyón*
espartir: to divide.
6 ÷ 2 = 3: *sesh espartir por/kon dos sale tres.*

Store advertisements

גראנדי ליקידאסיון אל מאגאזין
" איל סול "
סיטואדו סאברי פאשה

ב'ינימוס די טראיר אלה אוקאזיון די לאס פ'ייסטאס און
גראנדי אסורטימיינטו די קאמיזיס די טודו מודו ריזיוס
אי באראטום דיספ'יאמדו טודה קונקורינסייה אונה סולה ב'יז'יטה
אין מואיסטרו מאגאזין פור קונב'ינסיד'ום.
פריסיו פ'יקסו מיג'יד *19*
פראטילי שלטיאל

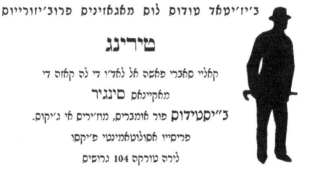

ב'יז'יטאד' טודוס לום מאגאזיניס פרוב'יזוריוס
טירינג
קאלי סאברי פאשה אל לאד'ו די לה קאזה די
מאקיינאס סינגיר
ב''יסטידום פור אומבריס, מוח'יריס אי ג'יקום.
פריסיו אסולוטאמינטי פ'יקסו
לירה טורקה 104 גרושים

קורידו טודום אל מאגאזין די דראפירי
☞ פ''ראנסיס אי ארדיטי
סיטואדו אין ג'אמלי חאן
(ב'יזאב'י אורוחדי)
איי סי טופה ריאונידו סולידיטה, בואין גוסטו
אי פריסייום באראטום.

Advertisements taken from *La Solidaridad Ovradera*,
in Nicole Cohen-Rak, ibid., *cf.* p. 76.

The same advertisements transcribed into Latin characters

GRANDE LIKIDASYON AL MAGAZEN
"EL SOL"
situado Sabrí Pashá

Venimos de trayer ala okazyón de las fyestas un grande asortimyento de kazmires de todo modo de djénero rezyos i baratos desfyando toda konkurensya una sola vijita en muestro magazen por konvenservos.

PRESYO FIKSO MEDJID 19

FRATELI ŞALTIEL

Vijitad todos los magazenes provizoryos
TIRING
Kaye Sabrí Pashá al lado de la kaza de makyinas **SINGER**
VESTIDOS por ombres, mujeres i chikos.
Presyo asolutamente fikso
Lira turka 104 groshes

5b

KORRED TODOS AL MAGAZEN DE DRAPERI
☞FRANSES I ARDITI
SITUADO EN DJAMLI HAN
(vizaví Orozde)

Ayí se topa reunido soliditá, buen gusto i presyos baratos.

Glossary

likidasyón (F.): clearance sale.
el magazén (F.): general store.
kazmir: cashmere.
el djénero: the type, sort.
rezyo, a: solid, strong.
desfyar (F.): to defy.
asolutamente: absolutely.
el grosh (T.): the piastre (1/100th of the Turkish pound).

presyo fikso (F.): fixed price.
draperí (F.): bedlinens and curtains.
vizaví (F. vis à vis): across from.
la soliditá (F.): solid quality.
konkurensya (F.): competition.
konvenser: to convince.

Note: *estar trinka:* to be dressed smartly.

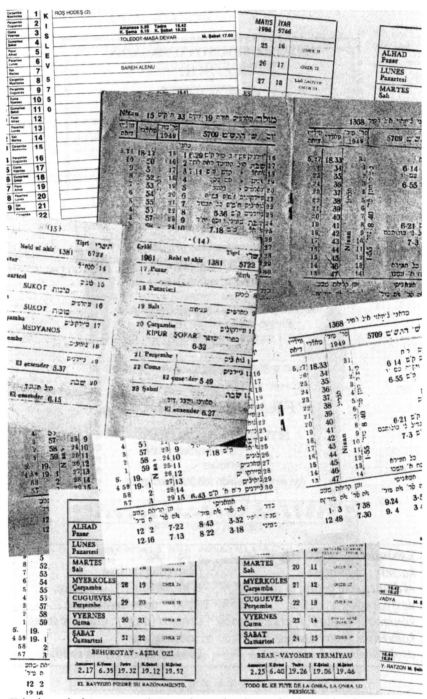

Kalendaryos djudyós, anyo 5750 (1989-1990); 5709 (1949); 5722 (1961); 5746 (1986).

LESSON 6

Al tyempo era al tyempo

Objectives

Communication skills: Asking, explaining, the forms of "you" (continued), recounting memories, speaking of the past.

Vocabulary: Verbs for recounting (indirect discourse), words for animals, technical terms borrowed from Turkish.

Conjugation: Formation of the imperfect tense, irregular imperfect verbs, formation of the past tense, irregular past verbs; the present perfect and pluperfect tenses.

Grammar: Which form of the past tense to use; elliptical syntax, Hebrew plurals, using the reflexive verb as a passive voice, *estar* + common nouns.

Culture: Life in the Jewish neighborhood: volunteer firemen, *aventar kantikas,* the mania for singing songs, satirical songs, a Passover song.

---

26 🎧 *Kóntame la konseja…*

Diya de alhad en París. Izí está en la kaza de su prima la grande ke tomó tambyén en su kaza a su nono de Estanbol. No pueden salir a la kaye i s'está enfasyando.

Michèle:	Izí, saviyas ke el onkl Shemuel fue tulumbadjí en Balat, al tyempo de la mansevéz?
Izí:	Tulumbadjí, kuálo kijo dizir?
Michèle:	Onkl Shemuel ke le konte lo ke me kontó a mí el otro diya… Le rogo…
Onkl Shemuel:	Uuy! Koza grande! I es ke antes no aviyan komo akí agora itfayés del governo, kon arabás koroladas. Para amatar fuegos, estávamos mozós, los tulumbadjís djudyós de ahuera Balat!
Izí:	Ya m'akodro… Balat es la mallé ande morava él… Ma no me disho ke teniya una kavané ayá?
Onkl Shemuel:	Kómo no?! La mijor kavané de ahuera Balat! Ma i era tulumbadjí… Kijo dizir ke fuego kuando aviya, deshávamos el echo, yo serrava la kavané, i korríyamos a amatarlo kon la kitá miya, kon la tulumba de agua i el fener.

145

Izí:	I vos davan paga para esto los Djudyós de la mallé?
Onkl Shemuel:	No solo los Djudyós! I los Turkos, i los Gregos… Todos los ke eran los patrones de las kazas ke se kemavan. Arogavan i pechavan para ke se amataran sus kazas en primero. A todo modo de mallé mos ívamos. Todo tavlas, aviyan fuegos grandes. Komo el ke uvo en Selânik, no sé si sintites la kantika del fuego de los Selaniklís?
Izí:	Sí, ésta mo la aviya kantado la nona un diya de tisha beav.
Onkl Shemuel:	Kada mallé teniya su kitá. Kaliya yegar el primero i por modo d'esto mos peleyávamos kon todos. Mas muncho kon los Gregos!
Izí:	Aviyan i Gregos?
Onkl Shemuel:	Sí. En Fener estavan los Gregos. Un diya mos topimos endjuntos, mozós korríyamos mas presto i eyos no mos desharon pasar, abashimos la tulumba i los aharvimos bueno.
Izí:	I el fuego?!
Onkl Shemuel:	Kuálo el fuego! El fuego ya s'olvidó! De los Gregos tomimos el fener kon el hach i lo enkolgimos en mi kavané. Duspués vinyeron a demandarlo i mos izimos paz. Na, te amostraré fotografiyas.

GLOSSARY

Spanish origin

arogar: to pray, beseech (= *rogar*).
amatar: to extinguish.
akodrarse de: to remember.
pechar, pagar: to pay.
yegar: to arrive.
la tavla: wooden plank, board.

peleyarse: to have a fight or argument.
aharvar: to strike, hit.
olvidar: to forget.
enkolgar: to hang.
azerse paz: to make peace.

Other origins

el onkl/el onkli (*la tant/la tanti*) (F): uncle and aunt.
un tulumbadjí (T.): a volunteer fireman.
los itfayés (T.): modern firemen.
la kavané (T.): the café.
la kitá (T.): the team.
la tulumba (T.): the water pump.
el fener (T.): the lantern (Fener is the Greek quarter, Phanar).
el hach (T.): the cross.

Communication skills

1. Asking

◆ To ask politely for something:

Le rogo… Please, "I beg you" (for use of the polite form of **you,** see below).

◆ To ask for explanations:

Kuálo kere dizir? Or *Kuálo kijo dizir?* What does that mean?

Ma no me disho ke…? But didn't you tell me that…?

◆ To ask for information on the cause of something:

Kuálo afitó (from *afitar*)*?* What happened? [perhaps expecting bad news].

Kuálo akontesyó? What happened [neutral]?

2. Explaining

Sí, amá… Yes, but…

Kómo no?! What do you mean! Of course!

Ya s'olvidó: It's over and forgotten (literally "it already forgot itself).

Kuálo el fuego?: What fire are you talking about! Oh yes, the fire!

Afitó un kavzo (ke): Something happened (and that is…).

I es ke: And it's that…

3. The "You" forms in Judeo-Spanish

Observe: *I no me disho ke tiniya…?* Literally: Didn't **he** tell me that **he** had…, but meaning here: But didn't **you** tell me **you** had…

The young man here is using the polite form of **you** with his old great-uncle. This form was studied in Lesson 1, "*avlar kon mersé.*" It was formerly used by children to address their father, and sometimes by a wife to address her husband. It is still used to address one's parents-in-law. It is formed by using the 3rd person singular without a specific pronoun, or if there is ambiguity by adding *él* or *eya*. The possessive is *su.*

Conjugation

1. The Imperfect tense

Observe: *korríyamos, aviya, saviyas, kaliya, moravas, dava, estávamos, arrogavan, mos peleyávamos, pechavan; deshávamos, estavan.*

All the above are in the imperfect tense—that is, the tense that denotes *continuous* action in the past. *Korríyamos,* for example, can be translated into English as "We were running" (a process going on in the past) or "We used to run" (a

147

regular event in the past) or "We would run" (a habitual action in the past done over and over). *Tú saviyas* means "You used to know" or "You knew" (an ongoing state in the past).

The imperfect is formed by replacing the infinitive endings as follows:

Verbs in -*ar* take the imperfect in -*ava*.

Verbs in -*er* and -*ir* take the imperfect in -*iya*.

Most verbs are perfectly regular in the imperfect tense. For ex.:

Dar	Estar	Saver	Tener	Vinir
dava	estava	saviya	teniya	viniya
davas	estavas	saviyas	teniyas	viniyas
dava	estava	saviya	teniya	viniya
dávamos	estávamos	savíyamos	teníyamos	viníyamos
davash	estavash	saviyash	teniyash	viniyash
davan	estavan	saviyan	teniyan	viniyan

Very few verbs are irregular in the imperfect. Here are *ir* and *ser:*

Ir	Ser
iva	era
ivas	eras
iva	era
ívamos	éramos
ivash	erash
ivan	eran

Notes:

1. In every case the *we* form is accentuated on the syllable that is third from last (the antepenultimate). Be sure to write the accent mark and pronounce the form correctly.

2. In Bulgaria, many verbs in -*er* and -*ir* have an ending in -*iva* in the imperfect. For ex., *teniva, tenivas,* etc.

3. In verbs that have -*e* in the stem, such as *tener,* the *e* tends to become -*i* in the imperfect: *teniya* or *tiniya, teníyamos* or *tiníyamos.*

4. In a number of areas, notably Salonika, the imperfect of the verb *ir* is completely regular: *iya, iyas, iya,* etc.

2. The Past tense

Observe: *kantó, s'olvidó, mos topimos, desharon, abashimos, mos peleyimos, enkolgimos, arekojyó, sintites.*

All the above verbs are in the **past tense**—that is, the tense that denotes *completed* acts in the past. (In modern Spanish grammar this tense is called the Preterite.) *Kantó,* for example, can be translated into English as "He sang," where the speaker depicts the action as a discrete act that took place once in the past. If he had wanted to stress, rather, that the singing took place on an ongoing basis or was going on when some discrete act took place, he would have used the imperfect, *kantava.*

The past tense is formed by replacing the infinitive endings as follows:
Verbs in -*ar* take the endings: **-í, -ates, -ó, -imos, -atesh, -aron**.
Verbs in -*er* and *ir* take the endings: **-í, -ites, -yó, -imos, -itesh, -yeron**.
Following are models of verbs that are regular in the past tense:

Kantar	Amatar	Arekojer	Sintir
kantí	amatí	arekojí	sintí
kantates	amatates	arekojites	sintites
kantó	amató	arekojyó	sintyó
kantimos	amatimos	arekojimos	sintimos
kantatesh	amatatesh	arekojitesh	sintitesh
kantaron	amataron	arekojyeron	sintyeron

Notes:
1. The final -*i* is characteristic of the 1st person singular in *all three* conjugations of regular verbs. This -*i* is found again in the -*imos* ending for the *we* form of *all* verbs in the past. This is an important difference from modern Spanish.
2.   The 1st and 3rd persons singular are accented on the final syllable.
The past tense thus comes across as being a very strongly accentuated form in oral speech.
Unlike the imperfect tense, verbs in the past tense show many irregularities, sometimes to the point of being difficult to recognize as being related to the infinitive. Following are some of the most common:

Aver becomes: *uvo, uvyeron* (3rd person forms only).

Estar	Azer	Kerer	Tener
estuve	ize	kije	tuve
estuvites	izites	kijites	tuvites
estuvo	izo	kijo	tuvo
estuvimos	izimos	kijimos	tuvimos
estuvitesh	izitesh	kijitesh	tuvitesh
estuvyeron	izyeron	kijeron	tuvyeron

Ser/Ir	Dizir	Vinir
fui	dishe	vine
fuites	dishites	vinites
fue	disho	vino
fuimos	dishimos	vinimos
fuitesh	dishitesh	vinitesh
fueron	disheron	vinyeron

Note that **ser** and **ir** share the same form in the past: *fui* can mean "I was" or "I went." The reflexive form, *irse,* means "to leave, go away." *"Me fui":* I left, went away.

3. The perfect tenses

The **present perfect tense** of verbs (*I have seen,* etc.) does not exist in traditional Judeo-Spanish. A form using the auxiliary verb *aver* once existed, and a form using the auxiliary *tener* still exists but in a very limited sense. Among western Judeo-Spanish communities, under the influence of French, modern Spanish or American usage, this form may be found by conjugating the auxiliary verb *tener* in the present tense plus the past participle of the main verb. For example, *tengo estado, tengo dicho.* Further examples will be studied in Lesson 9.

The **pluperfect tense,** as in English, consists of the verb *aver* conjugated in the imperfect + the past participle of the main verb. For example, *aviyas kantado* (you had sung), *aviya komido* (he had eaten), *aviyan sintido* (they had heard). The helping verb *aver* exists with a complete conjugation only in the imperfect tense and allows for the formation of the pluperfect tense. Its conjugated forms are regular: *aviya, aviyas, aviya, avíyamos, aviyash, aviyan.*

GRAMMAR

1. Using the various past tenses

♦ The **imperfect**, as we have seen, expresses habitual actions and circumstances suspended in the past, gives explanations about events that are reported in the past tense and comments on them, reports what time it was, serves to introduce stories, etc. Consider these examples:

*Antes, al tyempo, la djente **era** ansina…* People used to be like that.

***Era** la ora la sinko de la tadre…* It was five o'clock.

***Era** un diya de semana, **aziya** sol…* It was a weekday, the sun was shining.

*Mi padre me **disho** ke estava hazino…* My father told me (past) that he was ill (imperfect).

***Era** la vizina ke **viniya**…* "It was the neighbor who was coming over…"

150

An old *romanse* begins as follows:
Ay **aviya** un rey de Fransya
Ke **tiniya** tres ijikas…

Aviya de ser un buen de naser, el padre en la fasha, la madre sin naser: This is an example of one of those humorously absurd formulas one finds at the beginning of *konsejas*.

The **past** tense, as we have seen, expresses an act that happened and is over and done. *Era la sinko de la tadre kuando **yamaron** a la puerta. Presto **m'alevantí. Avrí** la puerta.*

The past tense can often replace the pluperfect: *Ya s'olvidó!* It had already been forgotten!

♦ To summarize: Situations and circumstances "suspended" in the past, along with background explanations, are expressed by the imperfect tense. The main action that takes place against this backdrop is expressed by the past tense.

♦ The **pluperfect** expresses a past that took place before some other past. For ex.: *La nona aviya kantado la kantika (muncho antes):* Grandmother had sung the song (long before). *En 1875, ya se aviya fondado la Alyansa:* In 1875, the Alliance had already been founded.

2. Elliptical syntax: Very often in Judeo-Spanish, for reasons of expressivity, speakers will eliminate what is not essential to understanding a statement. This concision, similar in nature to the way proverbs are constructed, makes expression very efficient. The verb is the first such element to disappear: *Todo tavlas: todo estava fraguado kon tavlas.* All wooden planks: everything was built with planks. *(Es) Koza grande!* (It's) A long story!

3. The meanings of "i"

Observe: *I no me disho ke teniya una kavané ayá? Ma i era tulumbadjí. I Turkos aviya i Gregos. I el fuego?*

As in biblical Hebrew, ***i*** can have meanings other than *and:*
—In general, it underscores the sense of "and moreover, further…"
—But it can also mean "also, likewise, even": *i Turkos aviya i Gregos* (and there were even Turks and Greeks, too);
—it also emphasizes the adverb "but": *ma i era tulumbadjí* (but you were also a fireman);
—or it can simply mean "but": "but didn't you say you had…?"

EXERCISES

Exercise 1: Redo the first five sentences of the dialogue at the beginning of the lesson, replacing the polite form of you *with the familiar form* **tú**.

Exercise 2: Conjugate the verbs you already know in the imperfect.

Exercise 3: Redo the following story using the imperfect.

Ex.: Antes kuando **era** un mansevo de vente anyos, me *alevantava*.

So un mansevo de vente anyos. Me alevanto a las sesh de la demanyana porke lavoro leshos de mi kaza. Me vo al echo kon la arabá, komo i bevo en mi büró, i torno a kaza a las syete. Tengo munchos amigos i kon eyos miro la televizyón, vo al match de futbol, djuguo kartas. En vezes vamos al sinemá, bevemos un chay en una kavané, nunkua no mos pelcyamos. Semos buenos amigos, mos avenimos, mos engleneamos i esto es tener buena vida.

Exercise 4: Put the verb in parentheses in the imperfect for the appropriate person.

1. Mozós (bivir) en la Bulgariya. 2. En Varna (aver) un kal muy ermozo ande mi padre i mi ermano (ir) para la tefilá. 3. Mi nona (saver) munchas kantikas i las (kantar) noche de alhad, (tener) una boz muy ermoza. 4. Tú me kontates ke (bivir) kon tu famiya en Sofia i ke (estar) muy kontentes ayá. 5. Tu ermana i tú (dizir) ke la vida (ser) fasil antes de la gerra. 6. Para mozós tambyén: kon mi ermano (meldar) en una skola ande (ambezarse) el fransés. 7. A mí me (plazer) muncho avlar, ma mi ermano no (pueder) o no (kerer) avlar esta lingua. 8. En kaza (avlar) todos en djudyó komo ande vozós ma i (saver) el bulgaro.

Exercise 5: Conjugate the regular -ar, -er *and* -ir *verbs you already know in the past tense.*

Exercise 6: Put the verb in parentheses into the past tense for the appropriate person. Watch out for the irregular verbs.

1. Ayer yo me (ir) kon mi mujer a kaza de mi es-huegra. 2. (komer) endjuntos i (avlar) de su ermana ke (irse) a Israel un mez antes. 3. Mi mujer (bivir) ayá antes de kazarse i (ambezarse) en ivrit. 4. Kuando mos (kazar), (kerer) ir a morar ayá, ma mi padre no mos (deshar): (dizir) ke él estava hazino i no mos iva a ver mas. 5. Mi madre (yorar) i yo (ampesar) a trokar de idea, no (tener) el koraje de amargarlos. 6. Mi mujer i yo (meldar) en la universitá amerikana

i (topar) un buen echo. 7. Yo en primero (lavorar) en una gazeta, duspués (azer) otro lavoro ke no me (plazer), i (empyegarse) en la fabriká de mi padre. 8. Mi mujer (deshar) el echo kuando (tener) una kriyatura. 9. Duspués (estar) desrepozada, ma agora (azerse) buena.

Exercise 7: Put the following text into the past tense.

Ex.: *Ayer m'alevantí a las syete i…*

M'alevanto a las syete i me vo al echo kon otomobil. Kuando salgo del echo, kuando eskapo, merko rozas i me vo a vijitar ande Flory/Florí. Su madre me aze un kavé i Flory i yo avlamos en el salón. Mos peleyamos porke eya kere ir al tiyatro i a mí no me plaze. A la fin vamos al restorán i mos topamos kon amigos. Van todos los mansevos al mezmo bar. Syenten muzika ingleza, avlan, beven vino, yo me durmo un poko i tornamos tadre a kaza. La madre de Flory no está kontente.

Exercise 8: For each verb in parentheses, choose the appropriate verb form in the past, the imperfect or the pluperfect.

1. Antes los tulumbadjís (vistir) kalsados livyanos i (korrer) mas presto. 2. Me akodro ke un diya (estar) asentados en la puerta, en súpito (vinir) un ombre i (dizir) ke (aver) fuego en una mallé muy leshos. 3. Mozós lo (mandar) a dar haber a la kavané de al lado. 4. Presto (alevantarse) tres mansevos, (entrar) aryentro i (salir) enteramente vistidos. 5. Estos tres (ir) a bushkar a los otros. 6. Mozós (mirar) kómo (yevar) la tulumba i el fener i (ampesar) a korrer. 7. En dos puntos (estar) a la punta de la kaleja i (espareserse). 8. Mozós (kedar) enkantados. 9. A la noche kuando (tornar), (kontar) ke el fuego (amatarse) kuando (yegar).

Exercise 9: Complete these sentences either by telling about some action that happened or by giving the circumstances in which it happened.

1. …kuando un ladrón entró en su kaza.
2. Yo morava en Izmir kuando…
3. …i en súpito lo vide en la plasa.
4. Aziya muncha luvya i por esto…
5. Un diya ke iva a vijitar a mi madre…
6. …i topí un livro muy enteresante.
7. …vino su ermana i no le avlí.
8. …ma topí su puerta serrada.
9. Kije avlar kon Marko ma…

Exercise 10: Translate the meanings of "i" in the following sentences.
1. Meldo i matematikas i literatura. 2. I yo so djudyó. 3. Kere ir al sinemá i eya. 4. El marido i la mujer se peleyan muncho i esto no es vida. 5. Los asperimos noche entera i no vinyeron. 6. Elí keriya merkar kalsados i no vino a mi butika; i tengo sapatos muy ermozos. 7. Mösyó Nahum era i moel i shohet. 8. Viní i vozós. 9. "De ké no le dishites bonjur?" —"I no lo vide."

Exercise 11: Tell a story about Marko and Ester Danon based on the photographs below.

Readings

Proverbos i dichas

No es ni tyempo de berendjena
(It's not even the season for eggplant).
This is said when people behave crazily, without reason. One speaker used this expression when she explained: *En enverano aze kalor, la djente sale a kozinar en las tarasas; de esto saliyan munchos fuegos* (In summer it's hot, people go out to cook on their terraces; many fires started that way).

Se alevantaron los pipinos, aharvaron a los bahchevanes
(The cucumbers rose up, they beat the gardeners).
This is said of students or children who think they can teach their teachers or parents.

Es un amatakandelas
(He is a candle extinguisher).
He is a killjoy, party pooper.

Kantikas

27 🎵 *1. Asperar i non vinir*

T'asperí i non vinites
ich no me kijites?[15] (repeat)
Dime, dime, ich no me kijites? (repeat)

2. Satirical songs

In the Jewish quarters of large cities everyone knew each other, and gossip was flagrant. It was common to lampoon one figure or another from the neighborhood for some failing or ridiculous trait, or to publicize a case of adultery, or compose humorous songs. People would say *"le aventí kantika,"* I made up a song about him or her. As certain highly placed figures might well be the butt of such satire, or because certain songs did not have good intentions, the rabbis or community authorities would periodically have to intervene to call for a stop. To no avail…

---

15. past tense of *kerer*.

Here is a satirical song about a certain teacher at an elementary school—a *mestra*—who taught a little French and was reputed to be mean.

A madam Aneta
le kayó la teta
la bushkó
i no la topó

Glossary

la teta: the breast (but perhaps a pun using the French word for head, *tête*).

28 ◎ *This one pokes fun at a mother who, too hasty in her concern about her daughter Solucha, runs from the school to the synagogue.*

El chan ya dyo
Solucha no eskoló
Guay de su madre!
Ke la ija ya boló
Al kal me hui
La mezuzá bezí
I de ver al haham
kayí me desmayí.

Glossary

el chan ya dyo: the bell has already rung.
eskolar: to get out of school.
guay de: poor…
bolar: to fly off
me hui/fui: I went.
bezar: to kiss.
kayer: to fall.
desmayarse: to faint.

29 ◎ *3. Tu madre kuando te paryó*
(A contemporary song with a tango beat).

Tu madre kuando te paryó,
I te kitó al mundo,
korasón, eya no te dyo,
para amar sigundo.
 (Repeat last two lines)
Va búshkate otro amor,
aharva a otras puertas,
va búshkate otro ardor,
ke para mí sos muerta.

Glossary

parir: to give birth to.
kitar al mundo: bring into the world.
sigundo: here, a second person, a loved one.
tomar sigundo: to take a lover.
bushkar: to seek, look for.
aharvar (H.): to beat, strike.
el ardor: the passion.
amargar: to embitter.

Refrain:
Adiyó adiyó kerida,
non kero la vida,
me l'amargates tú.
(Repeat refrain).

Note:

Sos muerta: normally *estás muerta.* (The verb *ser* makes the statement more absolute).

Vittorio Isacco, engineer, at the command of the "helicogyre" he invented (Le Bourget, Paris, 1926).

Salonika, 1916; Jeanno and his grandparents.

Jewish quarter of Kirklissé (*Kirlareli*), Thrace, 1900.

Mr. Daniel Bardavid on a pilgrimage to Jerusalem (1920).

Salonika, August 19, 1917, 7:00 a.m.: The fire as seen from the docks.

A group of victims of the fire, Champ-de-Mars Square (Salonika, 1917).

Firefighters Squad (Salonika, 1917).

Victims housed in tents at the Zeltennik camp (Salonika, 1917).

Kantika del fuego de Selânik (1917)

Diya de shabad la tadre
La orika dando dos
Fuego salyó a l'Agua Mueva
A la Torre blanka kedó

Mos dyeron unos chadires
Ke d'el ayre se bolavan
Mos dyeron un pan amargo
Ni kon agua no abashava [...]

Tanto proves komo rikos
Todos semos de un igual
Ya kedimos arrastando
Por kampos i por kishlás

Entyendeldo mansevikos
De los pekados de shabad
S'ensanyó el Patrón del mundo
I mos mandó a tal luguar.

En su livro *En torno de la Torre blanka,* Enrique Saporta y Beja eskrive sovre el fuego [original spelling used]: "*Este fuego ke aviya turado mas de tres dias fizo mas de 200 milyares de la epoka, de danyos, i asolado 128 ektares kuadrados. Uvo mas de 75,000 personas ke avian pyedrido todo [...]. Komo los djidyos formavan la majorita de la povlasyon de la sivda (80,000 sovre 120,000), fueron eyos ke tuvyeron lo mas de danyos. Fueron destruidos 34 kales sovre 37 ke avia, 80 yechivas i todas las havras.*" Eskrive munchas kozas mas i da la kantika entera kon algunos trokamyentos.

Enrique Saporta y Beja, *En torno de la Torre Blanka,*
Paris: Vidas Largas, 1982, p. 317.

Notes:

1. In E. Saporta y Beja's text, note *fizo*. The Salonikan form of *azer* is *fazer,* hence *fizo* instead of *izo* in Istanbul and Izmir.

2. *Entyended + lo* ⇨ *entyendeldo:* Hear it, listen to this. *Entyended* is the imperative form for *vozotros.* When there is a pronoun object after this form, Judeo-Spanish inverts the order of the *d* and *l* (see p. 173).

Glossary

kampos: fields.
arrastar: to drag oneself.
una kishlá (T.): a military barracks.
un chadir (T.): a tent (but usually means "umbrella" in Judeo-Spanish.)
abashar: to go down
los pekados: the sins.
mandar: to send.
turar: to last.

la época: the period.
el danyo: the damage, the harm.
asoladar/asolar: to destroy, to ruin
la yeshivá (H.): Talmudic school.
la havrá (H.): the school, association.
ensanyarse: to become angry.
el trokamyento: the change, alteration.

Here is a romanse *that is very well known in the Hispanic world. It is sung in a virtually monotone fashion. The verse lines have eight syllables, with free verse alternating with an assonance in* a-a, *with only a few exceptions. Several versions of this tragic incest story exist. This one was sung by Mss. Rachel and Rika Vitas.*

Ay aviya un rey de Fransya – ke teniya tres ijikas.
La mas chikitika d'eyas – Delgadiya se yamava.
Una noche en la meza – su padre ke la mirava:
"Ké me mira sinyor padre – ké me mira i ké me mata?"
"Yo te miro Delgadiya – ke de ti m'enamorava."
"Nunkua kera el Dyo del syelo – tal ayege ni tal aga,
ser kondesa de mi madre – madrasta de mis ermanas."
"Arremata Delgadiya – arremata perra mala!"
En el medyo del kamino – un kastiyo le fraguava.
A komer ké le dariyan? – karne kruda i byen salada;
a bever ké le dariyan? – sumo de narandja amarga.
Pasó tyempo vino tyempo – prinsipyo de dos semanas,
por ayí pasó su madre – en siya de oro asentada:
"Madre miya mi kerida – deshme deshme un poko d'agua,
ke de sed i no de ambre – al Dyo vo a dar la alma."
"Kaya kaya Delgadiya – kaya kaya perra mala,
si tu padre el rey lo save – la kavesa mos kortava."
Pasó tyempo vino tyempo – por ayí pasó su ermana:
"Ermana miya mi kerida – dame dame un poko d'agua,
ke de sed i no de ambre – al Dyo vo a dar la alma."
"Kaya kaya Delgadiya – kaya kaya perra mala,
si tu padre el rey lo save – la kavesa mos kortava."
Pasó tyempo vino tyempo – Delgadiya se ezmayava;
fin a ke trusheron l'agua – Delgadiya dyo la alma.

Glossary

el rey: the king.
enamorarse: to fall in love.
ayegar: to reach the point.
kondesa: countess (here: rival).
madrasta: stepmother.
arrematar: to die.
la perra: female dog, bitch.
un kastiyo: a castle.
la karne: the meat, flesh.
krudo, a: raw.

pasar: to come by.
el sumo: the juice.
narandja amarga: bitter orange.
(en) prinsipyo: at the beginning.
siya: chair, seat.
la sed: thirst.
la ambre: hunger.
kayar: to be quiet, to hush.
ezmayarse/esmayarse/desmayarse: to faint.
trusheron: past tense of *traer.*

Notes:

1. dariyan (from *dar)* is the conditional form of the verb, to be studied later. *A komer ké le dariyan:* "What would they give her to eat," but used poetically here for "What did they give her to eat."

2. Si tu padre el rey lo save, la kavesa mos kortava. If your father the king knows (knew) it, he will (*or* would) cut off our head. The verb tenses here are subject to poetic license; note that the imperfect tense is sometimes used in a conditional sense.

3. deshme = imperative of *dar* using the subjunctive (variant of *dadme*).

Exercise: Recount the sad story of Delgadiya by summarizing it in the past tense.

31 🎵 *El kavretiko (Had gadya)*

This is the second cumulative song sung at Passover, at the end of the Seder, *after the meal. It takes the chain of causes and effects all the way up to God.*

Un kavretiko ke me merkó mi padre por dos levanim
I vino el gato
i komyó a el kavretiko
ke me merkó mi padre por dos levanim
I vino el perro ke modryó a el gato
ke komyó a el kavretiko
ke me merkó mi padre por dos levanim

I vino el palo ke aharvó a el perro …
I vino el fuego ke kemó a el palo …
I vino la agua ke amató a el fuego …
I vino el buey ke bevyó a la agua …
I vino el shohet ke degoyó a el buey…
I vino el malah amavet ke se yevó a el shohet…
I vino el Santo Bendicho El ke mató al malah amavet…

Glossary

levanim (B. + H. plural): a type of money, a white coin.
modrer: to bite. *el palo:* the stick.
kemar: to burn. *amatar:* to extinguish.
degoyar: to slaughter, slit the throat.
el malah amavet (H.): the angel of death.
matar: to kill.

Vocabulary

Animals

Vocabulary relating to animals is very limited. Living in cities, the Spanish Jews do not often know the names of animals they do not see or eat or that do not appear in their books—for example, *el taushán* (T.): rabbit.

General terms: *las alimanyas* (wild animals), *las kuatropeas* (Ladino for quadrupeds), *las hayot, las hayás* (H., animals in general), *los pasharós* (the birds), *los guzanos* (insects).

la vaka

el buey

el puerko/ el hinzir/ el hazir

el azno/ el hamor

la palaza

el kavayo

el pato

la gayna

el pishkado/ el peshe

la gruya

el gayo

la palomba

el kulevro

el kavretiko

el león

el gameyo

la rana

el kodredo   la oveja

el ratón

el lonso

el gato

el perro

Notes:

1. The Bible provides a few other names (in Hebrew).

2. Animals are not highly valued. They symbolize negative characteristics. For example, *puerko* is something or someone repugnant, *kavayo* and *gameyo* are said of coarse persons, *lonso* is a heavy, slow-witted person, *hamor!* is an insult, and the same holds true for *hayá!* as well as *es una beemá* (H. beast, animal, head of cattle).

3. In certain cases, the Hebrew plurals can be used interchangeably with the Judeo-Spanish plural: *la hayá, las hayot* or *las hayás*. In the text above, *dos levanim* is the plural of *levá* or *leván*. One can also find *los ladrones* or *los ladronim* and even *los ladronimes*, with a double sign of the plural.

6b

32 🔊 *Memoryas de un tulumbadjí*

Avlan dos personas, Marí i Sabetay, kon Izak Azuz, tulumbadjí djudyó de Balat, nasido en 1908:

Marí:	Ké modo de persona era Perendeoğlu?
Izak:	Una persona normal. Un blondeado ortá de boy, ma si le viniyan dyez personas, a todos kaliya ke les kitara los ojos. Los ojos les kitava. Te djuro! Kon ridá!
Marí:	I ké aziya éste ayá?
Izak:	Kavedjí, era kavedjí. Ande él ívamos… asperávamos ke uvyera fuego para irmos. Para pasar la ora djuguávamos kartas. Mos viniyan polís, mos davan haber (kuando aviya fuego).
Sabetay:	I kómo estavash vistidos?

Izak:	Vistidos no ay. Una fanela, atlet, i un… un shalvar de amerikana. Akí era apretado, akí era flosho. Esto era, i deskalso.
Sabetay:	Invyerno i enverano?
Izak:	En invyerno teníyamos unas sapatikas, se yamavan "tulumbadjí yemenisi," delgados, syen gramos veniya un par.
Sabetay:	De kuero?
Izak:	Sí, de videlo.
Sabetay:	Kén es ke se los dava? Kada uno se lo merkava?
Izak:	No. Mo lo aziyan. El reis mo lo aziya. I él tomava de akí de ayá parás i mo lo aziya.
Marí:	Los tulumbadjís otro echo no teniyan?
Izak:	Hamallik aziyan.
Marí:	Aaa… I de esto ganavan?
Izak:	D'esto… i duspués de esto kuando mos ívamos a los fuegos, veniya el patrón de kaza. *"Amán, la kaza miya kurtárame! Te vo a dar vente liras!"* Akel tyempo vente liras era komo kinyentas mil de agora. Amá se kemó, se kemó.
Marí:	Si se kemó yiné vos dava?
Izak:	Siguro!

Interview with Mr. Izak Azuz.

Glossary

nasido: born.

blondeado: blondish.

ortá de boy (T.): average size.

kitara: (imperfect subj. of *kitar*).

djurar: to swear.

la ridá (T.): a rag, handkerchief.

asperar: to wait.

ke uvyera (imp. subj. of *aver*).

un polís (T.): a policeman.

dar haber (T.): to inform, warn.

fanela (flannel) = *atlet* (T.): undershirt.

un shalvar (T.): baggy trousers.

amerikana: cotton cloth.

deskalso: barefoot.

apretado: tight.

flosho: loose.

delgado, a: thin.

sapatika: slipper, little shoe.

kuero: leather.

videlo (I.): calf, calfskin.

un par: a pair.

el reis (T.): the chief.

hamallik (T.): porter's work, loading and hauling.

kemarse: to burn up.

yiné (T.): anyway, just the same.

siguro: of course.

Questions: *1. Los tulumbadjís, solo un echo teniyan? 2. Ánde asperavan el fuego? 3. Kén era Perendeoğlu? 4. Kén pagava a los tulumbadjís? 5. Kén les merkava sapatos? 6. Ganavan muncha pará?*

Las kazas de Perendeoğlu

Eran sinko kazas a la sirá. Son kazas de dos kates, de tavlas. Abasho de la primera aviya una kavané. Está en la köshé de dos kalejas. A la punta de la kaleja de la derecha se topa la skala de los kayikes para Hasköy.

En la kavané de Perendeoğlu viniyan tulumbadjís djudyós. Se arekojiyan asperando ke uvyera fuego. Ayí djuguar tavlí aviya, djuguar kartas, peleyar muncho, ma matar, no. Estas kazas s'estruyeron en 1980, kuando izyeron de muevo los kenares del Halich. Ayí agora está guerta.

Recounted by Mr. Izak Azuz.

Glossary
un kat (T.): a floor (of a building).
la skala: docking area.
el kayik (T.), *la barka:* small boat.
el tavlí (T.): backgammon.
peleyar(se): to get into a fight, an argument.
estruirse/estruyirse: to be destroyed.
el kenar (T.): the edge.
el Halich: the Golden Horn (estuary flowing into the center of Istanbul).

6b

Las kazas de Perendeoğlu kon la kavané en la kyöshé (Balat, 1980).

Notes:
1. Ay/aviya + infinitive (syntax modeled after the T.).
Djuguar tavlí aviya, people played backgammon (literally: "playing backgammon there was").
djuguar aviya: people played ("there was playing").
peleyar aviya: there was fighting.
2. ayí is between *akí* (here) and *ayá* (over there).
ayí means "there," but is used much less often than *ayá*.

Grammar

1. *Estar* + common noun

In Judeo-Spanish, *estar* before a common noun means:

to be transformed into, become…

to be ready to…

to be reduced to the state of…

to be like…, etc.

Together, such constructions are highly expressive, often figures of speech and metaphors.

está guerta: it's become a garden, it's like a garden.

está grano para patladar! ("it's a blister about to burst open"), a common expression meaning something or someone ready to explode.

Estó polvo: ("I am dust, powder"), I feel all in pieces.

2. The reflexive verb used for the passive voice

Observe: *S'estruyeron en 1980.*

The passive voice is used infrequently in Judeo-Spanish. Instead of saying *fueron estruidas* (they were destroyed), the reflexive form of the verb is used, whenever the agent is not expressed or highlighted: *s'estruyeron* (literally, they destroyed themselves, but meaning "they were destroyed").

Ex: *Se kemó,* he was burned.

Mr. Izak Azuz, former *tulumbadjí djudyó*, in the Galata tea garden.

LESSON 7

Viní, komeremos

OBJECTIVES

Communication skills: Affirmative and negative commands, expressing purpose, *before* and *after* situations, describing what things are made of.
Vocabulary: Food, kitchen utensils, cooking techniques, tastes, more borrowings from other languages.
Grammar: Indirect object pronouns, the order of pronouns in a sentence (continued), joining pronouns to verbs, special usage of the future tense, using the subjunctive in subordinate clauses.
Conjugation: The imperative, the verbs *trayer* and *kozer*.
Culture: The role of cooking and meals, religious taboos and the laws of *kashrut,* holiday recipes.

---

33 🎧 *Para mezas de alegriya.*

Luna está kon su nona en el mupak. S'está ambezando a azer tishpishtí.

Nona: En primero, antes de empesar, lávate las manos i vístete esta prostelika.
Luna: No embarasa nona, es un fostán vyejo ke tengo.
Nona: Aze lo ke t'estó dizyendo, ijika. Syempre kale prostela; la tyenes menester para enshugarte las manos, para kitar el tefsín del orno, todo modo de kozas…
Luna: Pekí, pekí, ya sta bueno…
Nona: Agora toma dos findjanes de azeyte i uno de agua, mete sesh findjanes de arina.
Luna: Guevo no se kere?
Nona: No, guevo, no. Un pokitiko sal.
Luna: Amá es dulse?!
Nona: En kozas de orno syempre se kere sal en la masa. Agora vas a finyirla, adjustando la arina avagar avagar.
Luna: Ké karar se mete?
Nona: El karar ke areyeve. Metes kashka de limón rayada, la levadura ke te aparejí. Agora la vas a aresentar esta masa en el paylón… i le metes la muez majada por enriva. Ma kale apartar un pasiko para tapar enriva. Agora al orno…

(7a)

167

Luna:	Ké karar kale ke esté?
Nona:	Medya ora en el orno kayente. Ma antes lo vamos a kortar ansina para ke beva byen el shurup de asukuar ke vamos a aparejar antes ke eskape de kozer. No te asentes!
Luna:	Uuf! Me kansí de estar en pyes. Tomaremos un kavé?
Nona:	Aspérate un puntiko. Tomaremos un kavé después de eskapar.
Luna:	Aora echaremos el shurup.
Nona:	No. No lo metas! Kale asperar ke se yele.

Glossary

Spanish origin

embarasar: to get in the way.

l'azeyte/azete: the oil.

la arina: the flour.

un guevo: an egg.

la sal: the salt.

la masa: the dough.

finyir: to knead.

adjustar: to adjust.

areyevar: to take, hold, absorb.

la kashka: the peel.

la muez: the walnut.

rayar: to grate.

la levadura: the yeast.

aresentar: to place, put.

el paylón: baking pan, tray.

majar: crush.

apartar: to put aside, to separate.

un pasiko: a piece.

kortar: to cut.

aora = agora.

yelar (se): to get cold.

Other origins

la prostela (G.): the apron.

un fostán (T.): a dress.

pekí (T.): alright, very well.

un findján (T.): a cup.

el shurup (T.): the syrup.

el tishpishtí/tupishtí (T.): cake with syrup and nuts.

Communication skills

1. Affirmative and negative commands

♦ To give affirmative commands or advice, the **imperative** form of the verb is used:

Lávate las manos, vístete la prostela, aze, toma, mete, aspera!

♦ To give negative commands, the **subjunctive** is used. For example, *Ázelo!* means "Do it." *No lo agas!* means "Don't do it."
   Aséntate/No te asentes! Mételo/No, no lo metas!

♦ Also, when giving a command in the polite form *(él, eya, eyos, eyas),* the **subjunctive** is used, often following *ke:*
   Ke entre! Enter, come in (sir or ma'am).
   Ke s'asente, sinyora! Sit down, ma'am.

♦ For the **we** form, the **future** is used for the imperative:
   Komeremos: let's eat.

2. To express a purpose
Use *para ke* + **subjunctive**. *Lo vamos a kortar ansina para ke beva byen el shurup:* We are going to cut it this way so that it drinks up (soaks up) the syrup well.

3. Expressing *before* and *after* situations
Reminder (Lesson 5): *antes **de*** + infinitive, *duspués/después de* + infinitive. Ex.: *antes de empesar* (before beginning), *duspués de eskapar* (after finishing).

Now observe, when the following clause contains a subject: *antes **ke*** + **subjunctive**, *duspués ke* + subjunctive. Ex.: *antes ke eskape de kozer* (before it finishes cooking), *duspués ke eskapemos* (after we finish).

VOCABULARY

1. Fruits and vegetables: *Vedruras i frutas*

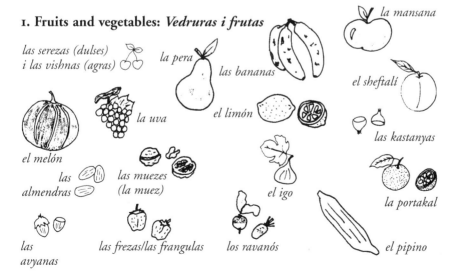

la mansana

las serezas (dulses) i las vishnas (agras)

la pera

las bananas

el sheftalí

la uva

el limón

las kastanyas

el melón

las almendras

las muezes (la muez)

el igo

la portakal

las avyanas

las frezas/las frangulas

los ravanós

el pipino

169

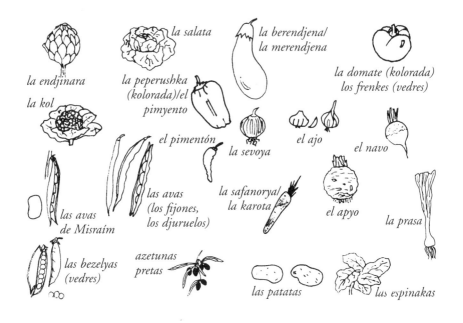

la endjinara

la salata

la berendjena/
la merendjena

la peperushka
(kolorada)/el
pimyento

la domate (kolorada)
los frenkes (vedres)

la kol

el pimentón

la sevoya

el ajo

el navo

las avas
de Misraím

las avas
(los fijones,
los djuruelos)

la safanorya/
la karota

el apyo

la prasa

las bezelyas
(vedres)

azetunas
pretas

las patatas

lus espinakas

2. Basic cooking ingredients

la manteka

la pimyenta

el/la sal

l'azete de
azetunas

la farina/la arina

la asukuar

l'azete

el agro/
el vinagre

kezo kasher

el myel

el kezo blanko

3. Cooking utensils

el mortero

el tripitón

la kasherola

el kapak

el sartén

el tefsín

la kaldera

la payla/el paylón
(mas grande)

la bimuelera
(para Pesah)

la oya
(de barro)

4. Cooking techniques

asar: to roast, grill.
pikar: to chop.
eskaldar: to scald.
rayar/rayer: to grate.
majar: to pound (foods).
friyir: to fry.
salar: to salt.
mundar: to peel.
machukuar: to crush.
kortar: to cut.
mesklar: to mix.

esprimir: to press (foods).
menear: to stir, shake.
buyir: to boil.
eskurrir: to drain.
karishtrear/-terear: to mix.
enhaminar: to braise.
abafar: to steam.
kozer: to cook.
enreynar/areyenar: to stuff.
untar: to grease, to dip.

5. Tastes

es dulse: sweet.   *dulse myel:* honey (very) sweet.
es agro: sour.   *agro vinagre:* vinegar (very) sour.
es amargo: bitter. *amargo fyel:* as bitter as gall (*amargo pulga:* "flea" bitter, meaning very bitter, is the comic twist on *amargo purga,* purge).
es salado: salty.   *salado pinya:* as salty as a pine cone (!), very salty.
es savrozo: tasty, flavorful.   *es shavdo:* flavorless, insipid.

GRAMMAR

1. Object pronouns

We have already seen the **direct object pronouns** (Lesson 2B). In the construction "to say something to someone," "something" is the direct object, while "to someone" is the indirect object—a noun in this case. Replacing that noun by a pronoun we get: "to say something to him/her" *dizirle una koza.*

The indirect object pronoun *le* replaces both masculine and feminine nouns. The plural form *les* is likewise both masculine and feminine: *dizirles una koza,* "to say something to them" (masculine and/or feminine). For emphasis, or especially to avoid ambiguity, the expression *a* + noun or pronoun is included **in addition to** *le* or *les:*

> *Le do una koza **a Izak**. Les disho una koza **a eyas**.*

Chart of 3rd person object pronouns:		Direct	Indirect
Masculine	singular	lo	le
	plural	los	les
Feminine	singular	la	le
	plural	las	les

Observe how the following nouns in parentheses have been replaced by either **direct** or **indirect objects:** *(La prostela)* **la** *tyenes menester.* **La** *vas a aresentar (esta masa).* **Le** *metes la muez enriva (a la masa).* **Lo** *vamos a kortar (el tishpishtí). No* **lo** *metas (el shurup).*

Note: In the expression *aze lo ke te estó dizyendo,* "do what I tell you," **lo ke** (direct object pronoun + *ke* to introduce a clause) is used in the sense of "that which," generally rendered in English as "what."

2. Joining pronouns to verbs

We have already seen how the pronoun can be joined to the infinitive: *finyirla, enshaguarte las manos.* Remember to distinguish between direct object pronouns and reflexive objects: *ambezarse* (reflexive pronoun) "to learn," and *ambezarle una koza a una persona* (indirect object pronoun), "to teach something to someone." Object pronouns are similarly joined to the imperative: *Vístete esta prostela, lávate las manos.*

In summary, the following pronouns are joined to the infinitive and imperative forms of the verb:

—the reflexive pronoun: *lavarse* ⇨ *lávate.*

—The direct object pronoun: *finye la masa* ⇨ *fínyela, kome la masa* ⇨ *kómela, melda los livros* ⇨ *méldalos.*

—The indirect object pronoun: *avla a Lina* ⇨ *ávlale.*

A. The order of the pronouns

♦ When there are two pronouns, the reflexive or the indirect object pronoun precedes the direct object pronoun. Ex.: *para ambezárselo: ambezar* (infinitive) + *se* (reflexive pronoun) + *lo* (direct object pronoun), "to learn it (for himself)." *Ambézamelo:* teach it to me.

♦ With a 2nd person pronoun, the indirect object *le* becomes *se.* *Dile/dízele lo ke saves* becomes *díselo/dízeselo. Ambézale la lisyón* becomes *ambézasela.*

B. Emphasis

The reflexive pronoun is often added to the imperative for emphasis. Instead of *kome el pan* one finds *kómete el pan, bévete la agua* (literally "eat the bread for yourself," "drink the water for yourself").

C. Consonant changes

♦ Before the *l-* of the direct object, the *s* has a tendency to drop: *dámo(s)lo,* give it to us (see Lesson 5A for an earlier example). *Vo lo va dar* (Lesson 6A). *Mo la kantó la nona.*

♦ **Metathesis**—that is, the inversion of two consonants—generally takes place when a command is given with the *-d* of the *vozós* form followed by a direct object. Instead of *ambezadlo* one often finds *ambezaldo* (see *entyendeldo,* p. 159).

3. Special functions of the future tense

Observe: *Viní komeremos. Agora echaremos el shurup. Tomaremos un kafé?*

In all these cases, we are dealing with the future tense, to be studied in Lesson 8. What is important to note here, however, is that in Judeo-Spanish the future tense may serve functions other than to denote future time. In the first example above, the future of *komer* is used in the sense of an invitation given in the *we* form, "let us eat," while in the second example the future of *echar* becomes virtually a command, again in the *we* form: "Let's put in the sugar now." In the third example the future of *tomar* is used to propose an action now: "shall we have coffee?," or "would you like us to have a coffee?"

This third example, asking if someone desires something, is particularly striking in Judeo-Spanish, and is differentiated from the ordinary function of the future tense in that it is asked as a question. A young girl might propose to help her mother pealing an apple in these terms: *Te la mundaré, mamí?* Shall I (do you want me to) peel it for you, mom? *Lo merkaré?* means "Shall I (do you want me to) buy it?

4. Function of the subjunctive in subordinate clauses

Observe: *(mete) el karar ke areyeve.* The speaker here has chosen to express the verb using the subjunctive to show that she is dealing with an indefinite, unknown quantity, difficult to evaluate beforehand.

7a

She could have also used the indicative in this construction: *el karar ke areyeva.* Unlike the statement in the subjunctive, here she is referring to a determined, known quantity that she has already evaluated.

Conjugation

1. The imperative

There are only two persons requiring the imperative form, the 2nd person singular (*tú*) and 2nd person plural (*vozós/vozotros*). Following are the forms for the regular verbs *kantar, komer* and *bivir*:

tú	kanta	kome	bive
vozós/vozotros	kantad/kantá	komed/komé	bivid/biví

Notes:

1. The final -*d* tends to drop from the *vozós* form, but the accent still falls on the last syllable, a particular characteristic of this form.

Certain irregular verbs have shorter imperative forms:

> *vinir* ⇨ *ven, viní/vinid.*   *tener* ⇨ *ten, tené/tened.*
> *dizir* ⇨ *di, dizí/dizid.*   *ir* ⇨ *va, (andá).*

2. The verb *ir* has only the *tú* form of the imperative. For the *vozós* form, the verb *andar* is used. *Andá* (or *Andad*): Go, leave! *Andávos:* get out, get away!

3. When rules or commands are given to a general audience, such as in recipe books, the infinitive form is used rather than the imperative; see Exercise 3. below.

4. In Salonika, the 2nd person plural imperative tends to disappear, and is replaced by the gerundive: *andando!* (let's move on, go on), *komyendo!* (eat, let's eat).

2. Conjugation of the verbs *saver, vinir* and *trayer*

Saver

Pres. subjunctive	Past	Imperfect	Imperative
ke sepa	supe	saviya	save
ke sepas	supites	saviyas	saved/savé
ke sepa	supo	saviya	**Pres. participle**
ke sepamos	supimos	savíyamos	savyendo
ke sepásh	supitesh	saviyash	**Past participle**
ke sepan	supyeron	saviyan	savido

Vinir

Pres. subjunctive	Past	Imperfect	Imperative
ke venga	vine	viniya	ven
ke vengas	vinites	viniyas	viní
ke venga	vino	viniya	**Pres. participle**
ke vengamos	vinimos	viníyamos	vinyendo
ke vengásh	vinitesh	viniyash	**Past participle**
ke vengan	vinyeron	viniyan	vinido

Trayer

Present	Pres. subjunctive	Past	Imperfect
traygo	ke trayga	trushe	traíya
trayes	ke traygas	trushites	traíyas
traye	ke trayga	trusho	traíya
trayemos	ke traygamos	trushimos	traíyamos .
trayésh	ke traygásh	trushitesh	traíyash
trayen	ke traygan	trusheron	traíyan

Imperative	Pres. particip.	Past participle	
traye	trayendo	trayido	
trayed/trayé			

EXERCISES

Exercise 1: Replace the words in bold by the appropriate pronoun (1 or 2 pronouns).
Ex.: *komé(d)* **el pan ke kozyeron** ⇨ *komélo* or *komeldo.*
1. Inche **las domates**. 2. Mete **el bonete a tu ermana**. 3. Merka **este fostán para ti**. 4. Mirá **la televizyón**. 5. Melda **los artíkolos para mí**. 6. Kortad **la karne para los ijos**. 7. Kanta **la kantika para la nona**. 8. Echa **la pará al zarzavachí**. [Note: In making this purchase, a basket attached to a cord is thrown out the window.]

7a

Exercise 2: Translate.
1. Listen to me. 2. Give me your hand. 3. Teach it to him. 4. Look at yourself in the mirror. 5. Read me these books. 6. Recount it to her. 7. Say it to them. 8. Sing it to me. 9. Arrange them on the plate. 10. Turn off (close) the television (for me).

Exercise 3: Put the following recipe into the imperative (tú form).
Ex.: *lava las domates…*
"Domates enreynadas o yenas"
Lavar las domates, mundarlas i kortarlas en dos, kitar lo d'en medyo i las pipitas. Aprontar el gomo (the stuffing). Inchir las domates i apretar el gomo kon el dedo. Untarlas en la arina i el guevo i friyirlas bueno en la azete. Aresentarlas en un paylón, echar por enriva la azete ke kedó, kaldo de domate kon sal i asukuar, tapar i deshar kozer. Komer kayente.

175

Exercise 4: **Kuálo dize la madre a sus ijikos?** *(Compose commands, affirmative or negative as appropriate.)*
– avrir el frijider – meter los dedos en la priz(a) *[electric socket]* – asentar – komer bombones – bever agua yelada – mirar la televizyón – azer el lavoro de la skola – meldar las lisyones – eskrivir una letra a la tiya Malka – djuguar kon top *[ball]* en kaza – saltar enriva de la kanapé – abokarse *[to lean out]* por la ventana.

Exercise 5: **Kuálo keren dizir estos sinyales?** *(Express affirmative or negative commands according to the drawings and the words in the glossary below.)*
Ex.: *3. Pasa enfrente/de enfrente a enfrente. No asperes.*

Glossary – bever sigaro – estar kayado – kayar – asperar – pasar – azer bruido – pasar enfrente – azer dikat – korrer – avlar – amatar el sigaro – tokar – echar al chöp – echar en basho.

Butika de zarzavachí en Estambol.

Readings

Proverbos i dichas

Pan para komer no ay, ravanikos para regoldar
(No bread to eat, little radishes to belch).
This is said of someone who buys superfluous things when there are not enough basic things.

Este arroz areyeva muncho kaldo
(This rice holds a lot of sauce).
This is said of an affair or deal in which many people have an interest.

Pan i azetunas ke seyan i buena veluntad
(May there be bread and olives and good will).
This expresses the desire for a simple and frugal life, an invitation to be happy with little.

Este pan para este kezo
(This bread for this cheese).
Choose what is in harmony, what goes together, the right price for a given quantity, etc.

Pan kon pan komida de bovos
(Bread with bread, a meal for idiots).
This contains a principle of good eating: pasta and potatoes, for example, are not eaten with bread because they are similar in nature.

(Pareserse komo) Guevos partidos
([To resemble someone like] two halves of an egg).
This is said of people who are the spitting image of each other.

Si tu sos ajo yo so pyedra ke te majo
(If you are garlic, then I'm a rock that can crush you).
You may be strong (like garlic) but I'm stronger.

Here are two Judeo-Spanish tongue-twisters:
Una vyeja kon ijada ke majó masá majada/mojada.
(An old woman with a urinary infection who crushed soaked/wet matzah).
Mueve uevos muevos muevos. (Nine eggs, all new).

177

♦ When children ask what food has just been served them, the mother may answer, to stop the complaining: *Es komekaya,* it's eat-hush.

♦ Blessings:
Para mezas de alegriya!
(For tables of joy!): inviting someone to enjoy a dish, a meal, a recipe.

Kon salud i berahá!
(With health and blessing!): to toast someone.

Azlahá en tus manos!
(Prosperity in your hands!): to the good cook (or worker)!

En kada dedo un marafet!
(In each finger a gift!): to the woman who is very nimble with her fingers.

♦ Here is a short version of the *birkat amazón* said by the women at the end of the meal: *Bendicho sea el Dyo ke mos dyo pan para komer, panyos para vistir i anyos para bivir.* God be blessed for he gave us bread to eat, clothes to wear and years to live.

Los guevos ruvyos

Para shabad, para moedes, syempre se keren guevos haminados, guevos ruvyos. Los mijores eran guevos de palaza o de indyana porke son mas godros de los de la gayna.

Se deshavan haminar endjuntos kon la gayna i tomavan la kolor i la golor de la karne, azyéndosen savrozikos. Si no se koziyan kon karne, para darles kolor kaliya una kashka de sevoya o una piska de kavé.

En Balat, el vyernes, vendedores proves arekojiyan guevos i los yevavan al orno en un teneké de fyerro kon samán aryentro para ke se kozyeran i tomaran savor de fumo, duspués los vendiyan por las kayes a los proves.

Memories recounted by Mrs. Rika.

Glossary

el moed (H.): religious holiday.

ruvyo: russet, reddish brown.

la golor: the smell.

savrozo: tasty.

la kashka: the peel, shell.

una piska/pishka: a pinch.

un teneké (T.): a can.

el samán (T.): the straw.

kozyeran, tomaran (imp. subj. of *kozer* and *tomar*).

el fumo: the smoke.

Notes:

1. Observe: *Azyéndosen.* Pronouns can be joined to the present participle just as they are to the infinitive and the imperative (see Lesson 7A). For example, *dizyéndomelo* (while saying it to me), *lavándose* (while washing herself).

2. The present participle (gerundive) of reflexive verbs tends to take on the sign of the 3rd person plural, *-n,* when the reflexive pronoun is joined to it. For ex., *Kanta en lavándose* (he sings while washing himself), *Kantan en lavándosen* (they sing while washing themselves). This is not done systematically but is found quite frequently, especially when reference to the subject is separated from the reflexive verb being used as a present participle.

34 ☺️ *Djohá ande la novya*

No dishimos ke Djohá era bovo? La madre lo mandó a vijitar ande la novya. Antes, le disho la madre ke no komyera demaziya. Le dyeron a komer i Djohá torró a kaza. La madre le demandó ké komyó. "*Albóndigas,*" respondyó el ijo. "*I kómo las komites,*" demandó la madre. "*A una a una,*" disho Djohá. "*Esto se aze!*" s'aravyó la madre, "*kuálo van a pensar! Kale kortar la komida pasikos menudikos i komer avagar avagar!*"

Una semana pasó yiné se fue Djohá ande la novya. A la tornada le kontó a la madre: "*Ize todo djusto komo me dishites. Mos dyeron a komer lentejas i las kortí pedasikos pedasikos i las komí avagar avagar!*"

179

Glossary

demaziya: too much.

una albóndiga: a meatball.

aravyarse: to get angry.

un pasiko/un pedasiko: a little piece.

menudo: small, minute.

yiné (T.): again.

a la tornada: upon returning.

lentejas: lentils.

Questions: *1. Ké aze Djohá en kaza de la novya? 2. Ké konsejos le da su madre? Porké? 3. A Djohá le sirven los konsejos de su madre? Porké?*

El gid para el pratikante

Apartar o mundar kozas en Shabat

[…] Es permetido de azer salata o semejantes en Shabat, a kondisyón de eskojer las ojas buenas i deshar las pudridas o suzyas. Todo esto es permetido kuando los munda por el menester de akea seudá, ma no para la de después, por egzempyo: ke munda o apronta salata la noche para el diya o la demanyana para midí, esto no syerve. […]

Esprimir

No puede esprimir uvas o semejantes para beverlas, solamente limones es permetido de esprimir aryento la komida, tambyén puede esprimir aryento la agua i asukar limones para azer limonada. […]

Kozer

Es defendido de kozer pan o alguna komida ke está kruda. Toda kayentura ke provyene de la lumbre es komo la lumbre mezmo: por egzempyo pozar un guevo krudo alado de una kaldera ke dejá ya está ensima la lumbre o semejantes… Tambyén es defendido de asar, friyir, buyir, sea ke es echo por la lumbre mezmo, sea por la vapör, sea kon elektrik, sea kon gaz o semejantes. […]

Excerpted from *El gid para el pratikante*, Nisim Behar, Güler Basımevi, Istanbul, 1967, pp. 108-109.

Glossary

el gid (F.): the guide.

permetido: permitted.

la salata (T.): the salad.

semejantes: similar things.

eskojer: to select.

la oja: the leaf.

pudrida: rotten.

suzyo, a: dirty.

la seudá (H.): the meal.

asukar: to add sugar.

limonada: lemonade.

midí (F.): noon.

esto no syerve: that won't do.

defendido, a: forbidden.

kayentura: heat (in this context).

la lumbre: the fire (for cooking or heating).

pozar: to pose, put.

alado = al lado: next to.

dejá (F.) = *ya:* already.

ensima: on top of.

el elektrik (T.): electricity.

Questions: *1. Kuálo es defendido en shabad? 2. Mas kuálo no se aze? 3. Ké puedésh azer asigún el gid? 4. Ké devésh de azer asigún la Ley djudiya?*

Vocabulary

Sirve/no sirve (syerve/no syerve): From the verb *servir/sirvir* (to serve), with a variable conjugation as indicated. It is also used in the 3rd person singular as an impersonal form meaning "that is done," "should be done," and in the negative, "that is not done, that won't do."

Exercises

Exercise 1: Fill in the following by adding **sirve** *or* **no sirve** *according to the sense.*

1. Entrar a la mar *(to go swimming in the sea)* en invyerno, ...

2. Pagar sus devdas a tyempo, ...

3. Ambezarse la Ley, ...

4. Azer lumbre en Shabad, ...

5. Komer en diya de Kipur, ...

6. Alegrarse diya de Shabad, ...

Exercise 2: Rewrite the 3 articles in **El gid para el pratikante** *using command forms, affirmative or negative as appropriate, for* **tú** *and* **vozós.**

Ex.: a.*(tú): eskoje las ojas buenas.*

   b. *(vozós): eskojé(d) las ojas buenas.*

COMMUNICATION SKILLS

The interplay of languages

In the preceding text, the influence of French can be seen even in the title (F. *le guide*). Instead of *pratikante* (F.), other words might have been used: *piyadozo, djudyado, hasid.* French *dejá* (*déjà*) reinforces Spanish *ya* for "already." *Vapör* (French *vapeur*, "steam") is used here instead of *bafo,* as in *abafar,* to steam, cook by steaming.

La seudá, a Hebrew term, connotes a meal for a religious festival or special occasion, distinct from a simple *pranso,* of Spanish origin, meaning a banquet.

El aharosi de Pesah

The haroset (el aharosi) *is a dish made with chopped ingredients symbolizing the mortar used by the Hebrews in the construction projects of ancient Egypt. It is prepared and eaten only for the Seder table at Passover, the commemorative meal of Pesah during which is read* la agadá, *the* Haggadah, *recounting the exodus of the Jews from Egypt under the guidance of Moses.*

Para sesh personas: 250 gr. de dátiles pikados sin kueshko, 250 gr. de mansana rayada, medya kupa de muez majada, una kashka de portakal (buyida, esprimida i machukuada), 125 gr. de asukuar, una piska de kanela, sinko klavos de komer mulinados, medya kupa de agua buyida, una kucharada de sumo de limón.

En una oya para dulse meter todo lo ke se disho sin el sumo del limón. Kozer avagar avagar meneando kon kuchara de palo durante dyez o dodje puntos, fin a ke se meskle todo bueno bueno, i se aga preto; echar el limón tres puntos antes de kitar de la lumbre.

From Meri Badi, *250 recettes de cuisine juive espagnole*, Paris, 1984.

Glossary

el datil: the date.	*molinado:* ground, passed through the mill.
el kueshko: the pit.	*el sumo:* the juice.
una piska: a pinch.	*avagar avagar:* slowly and gently.
la kanela: the cinnamon.	*el klavo de komer:* the clove.
de palo/de tavla: wooden.	*sin:* without.
azerse preto: to turn dark	

Sukot meal in the *Suká* of the *kal de Yambol* (Balat).

Seder de Pesah en kaza de M. Ben Adrete (Istanbul).

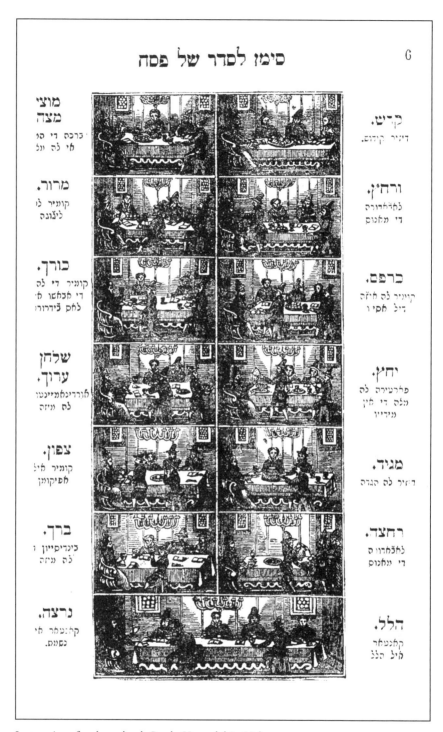

Instructions for the *seder de Pesah, Haggadah* in Hebrew and Ladino, printed in Vienna, end of the 19th century.

Questions: *1. Ké savor tyene el aharosi (es agro?, salado...)? 2. Kuálo sinyifika el aharosi en el seder? 3. Para kuálo sirve el sumo de limón?*

COMMUNICATION SKILLS

Describing what things are made of

Observe: *La kuchara está echa de palo:* the spoon is made of wood.
una kuchara de palo, a spoon of wood = a wooden spoon
una bombonyera de plata, a candy dish of silver = a silver candy dish.

A noun denoting the material something is made of is preceded by the preposition *de.*

de fyero: of iron.	*de hasé:* of cotton cloth, of fine cloth.
de oro: of gold, golden	*de pyedra:* of stone.
de barro: of clay.	*de vidro:* of glass.

CONJUGATION

The verb *kozer/kuezer* (to cook)

Pres. ind.	Pres. subj.	Past
kozgo/kuezgo	ke kozga/ke kuezga	kozí/kuezí
kozes/kuezes	ke kozgas/...	kozites/...
koze/...	ke kozga/...	kozyó/...
kozemos/...	ke kozgamos/...	kozimos/...
kozésh/...	ke kozgásh/...	kozitesh/...
kozen/...	ke kozgan/...	kozyeron/...

Imperative	Past participle
koze/kueze	kozido/kocho
kozé(d)	

Los yaprakitos de karne de Tant Ester

Tant Ester: Ay espinakas ke tyenen las ojas grandes. Las vas a apartar. Estos yaprakes ke son grandes los vas a eskaldar ansina. No los eskaldes kon la agua endjuntos, se te despedasan; les vas a echar la agua

185

kayente enriva. Peshín los vas a kitar i se izo. Vas a tomar la karne kruda, la vas a menear kon un poko de pan mojado i sal, un poko de pimyenta. Ken kere echa sevoya, amá no eches. Para este modo de yaprakitos no sirve. Estas ojas vas a inchir. Yaprakes, apretadikos ansina. Les vas a meter kon un poko de kaldo de karne, sino un poko de agua i azete. Ke se kozgan.

Marko: I armí?!

Tant Ester: Tyempo de domates vas a mirar las muy koloradas i blandas. El kuero i el mijo, lo de aryento, lo vas a kitar. Las vas a azer pedasikos pedasikos. Un kilo de domates tomas, por egzempyo. Echa aryento sal, azete, maydanó un demetiko, i una sevoyika pedasos pedasikos. Lo vas a meter sin agua porke ya tyene agua la domat. Lo vas a meter a poko a poko. Kon asukuar, siguro.

Recipes as given, word for word, by Mrs. Ester Danon.

Glossary

ensegida: immediately.
la espinaka: the spinach.
menear: finyir.
mojado: wet.
el yaprak (T.): grape leaf (for stuffing), stuffed grape leaf or leaf in general.
(d)espedasar: to tear into pieces.
no sirve: that won't do (Lesson 7B).
inchir: to fill, stuff.
apretado: tight.
el kaldo: the gravy, sauce.
sino: otherwise.
el armí (G.): dish based on tomato purée.
blando: soft, tender.
el kuero: the skin.
el mijo: the soft inside of bread.
el maydanó (G.): the parsley.
un demet (T.): a bunch.

Questions: *1. De ké no se echan las ojas de espinaka en la agua kayente? 2. De ké no se mete sevoya en los yaprakitos de karne? 3. Kuálo se aze para gizar armí? 4. De ké se mete asukuar? 5. Ké es lo ke se kita?*

El bokaliko de vino

איל בוקאליקו די ב'ינו די
און בוראג'ון.

————

קואנטו בואינו
מי סום
טו , בוקאל מיאו יינו
אמאדו מאס קי מי אירמאנו
אה מי טום
אממאחאס
אה מי בום
אקלאראס
נו דישאס
ני ייורוס
ני אנסייאס
סום מי אמיגו
אי מי גראנדי אבריגו
קואנטו טו ב'ינו אים אירמוזו
אי קואנטו מי קוראסון סי אזי גוסטוזו
און מיג'ידיאי ב'אלי קאדה גוטיקה אי גוטיקה
אונה לירה ב'אלי קאדה קופיקה אי קופיקה
טודו טיימפו קי ייו איסטו אי ב'ו אה ביב'יר
די טי נו מי ב'ו נונקה אה דיספארטיר
אי טי ב'ו גואדראר דיינטרו מי פינ'ו
קומו און גראנדי פרוב'יג'ו
ב'ינו מיאו איל מי קירידו
ני מי טומים איל סינטידו
איסטאטי ביין קונטינטי
סיגון ייו איסטו אלינגריטי
א. ז' ניאת.
(טיליגראפ'ו, אידיסייון די מארטים 5649)

Glossary

un bokal: a pitcher.   *las ansyas:* the worries.
bor(r)acho, a: drunk.   *el abrigo:* protected shelter.
yeno, a: full (≠ *vaziyo:* empty).   *un medjidiyé:* an Ottoman coin.
la tos, toz: the cough.   *una gotika:* a little drop.
amahar: to alleviate, relieve.   *despartirse (de):* to separate (from).
amar: to love.   *el pecho:* the breast.
la bos/boz: the voice.   *el provecho:* the profit, benefit.
aklarar: to clarify.   *el sintido:* the mind.
deshar: to allow, leave.   *alegrete:* joyful.
los yoros: the sobs, tears.

El bokaliko de vino de
un borachón.

———

kuanto bueno
me sos
tú, bokal miyo yeno
amado mas ke mi ermano
ah, mi tos
a m a h a s
ah, mi bos
a k l a r a s
no deshas
n i   y o r o s
n i   a n s y a s
sos mi amigo
i mi grande abrigo
kuanto tu vino es ermozo
i kuanto mi korasón se aze gustozo
un medjidiyé vale kada gotika i gotika
una lira vale kada kupika i kupika
todo tyempo ke yo estó i vo a bivir
de ti no me vo nunka a despartir
i te vo guadrar dentro mi pecho
komo un grande provecho
vino miyo el mi kerido
no me tomes el sintido
estate byen kontente
sigún yo estó alegrete

A. N. Giat

(*Telegrafo,* edisyón de martes, 5649-1889)
Reproduced in the journal *Aki yerushalayim.*

Notes:

♦ *Kada kupika i kupika. Kada gotika i gotika.*
Kada … i … means "every…" (see Lesson 2A).
♦ *Sigún yo estó alegrete:* just as I am joyful.
Sigún (or *asigún) tú, él, eya, mozós, vozós, eyos, eyas.*
Asigún mi amigo, according to my friend/like my friend (more or less the same as *komo mi amigo).*

188

Grammar

Possessive adjectives and pronouns
Observe: *bokal miyo; vino miyo,* lit. bottle of mine; wine of mine.

el/lo (neuter)/*los*	*miyo(s)*	*la/las*	*miya(s)*	mine
	miyo(s)		*tuya(s)*	yours
	suyo(s)		*suya(s)*	his, hers
	muestro(s)		*muestra(s)*	ours
	vuestro(s)		*vuestra(s)*	yours
	suyo(s)		*suya(s)*	theirs

Lo muestro: what belongs to us; *Los muestros:* those which belong to us.

Komidas i kostumbres

1. *Otras komidas de moedes*
For Pesah, special sweets are prepared, one of which is *sharope blanko de Pesah,* a kind of white confection that requires a veritable mastery for cooking sugar. This sweet, offered to visitors, is perfumed with vanilla with orange peel or *mastiká,* aromatic mastic. In Izmir, *la sodra* (literally, the deaf woman) is a typical Passover soup in which *la masá*—cooked in a broth to which has been added an *agristada,* a sauce made with egg and lemon—takes on the consistency of pasta.

On Purim, fritters with honey are made in a pointed shape, called *orejas de Amán,* Haman's ears, in reference to the treacherous vilain who wanted to destroy the Jews. People also eat *folarikos,* made by wrapping strips of dough around a hardboiled egg to form a little basket. There were also street vendors selling small items made of sugar.

For Simhat Torá, which celebrates the giving of the Law to *Moshé rabenu,* Moses, people eat white foods—that is, milk products. Rice with milk and cream of rice, *el mallebí,* are the most common dishes.

2. *El gostijo*
When someone cooks a dish and has created a particularly good desert, it is a custom to send a little over in a dish for the neighbors to taste. This is what is called *el gostijo.* Indeed, since cooking odors spread widely, if neighbors smell a particularly appetizing dish they might develop a jealous envy for it, and that would be considered inauspicious for the family. If there is a pregnant woman in the neighborhood the sin becomes even greater because her envious desire might harm her child.

Gazetas i revistas en djudeo-espanyol: El Pregonero and *Aki Yerushalayim* (Israel), *Ererensia Sefardi* (U.S.A.), *Şalom* (Turkey), *Los Muestros* (Belgium), *La Lettre Sépharade* (France).

Kozas de tresalir

OBJECTIVES

Communication skills: Expressing feelings, probabilities and possibilities, future time, conditional situations; writing a letter.

Vocabulary: Verbs of feeling.

Grammar: Constructions with verbs of fear, usage of the future and conditional tenses, usage of *ser* and *estar* (continued).

Conjugation: The forms of the future and conditional tenses, variations in conjugations.

Culture: Songs about births, the Haggadah of Passover, the dispersion of the Spanish Jewish community.

---

35 🔊 *...ke te saludo de alto de mi korasón.*

Avlan Ida i Rubén.

Ida: Rubén, aresivimos una letra de l'Ameriká, de tu tiyo Mordo i la Tant Malka.

Rubén: Ya mos eskarinyimos. Kuálo kontan?

Ida: Van a vinir ande mozós, i vijitarán a tu madre, povereta, tanto tyempo sin verlos, se bolará de la alegriya.

Rubén: Van a vinir kon los ijos?

Ida: Sí. Faní kon el ermaniko i kon un novyiziko parese. Kuando se fue a ambezar ivrit a Israel se beyeneó kon un ijiko de Kanadá. Ya s'espozariyan ayá.

Rubén: Faní teniya dyez anyos kuando se fueron, ya teneriya dyez i mueve. I el chikitiko ocho. Kómo se van a gustar los ijos! Me demandaron si viniriyan o no viniriyan i no topí koza para dizirles. Dyez anyos sin vermos las karas!

Ida: Atyó lo vyera tu nona, en ganedén ke esté, tanto ke yoró ke se le fue el ijo regalado.

Rubén: Mi madre yorava ma la nona no amostrava...

Ida: Kómo no! Afilú yo m'estó akodrando, ke éramos rizín kazados. Guay de mí! En tu kaza todos yorando i mauvyando. Es del penseryo i de ke se kedó en kudyado ke se le fuyó el meoyo a tu nona i se izo hazina. Si no se ivan eyos, puede ser dainda estariya en vida!

Rubén: Si mi madre los ve al ermaniko i los sovrinos puede ser ke esté mijor. Si es ke van a vinir presto, pishín le daremos haber ke se le achilee el korasón. Le avriré el telefón?

Ida: Sí, ma dizéselo avagar avagar, porke tyene korasón.

Rubén: No te merekiyes… Ya verás kómo se va a alegrar!

GLOSSARY

Spanish origin

tresalir: to be thrilled, overcome (with joy).

saludar: to greet.

eskarinyarse: to miss, long for someone.

bolarse: to fly off, to boil over (milk), disappear.

la alegriya: the joy, happiness.

gustarse: to be happy.

la kara: the face.

Atyó!: My Lord!

el ijo regalado: the only son.

amostrar: to show, display.

rizín espozados: recently engaged, new fiancés.

mauvyar: to complain (influence of *mauyar:* to meow, howl).

el penseryo: the worry.

kedar en kudyado: to be worried.

se le fuyó el meoyo: she lost her mind.

mijorar/mijorear: to feel better, to improve.

tener korasón: to have a heart condition.

avrir el telefón: to telephone, pick up the receiver.

Other origins

povereta (I.): poor dear.

beyenearse (T.): to be in love, to like each other.

en ganedén (H.): in paradise.

afilú (H.): even, even though.

pishín (T.): immediately.

achilear (T.): to open up, light up.

merekiyarse (T.): to worry.

Communication skills

1. The expression of feelings

♦ To express worries and concerns
Estó en kudyado (por…): I am worried (about…).
Estó penseryozo, merekiyozo (a kavza de…): I am concerned, worried (because of…).
Guay de mí: dear me, oh my! (expressing concern for someone).
Echar guayas: to wail. *Fazer guayas* (Salonika): to cry, express regrets.

♦ To express fear
Me tomó sar: I took fright. *Me asarí:* I became afraid.
Bolarse del sar: to be scared to death.
Batires i firires!: [beatings and blows!] expresses intense emotions due to fear or anger.

♦ To express surprise
Kedí enkantado (enkantarse): I was astonished.
M'enkantí: I was surprised/I was thunderstruck.
Me kedí kuryozo: I was agape.

♦ To express joy
Me se achileó el korasón (T.): my heart lit up, was gladdened.
Se beyenearon los dos/se plazyeron: they liked each other/they fell in love with each other.
Estó kontente: I am happy.
Me alegro: I am delighted, full of joy.
Me gustí: I liked that.
Es koza de tresalir: It's something to fill one with joy.
Tresalirse de alegriya: to be overjoyed.
Me se embreneó la alma (T.): I became enraptured.
Reminder: *a mi me plaze* + infinitive = I like to (…do something).

♦ To express sadness
Mos eskarinyimos (eskarinyarse): We longed for, missed, had nostalgia (for someone).
Estar sehorento: to be sad, distressed.
Manziya i dolor!: Repeating the same notion intensifies this expression of compassion for someone's troubles.

193

Estó triste: I am sad.

Me adjideo de sus sufrimyentos (adjidearse de) (T.): I feel sorry for his suffering, his suffering moves me deeply.

Me se amanziyó la alma al ver… (amanziyarse): I was overcome with pity when I saw…

♦ **To express anger**

Me aravyí (aravyarse): I became angry.

Inyervarse: to become irritable, show bad temper.

Kizdere(y)arse (T.): to become angry.

Me kizdere(y)í muy muncho: I became very angry.

Embirrarse: to fume with anger.

Tomar kolorá/birra: to get angry.

Pletos, males!: [arguments, ills!] expresses the fury or violence of a fight or argument.

2. Expressing a possibility or probability

(Also refer to the use of the conditional, below).

♦ **Puede ser ke + subjunctive:**

Puede ser ke mijore: it's possible that she will get better. The fact that this is a possible eventuality that is still unknown is expressed here by the use of the subjunctive. Since this event will go on into the future, the subjunctive in fact can take on the function of the future tense and be translated into English as "maybe she will get better." The *ke* may be omitted: *puede ser mijore.*

In the past tense the indicative would be used: *Puede ser ke mijoró* (maybe she got better). In the present tense, however, the degree of probability can be expressed with nuances of meaning by the choice of the indicative or subjunctive:

Indicative = *Puede ser ke tyene este livro:* Maybe he has this book (he probably has it).

Subjunctive = *Puede ser ke tenga este livro:* He may have this book (but I doubt it).

GRAMMAR

1. Expressing verbs of fear

♦ *m'espanto de* + noun.

   M'espanto del doktor: I am afraid of the doctor.

♦ *M'espanto ke* + indicative, when the thing feared is real or thought to be so. Often the fear has a cause that is expressed.

m'espanto ke va a vinir: I am afraid that (because) he is going to come.

m'espanto ke kome todo: I am afraid he is going to eat everything. This could also be expressed: *M'espanto porke kome todo*.

♦ *M'espanto ke* + subjunctive when there is fear caused by the uncertainty of a future event.

m'espanto ke no venga: I am afraid that he might not come.

m'espanto ke koma todo: I am afraid he might eat everything.

Note: *ke* can be dropped and be replaced by the word *no* that does not negate (*cf.* the "pleonastic *ne*" in French grammar). This construction is similar to the somewhat archaic use of the word *lest* in English.

*M'espanto **no** koma todo:* I am afraid he will eat everything (I fear **lest** he eat everything). However, the *no* may have a truly negative function; the sense can only be determined by the context. For example:

*M'espanto **no** tengas tyempo para verlo:* I am afraid that you **won't** have time to see him.

There may be situations where the sense is ambiguous. *M'espanto no me aspere* can mean "I am afraid he **will** wait for me" or "I am afraid that he **won't** wait for me." Some other comment or a clear context is needed here to specify the exact meaning. For example:

M'espanto no me aspere i se vayga: "I'm afraid he **won't** wait for me and will leave.

M'espanto no me aspere i se kizdereye ke no vine presto: "I'm afraid he **will** wait for me and get angry because I didn't come right away."

2. Uses of the future tense

Formerly the future tense was sometimes used in speech and always used in writing. In modern times it has been systematically replaced in the spoken language by the use of the immediate future (*ir* + infinitive) to denote future time. *Vo a vinir para Roshashaná* is more natural than *Veniré (verné/vendré) para Roshashaná*.

In this respect, even if the immediate future (*ir* +...) does not have the same degree of certainty or firmness as the future tense, and even in situations where the future would sound perfectly normal, the future is replaced:

Vijitarán a tu madre ⇨ *Van a vijitar a tu madre.*

Se bolará de la alegriya ⇨ *Se va a bolar de la alegriya.*

Ya verás komo se va a kontentar ⇨ *Ya vas a ver komo...*

195

The future tense is, however, used to serve other functions, as we have previously seen:

—to soften a command. *Serrarésh la puerta:* [You will close…] Close the door.

—to propose an invitation. *Tomaremos un kavé?:* Shall we have coffee? (see Lesson 7A). *Le aviré el telefón?:* Would you like me to telephone him?

—to make a decision for the *we* form. *Mos asentaremos:* Let's sit down!

—to express doubt. *Kén será?* Who could that be?

3. The conditional tense

Observe: *Ya s'espozariyan ayá. Ya teneriya dyez i mueve.*
        Me demandaron si viniriyan o no viniriyan.
        Si no se ivan eyos, dainda estariya en vida.

Above are examples of the conditional tense in Judeo-Spanish, used mainly for **three** types of situations:

♦ **Probability**. The conditional is frequently used to speculate about some possible happening.

Ya s'espozariyan ayá: They must have already become engaged over there.

Ya teneriya dyez i mueve: She must already be 19 years old.

This is the only type of situation where the conditional tense is likely to be used in a natural manner in speech. Expressions with *dever* are also used in such situations, but are less hypothetical. *Deve tener dyez i mueve:* She is probably 19 years old. The emphasis on this construction is on the fact of her being around 19 years old, while the emphasis on *teneriya…* is more on the speculative nature of the statement.

Note: The conditional perfect is not used, only the present conditional.

♦ **Future time when reported in the past**. The nature of the conditional (the future stem + the imperfect endings) makes it particularly suitable for expressing future time when talking about a past situation.

Dize ke vendrá ⇨ *Disho ke viniriya/vendriya.*

Like the future, however, it is often replaced by the construction *ir* + infinitive.

Dize ke va a vinir ⇨ *Disho ke iva a vinir.*

Thus, the general abandonment of the future tense for this usage also applies to the conditional.

♦ **Expressing unreal situations.**

Si no se ivan (aviyan ido) eyos, dainda estariya en vida: If they had not left, she would still be alive. When a statement is made that is contrary to fact, unreal, wishful thinking, etc., there is generally an *if* clause (*si no se ivan…*) followed by a clause with the conditional tense (*estariya*). Even in this usage, however, the construction *ir* + infinitive may replace the conditional tense. The speaker could therefore have said: *Si no se ivan (aviyan ido) eyos* (an unreal hypothesis, a wish that is contrary to fact), *puede ser dainda iva a estar en vida.* The true conditional tense is still maintained in writing by older persons, cultivated people, or those who have a good knowledge of French or Spanish.

CONJUGATION

1. Formation of the future tense

♦ **Regular verbs**. Infinitive + endings: *-é, -ás, -á, -emos, -ésh, -án.*
Almost all verbs are regular in the future tense. Following are model forms:

kantar	komer	bivir
kantaré	komeré	biviré
kantarás	komerás	bivirás
kantará	komerá	bivirá
kantaremos	komeremos	biviremos
kantarésh	komerésh	bivirésh
kantarán	komerán	bivirán

azer	saver	ir
azeré	saveré	iré
azerás	saverás	irás
azerá	saverá	irá
azeremos	saveremos	iremos
azerésh	saverésh	irésh
azerán	saverán	irán

8a

There are a few irregular forms. *Aver,* for example, begins: *avrá* (and see also 8B). There are also frequent fluctuations in verbs that are normally regular, for example:

Saver: savré, savrás, etc.

Azer: aré, arás, etc.

Notes:

♦ Placing the accent on the final syllable is a characteristic of the future (except for the *we* form).

♦ The verb *vinir* has three possible forms:

Regular: *viniré, vinirás, vinirá,* etc.

An intermediary form with metathesis of r/n:

verné, vernás, verná, vernemos, vernésh, vernán.

Irregular: *vendré, vendrás, vendrá, vendremos, vendrésh, vendrán.*

2. Formation of the conditional tense

This tense is even more regular than the future. It is formed by adding to the infinitive the endings of the imperfect tense of *-er* / *–ir* verbs:

-iya, -iyas, -iya, íyamos, -iyash, -iyan.

kantar	komer	bivir
kantariya	komeriya	biviriya
kantariyas	komeriyas	biviriyas
kantariya	komeriya	biviriya
kantaríyamos	komeríyamos	biviríyamos
kantariyash	komeriyash	biviriyash
kantariyan	komeriyan	biviriyan

azer	saver	ir
azeriya	saveriya	iriya
azeriyas	saveriyas	iriyas
azeriya	saveriya	iriya
azeríyamos	saveríyamos	iríyamos
azeriyash	saveriyash	iriyash
azeriyan	saveriyan	iriyan

Exercises

Exercise 1: Translate into Judeo-Spanish using **puede ser ke** + *the indicative or + the subjunctive.*

1. He has probably gone to bed. 2. It's possible they don't know where to go. 3. Maybe they are coming/going to come. 4. It's possible you'll find a bus [use *vozós*]. 5. Maybe we're crazy. 6. It's possible that we are crazy. 7. Maybe she'll read this book. 8. It's possible she'll read this book.

Exercise 2: Rewrite the verbs using the future tense.

Ex.: *van a vinir = venirán* (or *vernán* or *vendrán*).

1. Mis amigos van a vinir alhad. 2. Mi nona va a salir del ospital. 3. Vamos a ir al tiyatro. 4. Vo a dizir la berahá. 5. Vash a tener un muevo haham. 6. Vas a azer la kolada? 7. Vamos a komer endjuntos. 8. Va a azer luvya. 9. Vash a bever un kaviko. 10. Se van a alevantar.

Exercise 3: Put the verb in parentheses into the conditional tense.

1. Me disho ke su padre (vinir). 2. Tu ya lo (saver). 3. Te kontaron ke yo (ir) a Yerushalayim. 4. Si mos dava la lisensya, mozós (azer) un vyaje. 5. Yo te (dar) la gazeta de oy ma tu ya la (meldar). 6. Mozós (salir) de kaza i mos (ir) al sinemá kon ti, ma la mamá (kizderearse).

Exercise 4: Translate into English the sentences composed in Ex. 3.

(Note: *vyaje:* trip; *gazeta:* newspaper).

Exercise 5: Translate into English.

1. M'espanto no tengamos haber. 2. S'espantaron ke no viniya. 3. No t'espantates ke no te yamí? 4. Mos espantamos porke vyene kon arabá. 5. S'espantan ke tyene kuchiyo. 6. S'espantan no tenga kuchiyo. 7. S'espanta ke su madre esté hazina. 8. M'espantí porke no saviya la lisyón i el rubí se arravyariya. 9. M'espanto no sepa la lisyón i ke el rubí lo konte a todos. 10. M'espanto no sepa ánde está i vayga a otro luguar. 11. S'espanta ke no vo a topar la repuesta.

Exercise 6: Translate into Judeo-Spanish.

1. I'm afraid of him. 2. We were afraid that the glass might break. 3. I am afraid that your brothers won't get out of school (*eskolar*) before seven o'clock. 4. Are you [polite] afraid that I'm leaving? 5. You were frightened because there was some noise. 6. I'm afraid you are going to eat everything (lest you eat everything). 7. She got scared because he was crying. 8. I am afraid to get burned.

Exercise 7: Translate into English.

1. Tomaremos un kavé? 2. Agora serraré la ventana. 3. Levantarán el plato de la meza i dirán la berahá. 4. Amanyana mos iremos al kal. 5. El anyo ke vyene vijitaremos la Spanya. 6. Aspera veremos. 7. Yamaré al doktor? 8. Ma savrésh ke la ija del rey estava espozada. 9. Si es ke vash a vinir, aparejaremos la kamareta. 10. Mos asentaremos! [Note: *aparejar:* to prepare; *asperar:* to wait).

Exercise 8: Translate into Judeo-Spanish.

1. He must have already brought it. 2. He must easily be fifty years old. 3. If you weren't going to tell it, I would have told you. 4. That must have cost a lot. 5. We would write him, but he won't know how to read our letter in French. 6. You asked (*pruntar*) us if we were going to make our *aliyá* but we would need some advice (*konsejos*). 7. Without his help, the old rabbi wouldn't eat every day.

Exercise 9: *Es diya de semana, k'estarán azyendo esta buena djente?* (It's a weekday; what are these good folks likely to be doing?) Answer by referring to the occupation shown in parentheses.

Ex.: *Madmuazel Marika (kuzandera)… estará kuzyendo un fostán para mi ermana.*

1. Mösyö Albert (empyegado de la banka)…
2. Madam Alegra (kazamentera)…
3. David (estudyante)…
4. Lina (eleva en la skola Aliansa)…
5. Mösyö Salomon (merkader)…
6. Madmuazel Suzan (trezladadora en la embasada)…
7. Madam Luiz (balabaya)…
8. Shimón Leví (jurnalisto)…
9. Avram Eskenazí (sarraf)…
10. Madam Merí (doktora de kriyaturas)…

Shastres, hamales, balabayas, isportadjís djudyós. (Balat, 19th century).

READINGS

Proverbos i dichas

♦ Expressions regarding psychological attitudes

Yorar ay, mauvyar ay
(There is crying, there is shouting).
This expression, modeled on the Turkish, denotes despair or affirms that life is but a valley of tears. *Mauvyar* comes from the confusion between *maulyar*, originally "to meow" and later "to howl," and of *mover*, to miscarry, abort, bring to a bad end. *Mauvyar la estreya:* to make the good star miscarry, to cause misfortune.

Las naves se te batearon en Yerushalayim?
(Did your boats sink in Jerusalem?).
This is an absurd adaptation of the Turkish expression "Did your boats sink in the Black Sea?," said to someone who looks as though he has been to a funeral.

Penso i arepenso i del penseryo salgo loko
(I think and keep thinking and my worries drive me crazy).
Meaning: You should not worry yourself crazy.

Está myedo teneré i no m'espantaré
(He/she says "I'll be afraid but I won't get scared").
This is said of someone who does not want to show he/she is afraid.

Guay del ke se fue
(Pity for the one who is gone).
The living remain and lament but it is the dead person who should be the one to be pitied.

Djohá ke no se echava kon sehorá vyeja
(Djohá who never went to bed with an old worry).
One meaning is: The fool manages to find a new worry every day. It is also used, however, to connote freedom from concern. Another expression goes: *Djohá ke no tyene kasavet* (T. for melancholy, worries), in reference to a simpleton who is happy despite causes for worrying, "the happy fool."

Meldó muy muncho salyó loko
(He studied [the Torah] too much and went crazy).
Studying is dangerous if it is not kept under control.

Un korasón espejo de otro
(One heart the mirror of another).
When two people think the same thought at the same time, they are very close to each other.

♦ **Good wishes**

Mankura ke no ayga! or *Ke no mos manke nunkua*
(May there be no loss *or* May we never have occasion to miss him/her).
Let no one we know die. The second expression is used in conversations to replace the name of someone who is away, often a husband, to protect him from misfortune. *Vino el ke no mos manke:* literally, He who should not go missing to us, came. This is a roundabout way of saying "My husband came" when the husband is not there.

Ugurlís i kademlís!
Two terms coming from the Turkish meaning "happy and fortunate;" a wish for good fortune.

Rikos i dovletlís!
Like the preceding, "rich and wealthy," joining a term of Spanish origin to a term of Turkish origin that means the same.

CONJUGATION

Fluctuation of forms in the future tense

When the Expulsion took place in 1492, the future tense had not yet stabilized on the Iberian peninsula. Several forms co-existed. Judeo-Spanish has retained the traces of this fluctuation. For example, in the same texts one can find the regular form *teneré* side by side with *terné* (based on the shortened form of *teneré, tenré,* with metathesis of the *n* and *r*), and even the form *tendré* which became the stable form in modern Castilian. This same lack of stability explains the fluctuations that we saw for *vinir, dizir, azer,* and *saver* in Lesson 8A.

La chosa del desesperado

For a word on the genre of the romanse, *see Lesson 6B. The following song of despair is the source of a popular expression, frequently used as a threat—to leave for good or to kill herself—by overworked housewives and mothers:* yo me vo a ir por estos kampos endelantre *(I am going to go out into these fields, straight ahead).*

Irme kero por estos kampos – por estos kampos me iré
i las yervas de los kampos – por pan yo las komeré
lágrimas de los mis ojos – por agua las beveré
kon unyas de los mis dedos – los kampos los kavaré
kon sangre de las mis venas – los kampos los arregaré
En medyo de akeyos kampos – una chosa fraguaré
por afuera kal i kanyo – por aryentro la entiznaré
todo ombre deskaminante – aryentro lo entraré
ke me konte de sus males – de los miyos le kontaré
si los suyos son mas munchos – a pasensya los tomaré
si los miyos son mas munchos – kon mis manos me mataré
kon mis manos me mataré – guay me mataré.

Text published by Guy Levis-Mano,
Romancero Judeo-espagnol, GLM, 1971. (Spelling adapted here).
New edition, Paris: Allia, 1994, *cf.* Bibliography.

Glossary

los kampos: the fields.
la yerva: the grass.
las lágrimas: the tears.
las unyas: the fingernails.
kavar: to dig.
las venas: the veins.
arregar: to water.
una chosa: a hut.
la kal: the whitewash.
el kanyo: adobe, mud.
entiznar: to cover with soot, blacken.
deskaminante: wandering off the path, lost.
entrar: (in this context) to have someone come in.
tomar a pasensya: to bear patiently.
matarse: to kill oneself.

Questions: *1. Kómo se ve la dolor del dezesperado? 2. Porké entizna su chosa? 3. Porké kere ke la djente le konte sus males?*

The birth of a child gives rise to all kinds of celebrations and festivities that we have already seen (Lesson 5B). The following song is always sung to a mother who has just given birth (la parida). *As the song indicates, the performance was left to a paid singer. Today it is the mother or mother-in-law of* la parida *who sings it. It would be considered a bad omen to sing it in the presence of a pregnant woman or in the absence of the newborn baby.*

Oh ke mueve mezes travatesh de estrechura
Vos nasyó un novyo de kara de luna
Mos biva la parida kon su kriyatura
Bendicho el ke mos ayegó a ver este diya
Ya es, ya es buen simán esta alegriya

Kuando la komadre dize: "Dale! Dale! Dale!"
Dize la parida "Ah Dyo, eskápame!"
Dize la su madre "Amén, amén, amén!"
Ya es, ya es buen simán esta alegriya.

Ke byen empleadas fueron las dolores
Vos nasyó un ijo de kara de flores
Syempre de kontino al Dyo demos loores
Ya es, ya es buen simán esta alegriya

Oh ké pino, pino revedrino
Mos biva el parido
Ke mos trayga vino
Por mezé likorino
Ya es, ya es buen simán esta alegriya

Kuando la komadre baruh abá le dishera
Se alegró el parido kon su kasta entera
A toda su djente muncho gusto le dyera
Ya es, ya es…

Parida, parida, desh me las estrenas
Para esta kantika ke es de las buenas
Vos alevantesh parida kon las manos yenas
A kriyar i a gozar ninyo en su vida

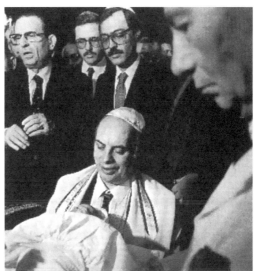

Berit milá del inyeto
de Şaul Kapeluto (Istanbul).

La nona traye al inyeto para la milá (Istanbul).

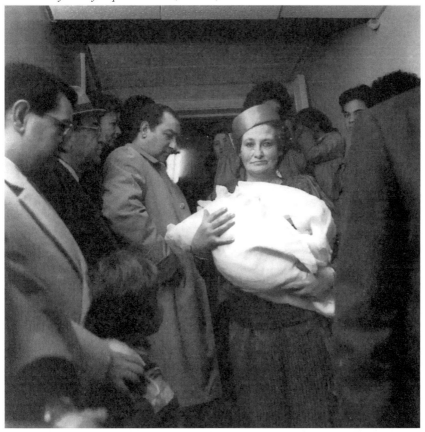

Salonika, 1910:
Madre kon su kriyatura
(Juda/Mondón family).

Congratulations on a birth;
in *La Luz de Israel*, Tel Aviv, 1977.

Oh ké pino …

Ya vyene el parido kon los konvidados
Traye en la mano resta de dukados
I en la otra mano vino i buen pishkado
Ya es, ya es …

Ya vino el parido a los pyés de la kama
Le disho la parida "Oy no komí nada"
Presto ke le traygan gayna enreynada
Ya es, ya es…

Oh ké parra parra revedrida
Mos biva la parida kon su kriyatura
A kriyar i a gozar ninyo en su vida
Ya es, ya es…

Glossary

travar estrechura: to suffer difficulties.
la luna: the moon.
naser: to be born.
ayegar: to bring (to a point in time).
un simán (H.): a sign, omen.
eskapar: (in this context) to deliver, release.
emplear: to use.
de kontino: constantly.
la loor: the praise.
el pino: the pine.
revedrido = revedrino: newly green.
el parido: the husband of the new mother.
el mezé (T.): hors-d'oeuvre.
el likorino: smoked mullet.
dar las estrenas: to give gifts, pay.
kriyar: to nurse, raise (a child).
gozar: to enjoy.
los konvidados: the guests.
una resta: a necklace, garland.
enreynada/areyenada: stuffed.
la parra: the trellis, grape arbor.
There are several versions of this song. Another one can be found in the book
by Manuel Alvar, *Poesía tradicional de los Judíos españoles,* Mexico: Porrua,
1979, p. 181.

37 🎵 *Durme, durme, ermoza donzeya* (lullaby)

Durme, durme, ermoza donzeya
Durme, durme, sin ansya i sin dolor (repeat)

Es tu madre ke tanto dezeya
ver tu suenyo kon grande ardor (repeat)

Syente djoya el son de mi gitarra
Syente ermoza mis males kantar (repeat)

Glossary

ermoza: beautiful.   *dezeyar:* to desire.   *la gitarra:* the guitar.
donzeya: young lady.   *la ardor:* the passion.   *el mal:* evil, sorrow.
la ansya: the worry.   *la djoya:* the jewel.   *los males:* the troubles.

Koplas de Yosef Ha-Tsadik

Composed in 1730 by Abraham de Toledo and published in Salonika and Constantinople, these 595 koplas recount the story of Abraham and Jacob but especially of Joseph. Several sections are in dialogue form and meant to be performed on stage, while others have notations for musical performance. The episode of Potiphar's wife is given a lengthy treatment (33 stanzas). She is given the name Segoviana. Here, rebuffed by Joseph, she sings a plaint in a stanza with a different form (the poem moves from an abab *rhyme scheme to* aaab, cccb, *etc., a verse form called* zehel*).*

"Yosef, mi alma i mi vida,
por ti yo ya so perdida
so yo tu syerva vendida
apiyádate de mí

Yosef, luzido i galante
pulido, mi diyamante
ke no seas tu kavzante
ke me mate de mí a mí

Yosef el pye kuanto te bezo,
ke el alma me tyenes prezo
no me agas perder el sezo,
así me enterres tú a mí

Yosef, kara de alegriya
no me mates kon manziya,
ke me apuro de diya en diya
amanzíyate de mí

Yosef, respóndeme agora,
sin myedo ni sin [p]avora
ke yo so tu esklava mora
kapará vaya yo por ti

Yosef, pye de buena estrena
porké me das tanta pena?
prezo me tyenes en kadena,
ke yo me muero por ti.

Yosef, mi kara de flores
me afinan tus kolores;
gozaremos de amores,
tú kon mí i yo kon ti

Yosef, troka esta suerte;
Ven, te bezaré la frente
no muramos de mala muerte
tú por mí, i yo por ti."

Published by Moshe Lazar, *Joseph and his Brethren*,
Culver City, CA: Labyrinthos, 1990, p. 206-208.

Glossary

perdida (pyedrida/pedrida): lost
syerva: woman servant, slave.
apiyadarse: to take pity on.
luzido/luzyo: handsome.
pulido: polished, handsome.
kavzante: person who causes.
matarse: to kill oneself.
bezar: to kiss.
la alma: the soul.
la manziya: pain, affliction.

amanziyarse: to take pity on.
la pavora: the fright.
mora: Moorish woman.
kapará (H.): sacrifice.
afinar: to refine.
gozar: to enjoy.
trokar: to change, exchange.
la suerte: luck, chance.
la frente: the forehead.
apurarse: to wear oneself out.

Letra

This letter, written in Solitreo (middle-eastern Hebrew cursive script used to write Judeo-Spanish) by an elderly man to his brother who emigrated to France, did not receive an answer because the family could not figure out how to read the script.

> *A mi muy kerido ermano,*
>   *resiví tu estimada letra kon los 100 frankos i me gustí ke ya vos topásh todos sanos i rezyos i yo tam[b]yén ya me topo bueno i syempre saveremos bueno de parte a parte, amén.*
>   *Te rogo mi karo ermano Behor ke me digas ké es este karar ke me tadrates la letra? No pensates ke ya pasó 6 mezes i no pensas en este ermano: bive? Muere? Hazino está? Syego está? Lavorando está? Kómo se topa este ermano noche de moedes i las noches de shabad. A la fin sávelo ke es un o[m]bre de 72 anyos ke estos anyos todo lo pasí en mizerya i en tu uerfandad.*
>   *[...] Yo penso syempre en ti porke sos o[m]bre hazino i no tengo mas de ti i del Dyo. Kuando me tadras la letra se me va el penseryo en mil lugares.*
>   *Mas no tengo otro ke sero mi chika letra. Selam para toda tu famiya i todos los ke son a tu lado.*
>   *Selam para ti mi karo ermano ke te bezo las manos komo ermano grande ke no me mankes. Selam de tu karo ermano Yontov.*
>   *Te mandí a dizir ke iva a vinir tu inyeto; ké es la kavza ke no vino? De ké lo asperí a ojos a ojos i no vino? [...]*
>   *Repuesta sin falta i no me deshes en penseryo i en merekiya. Si azes kuento de Pesah fin Roshashaná pasó de 6 mezes. Adyo bueno.*
>   *León*

Glossary

gustarse: to be happy, take pleasure.

toparse bueno: to be in good health.

rezyo: sturdy, in good health.

hazino: sick.

syego: blind.

moed (H.): religious holiday; *en moedes:* religious festival time.

uerfandad: fact or feeling of being an orphan.

serrar: to close, finish.

selam (T.): fond greetings.

asperar: to wait.

(asperar) a ojos a ojos: (to wait) impatiently.

pasar de: to go beyond.

Note the use of use of *ser* where we would normally expect *estar: los ke son a tu lado.* This use connotes a feeling of existence rather than a description of location: "those who are (who live) at your side."

Questions: *1. Ké le mandó su ermano? 2. Ánde bive el ermano Behor? 3. De ké se gustó el sinyor León? 4. De ké está en kudyado? 5. Porké se está keshando? 6. Tyene muncha paryentés el sinyor León? 7. Kén iva a vinir a verlo?*

COMMUNICATION SKILLS

How to write a letter

—Addressing a relative: *mi karo (ermano), mi kerido/kirido (ermano)…* To a more distant acquaintance: *mi estimado sinyor…*
—The first paragraph contains blessings, thanks, and wishes for good health.
—Formulaic expressions: *te mandí a dizir* is somewhat formal for *te rogí ke me disheras. te demandí ke. Resiví tu estimada letra* is a formula that would not be used in oral speech.
—Greetings: *adyó bueno, selam para toda la famiya, te bezo las manos* (in deference to an older brother).
—Formulas for signing off: *mas no tengo otro (ke dizirte* or *de alargar* understood), *ke sero mi chika letra.* Another frequent formula noted in correspondence: *Mas no tengo de alargar otro, ke te saludo de alto de mi korasón. Repuesta sin falta* calls for an urgent response. *Mas no vo alargar, espero haberes buenos de ti i de tu famiya. Te embiyo munchos bezos i abrasos.*
—Before the signature the relationship may be repeated: *tu kerido ermano, tu madre, tu amiga,* or simply *karinyozamente,* tenderly, with affection.

The letter itself constitutes a sign of caring. The contents may be completely impersonal. Its function is to maintain a relationship. People avoid announcing bad news in a letter, and even on the telephone. Only anodine or optimistic news should be given, although this does not exclude a few reproaches…

El gid para el pratikante

La ravya

1. La ravya i la sanya son tósigos muy perikolozos; perkura kon toda tu fuersa a alesharte de eyas, i por siguro ke eskaparás de munchos males.

2. El ke se inyerveya alkuruto (durmadan) se le akurta su vida.

4. No tomes kolora para ke no vengas a pekar.

5. Kual es el verdadero baragán, akel ke se save detener en ora de ravya.

10. La sanya i la ravya son la puliya de kaza ke destruye i deroka famiyas.

11. El ke se mete en kolora a parte ke danya a su alma, danya tambyén a su kuerpo, syendo en akea ora no tyene el meoyo en su kavesa vyene azer danyos. No respekta a ninguno, no konose padre i madre, i vyene has ve shalom a kafrar en el Dyo de Yisrael.

Nisim Behar, *El gid para el pratikante*,
Istanbul: Güler Basimevi, Istanbul, 1967, p. 252.

Glossary

la ravya: rage, fury.
la sanya: anger, relentlessness.
el tósigo: poison.
perikolozo: dangerous.
perkurar a (or de): to try to.
alesharse: to move away, keep at a distance.
eskapar: to finish, recover from.
inyerveyarse: inyervarse.
alkuruto: endlessly (the Turkish word in parentheses means the same thing: *durmadan*).
akurtar: to shorten.

el bar(r)agán: the strong person.
detenerse: to hold oneself back.
la puliya: the moth (fig. a destructive thing).
derokar: to knock down, destroy.
danyar: to damage, do wrong.
el kuerpo = el puerpo: the body.
el meoyo: the brain, mind.
has ve shalom (H.): God forbid.
kafrar (H.): to reject, blaspheme.

Questions: *1. Kuáles son los danyos (the damage, harm) de la sanya o la kolora? 2. El ke se inyerva o se peleya es un baragán? 3. Kómo peka el inyervozo?*

La Agadá de Pesah

As should be apparent, the following text will be difficult to understand if reference is not made to the Hebrew text of which it is a calque rather than a translation. In fact, while understanding the gist of the subject one would need a translation. This calque is what Haïm-Vidal Sephiha calls "Ladino." This artificial language allowed the holy text to be understood. Its particular purpose was to serve as an intermediary between the vernacular language (Judeo-Spanish) and the holy language (Hebrew), the latter being the object of study and training It therefore served an important pedagogical function. This calque-language—recited, learned, transformed into a liturgical language— also had an influence on Judeo-Spanish.

> *Bendicho el Guadran su feguzya a Israel bendicho El. Ke el Santo Bendicho El kontán a la fin, por azer komo lo ke disho, a Avram muestro padre en el firmamyento entre los espartimyentos. Ke ansí dize el pasuk: I disho a Avram saver savrás, ke pelegrino será tu semen en tyerra ke non a eyos, i sirvir los arán, i afriyirán a eyos kuatro syentos anyos. I tambyén a la djente ke servirán djuzgán yo. I después ansí saldrán[16] kon ganansya grande.*
>
> Izidor Baruh, *Haggadah shel Pessah*, Istanbul:
> Or-Ahayim hastanesi, 1981, p. 13.

Glossary

bendicho: blessed.

feguzya: faith, confidence.

el espartimyento: the separation.

el pasuk (H.): Biblical verse.

pelegrino: pilgrim, vagabond (noun and adj.).

semen: seed ⇨ descendants.

afriyir: to deprive, persecute, torment.

djuzgar: to judge.

saldrán/sarlán: they will go out, take out.

la ganansya: gain, retribution, profit.

Questions: *1. De ké avla este teksto? 2. Ké tyerra es la "tyerra ke non a eyos"? 3. A kén va a djuzgar el Dyo? 4. A kén sirvyeron los Djudyós? 5. Kén los kitó de Misraim? 6. Ké ganansya tuvyeron?*

Notes:

1. *Saver savrás:* this juxtaposition of the infinitive and the future constitutes a calque from the Hebrew, likewise the clipped present participles *djuzgán* and *kontán* for *djuzgando* and *kontando* and the ellipsis of the verb *ser* in the expression "*en tyerra ke non (es) a eyos.*"

---

16. The Salonika Haggadah gives *sarlán*.

2. The above is the transcription of a passage in *Ladino* written in square characters. In the Haggadah of Salonika—which contains passages in Hebrew, Ladino written in square characters, Ladino transcribed into Latin characters, and Greek—we find the expression *i servirlos an,* an archaic Spanish form for *los servirán.* In the text above we find *sirvir los arán* (they will make them serve).

3. *Saldrán* (*sarlán* in Salonika): this is the future of the verb *salir,* with the assimilation of a vowel and a metathesis between the *r* and *l: saliré* ⇨ *salré* ⇨ *sarlé, sarlás, sarlá, sarlemos, sarlésh, sarlán.* Regular forms also exist: *saliré, salirás, salirá,* etc.

The text of the Haggadah is known by heart more than any other. Many expressions and metaphors are appropriated into normal conversation for amusing effect. For example, a mother may refer to her children as *un bovo, un loko, i uno ke no save por demandar:* a simpleton, a crazy one and one who doesn't know how to ask questions. If something is hard to get, people will say *kon poder fuerte/kon mano fuerte i braso estendido:* [you can only get it] with strong force/with a strong hand and outstretched arm. *Ke ansí dize el pasuk* (As the verse says) is used as an amusing introduction to a general truth, a trite statement, or some personal comment that puts a distance between oneself and the expression. As for that promise that has been repeated for so long in the Diaspora, *Este anyo akí syervos **a el anyo el vinyén en tyerra de Israel** ijos foros,* the portion in bold is frequently used to mean "that will be the day," "you've got a long wait ahead." *Syervos fuimos a Paró?* I am not your slave; *demandas de Paró,* impossible questions; *las makás de Paró,* the plagues of Pharaoh, all the plagues of Egypt .

Some passages are used to create amusing parodies in other languages, through plays on words or by using a chanting intonation.

Passage from the *haggadah de Pesah.*

הָא לַחְמָא עַנְיָא דִי	אִיסְטֵי פָּאן דִי לָה אַפְלִירִי
אֲכָלוּ אַבְהָתָנָא בְּאַרְעָא	אִיסְיוֹן. קִי קוֹמְיֵירוֹן מוֹאִיסְ
דְמִצְרָיִם. כָּל דִּכְפִין יֵיתֵי	טְרוֹם פָּאדְרֵים אִין טְיֵירָה דִי
וְיֵיכוֹל. כָּל דִּצְרִיךְ יֵיתֵי	אַיְפְּטוֹ. טוֹדוֹ אֵל קִי טוּבְּיֵינְסִ
וְיִפְסַח. הַשַּׁתָּא הָכָא.	אַמְבְּרֵי אִינְטְרִי אִי קוֹמָה.
לְשָׁנָה הַבָּאָה בְּאַרְעָא	טוֹדוּ אִיל קִי טוּבְּיֵינְסִי דִימִי
דְיִשְׂרָאֵל. הַשַּׁתָּא הָכָא	נִיסְטִיר אִינְטְרִי אִי פָּאסְקוּאָי.
	אִיסְטֵי אַנְיוֹ אֵקִי. אָאִיל אַנְיוֹ
	אִיל בִּינְיֵין אִין. מְיֵירָה דִי

הגדה של פסח

כפי מנהג ספרדים יצ׳ו

ל׳׳ככ׳׳תשאדים קון ל׳יגרה לימנות לי לאריגאהרה עניי גין
הי קומפליהה אל סהר אינטירו הי לה כ׳׳׳.

ועם ציורים נאים ויפים הנדמרים למראה עין צנפים.

ל׳׳כנו אין טוניקא דיל ס׳ה יוסף ישלעווינגער אין לייהם
דישטענעכטעכ.אסהר׳׳ **6**

Made in Austria.

Cover page of the Passover Haggadah,
Vienna, end of the 19th century.

Kantika de Nisimachi el Ahchí

Here is another satirical song targeting some neighborhood character. This one is about the cook Nisimachi scurrying about the streets in a great rush, day and night, to satisfy the whims of his pregnant wife, who takes advantage of her condition to lead him on by the nose.

Sin kalevra i sin potín
Nisimachi el ahchí
se fue a merkar trushí
por la mujer k'está prenyada
s'espanta, no lo para

Glossary

kalevra, potín: types of footwear (origin ?).
el ahchí (T.): the cook.
el trushí (T.): pickled vegetables.
no lo para: subjunctive of the verb *parir*.
s'espanta, no lo para: he is afraid she won't give birth (to the child).

215

Yıldız (Estreya), volunteer of the *Matan Baseter* association, at the Or-Ahayim Hospital (Balat).

El haham León Ben Habib i su ermana, madam Rachel (Istanbul, 1982).

Sanos i rezyos

OBJECTIVES

Communication skills: Describing sickness and pain, illness, the body; expressing wishes, blessings and curses; explaining causes and reasons, expressing conditions and reservations.

Vocabulary: The human body, health, illnesses, meanings of the verb *kitar*, deriving words from the Turkish

Grammar: Uses of the imperfect subjunctive, *ke* clauses, compound sentences.

Conjugation: The imperfect subjunctive, conjugation of *morir* and *konsentir*.

Culture: Customs relating to illnesses and sick people.

---

38 💿 *Stamos holí i verem!*

Avlan Madam Röné i su marido Mösyö Salomón kon Madam Luiz i Mösyö Alber en un gazino, en tomando chay. Son aedados...

Mm. Röné:	Guay de mí! M'están tuyendo las pachás, barminán!
M. Salomón:	Si tomavas las kuras ke te dyo el doktor ya te aziyas sana i rezya, ma estás metyendo inat.
Mm Röné:	Toma kura desha kura, ya m'enfasyí! Ich no m'está amahando. Kaliya ke fuera ande otro doktor... Este doktor mueviziko ke metyeron en la hastané djudiya no s'entyende muncho de sangre... Mösyö Alber lo konoseriya!
M. Alber:	No, ayá ich no tengo ido... No sé kén es. Ma kale meter tino en esto, Madam Röné, las kuras afilú si no kitan la dolor, azen abashar la tansyón...
Mm. Röné:	Makare fuera! Ma a la rovés, me s'está pujando! Madem ki no ay hayre, de ké ke las tome?!
Mm. Luiz:	Para Alber lo ke disho el doktor, Ley de Moshé! Es de la kalor ke se le están auflando las pachás... Mos estamos atabafando... Keshke ke izyera luvya ke eskansáramos un poko!
M. Salomón:	Inshallá! Estos mezes de enverano son muy negros. Yo, noche entera sin durmir! Lo ke komo no m'espide, me se keda en la boka del korasón...

Mme. Luiz:	Mirá Mösyö Salomón, esto todo es de inyervos. Al tyempo diziyan ke era de sar o de aynará, mos aziyan las tres kupas o kaviko a la mezuzá i mos azíyamos buenos. Agora es de ograshar kon doktores i kon hapes, shurupes, kuras de inyervos…
M. Salomón:	Kaleriya ke vos izyerash mas modernas. S'alevantaron las kozikas de kaza i los prekantes. S'eskapó.
Mm. Röné:	No tyenes pasensya… T'estás keshando syempre! La novya de las syete fustanelas!
Mm. Luiz:	I Alber?! Tanto le enteresa ke ya s'azeriya doktor i él!
M. Salomón:	Mos estásh kitando alay, ma komo mos bolemos ya vos vash a azer pishmán.
Mm. Röné i Mm. Luiz:	Atyó santo! Leshos de mozós! El Dyo ke no mos trayga! Keshke ke no kitaras estos byervos de la boka!
M. Alber:	Ya vites ké modo de meoyo tyenen las mujeres… De hazinuras no s'espantan ma s'espantan de maldisyones!
Mm. Luiz:	Lo ke tenésh los dos es korasón en la pachá!

GLOSSARY

Spanish origin

tuyir: to hurt.
la kura: the cure, medicine.
amahar: to heal, relieve.
meter tino: pay attention, be determined.
auflar: to swell up.
atabafarse: to be stifled.
espidir: to digest.
la boka del korasón: (literally, the mouth of the heart), the entryway to the stomach.

el prekante: the incantation.
kesharse: to complain.
la fustanela: the skirt.
bolarse: to fly off, disappear ⇨ to die.
un byervo: a word.
el meoyo: the brain, "brains," the mind.
eskansar: to rest.
la maldisyón: the curse.
enteresar: to interest.

Other origins

barminán (H.): Away from us!, Horrors! How terrible!
la hastané = el ospital: hospital.
meter inat (T.): to be stubborn.
makare! (G.): How I wish!
madem ki (T.): since, inasmuch as.

hayre (T.): profit, good.
el aynará (H.): the evil eye.
el hap (T.): the pill.
ograshar (T.): to try hard, strive.
kitar alay (T.): to make fun of.
azerse pishmán (T.): to rue, have regrets.

Communication skills

1. Asking questions of a sick person

Kuálo te afitó? (*afitar,* regular verb): what happened to you?

Kuálo tyenes?: what's the matter with you?

Kómo estás?.: how are you, how do you feel?

Ánde t'está tuyendo?: where does it hurt?

Kuálo te está tuyendo/Kuálo te está duelyendo? (*tuyir, dueler/dugueler* are regular verbs): where do you hurt?

Tyenes batires?: is your heart beating hard/fast? (*el batir*)

Tyenes dolores?: Do you have any pain? (*la dolor*)

Tyenes friyos?: Are you having chills? (*el friyo*)

Tyenes kayentura?: Do you have a fever? (*la kayentura*)

Tyenes gongoshas?: Do you feel nauseous? (*la gongosha*)

Te yelates?: Literally, did you get cold, but meaning "Did you catch a chill?" (verb *yelarse*)

Ánde te indjide(y)a? (verb *indjide(y)ar,* from the T.: to hurt, wound): Where does it hurt you? Ex.: *El korsé me indjideya la tripa:* the corset hurts my stomach.

Kuálo te konsyentes? (verb *konsentir,* conjugated like *sentir,* Lesson 4A): What do you feel?

Ké doktor t'está mirando?: Which doctor is looking after you?

Ké kuras tomas?: Which treatment are you taking?

2. Expressing wishes

Observe: *Makare (ke) fuera! Keshke ke izyera luvya! Keshke ke no kitaras estos byervos…! El Dyo ke no mos trayga! Inshallá!*

♦ A wish may be expressed simply by using the subjunctive.

The present subjunctive expresses a wish for the present and the future:

Ke no mos manke nunkua!: May we never miss him!

Pasado sea! [lit. Let that be in the past]: Get well!

El Dyo ke no mos trayga!: May the Lord not bring us (such a misfortune)!

The imperfect subjunctive expresses a regret or a wish relating to the past or to some very hypothetical future:

Muryera yo, no! [literally, That I should die, no!] I swear on my life/Hope to die!

Vinyera él i mos salvara!: If he had only come and saved us!

♦ *Makare* (G.) (*ke*) + imperfect subjunctive.
This is especially used with the verb *to be: Makare fuera!* If it were only like that! I wish to heaven that it had turned out that way!

♦ *Keshke* (T.) (*ke*) + imperfect subjunctive.
Oh if only…! This expression is used frequently, with any verb.
It can relate to the present: *Keshke ke izyera luvya,* If it would only rain! (contrary-to-fact situation in the present).
It can relate to the past: *Keshke no kitaras estos byervos de la boka!,* Oh if only (I wish to heaven) those words had not come out of your mouth! (contrary-to-fact situation in the past).

♦ *Inshallá!* (T.): Thank Heaven! This expression accompanies all sorts of declarations. But note: *Inshallá ke* + present subjunctive: Provided that…

3. Explaining causes and reasons

Observe: *Madem ki no ay hayre de ké ke las tome?*

♦ *Madem ki* (T.): since, inasmuch as… is stronger, more expressive than *visto ke* (since), which has the same meaning but is more neutral. *Visto ke lo keres saver te lo dizeré:* Since you want to know it, I'll tell it to you/if you want to know it, I'll…
Madem ki no te kreyes no lo agas: since you don't believe it don't do it.

♦ *Inimás ke* + indicative: all the more so in that… *Kale azerlo entrar inimás ke es konosido:* We have to have him come in all the more so because he's an acquaintance.

4. To state a condition

Reminder from Lesson 8A (contrary-to-fact situations in the past): the sense of the conditional can be expressed by the imperfect.

Observe: *Si tomavas las kuras ke te dyo el médiko, ya te aziyas buena. Komo mos bolemos, ya vos vash a azer pishmán.*

♦ *Si* + imperfect indicative here indicates a situation in the present that is contrary to fact: "if you took the medicines that the doctor gave you, you would already be well." This is the most frequent form found in speech. One could also say *te azeriyas buena,* the present conditional, just as for a contrary-to-fact situation in the past.

♦ *komo* + the imperfect subjunctive in the *if* clause, and the conditional (present time) in the result clause: *komo mos boláramos, ya vos azeríyash pishmán/ya vos ivash a azer pishmán,* if we were to disappear, you would be sorry *or* if we had disappeared, you would have been sorry. It should be noted that if the supposition or the condition relates to the past (contrary-to-fact situation in the past) the same construction would be used. The context allows for ambiguities to be avoided.

♦ *komo* + the present subjunctive or the immediate future expresses possibility: "If we ever disappear, you are going to be sorry." To express a contrary-to-fact situation in present time in this same circumstance, one might say: *Si mos bolávamos, vos ivash a azer pishmán,* or better, in a more literary style: *Si mos boláramos, vos azeriyash pishmán.*

5. Expressing a reservation (clauses with *even if, although*)

Observe: *Las kuras, afilú si no kitan la dolor, azen abashar la tansyón.*

♦ *Afilú* (H.) *si* + indicative: even if, although. The reservation expresses a truth—that is, medicines, even if they do not remove pain, lower blood pressure.

♦ *Afilú si* + subjunctive in the *if* clause (to express a contrary-to-fact situation), with the conditional (present time) or imperfect in the result clause. *Afilú si lo supyera, no se lo dizeriya/diziya:* Even if he knew it, he wouldn't tell it to him; or: Even if he had known it, he wouldn't have told it to him.
Here, again, we could substitute the imperfect or the *ir* + infinitive construction in the imperfect, instead of the conditional, and substitute the imperfect indicative in place of the imperfect subjunctive. For example, the above could be expressed as: *Afilú si lo saviya, no se lo iva a dizir.*

♦ *No sea ke* + subjunctive: so that … not …
No le digas ke su ija está hazina, no sea ke se ezmaye: Don't tell her that her daughter is sick, so that she won't faint (in case she might faint).

Vocabulary

1. Health symptoms

(d)ezmayarse: to faint.

atabafarse: to smother.

sarnudar: to sneeze.

gomitar: to vomit.

un vedrugo: a bruise.

tener chapetas: to have red cheeks (fever, cold).

la shushurella/shushunera: diarrhea.

entezarse: to become stiff, frozen.

sudar: to sweat, perspire.

la durera: constipation.

2. Illnesses

la puntada: pneumonia.

el sarampyón: measles.

el sarilik (T.): jaundice.

la ijada: urinary infection.

tener korasón: to have a heart condition.

apanyar una hazinura: to catch a sickness, disease.

la sitmá (T.): malaria.

la grip (T., from F.): the flu.

la abashada: the cold.

kitar una hazinura: to get sick.

la viruelika: chicken pox.

3. El puerpo umano

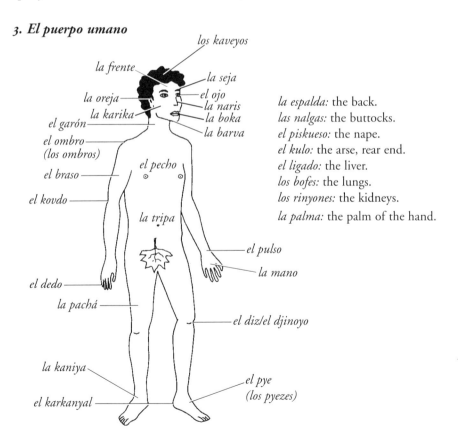

la espalda: the back.

las nalgas: the buttocks.

el piskueso: the nape.

el kulo: the arse, rear end.

el ligado: the liver.

los bofes: the lungs.

los rinyones: the kidneys.

la palma: the palm of the hand.

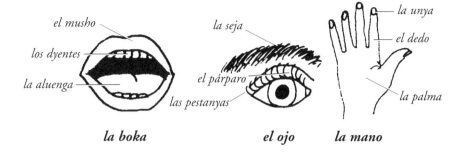

el musho

los dyentes

la aluenga

la seja

el párparo

las pestanyas

la unya

el dedo

la palma

la boka   **el ojo**   **la mano**

4. Meanings of the verb *kitar*

We have seen that the verb *kitar* may have different meanings depending on the various contexts.

Observe: *Kitarán el plato de la meza… Si no kitan la dolor azen abashar la tansyón. Mos estash kitando alay. Kitarse: estar kito, kita. Keshke no kitárash estos byervos de la boka! Kitar hazinura.* This verb often serves a semi-auxiliary function for which it is difficult to give a precise translation.

Its basic meaning is "to take off, take away, remove," and by extension "to have something removed." It also means "to have appear," "to publish." Translating the aphorism stated above, "*Syempre kale kitar byervos buenos de la boka, porke el Dyo kada diya aprova una koza,*" literally "One always has to take good words out of one's mouth, because…," Mrs. Lucie means: "You have always got to say harmless things, because…"

Kitar el plato de la meza: to take the plate off (away from) the table.
Kitar una koza de un luguar: to remove something from somewhere.
Kitar la dolor: remove the pain, make the pain go away.
Kitarse: to take leave of each other = to get divorced.
Kitar byervos de la boka: to declare certain words.
Kitarle alay a una persona: to "pull someone's leg," speak mockingly to someone.
Kitar hazinura: to become sick, have an illness.
Kitar un jurnal: to publish a newspaper.
Kitar loka a una persona: to drive someone crazy.
Kitar al mundo: to bring into the world, give birth to.
Lo kitó el nono: the grandfather sponsored him (the baby) at the circumcision.

94

223

GRAMMAR

1. Uses of the imperfect subjunctive (also see Lesson 4).

Observe: *Kaliya ke fuera. Kaliya ke vos izyerash mas modernas. Makare fuera! Keshke no kitarash estos byervos. Keshke izyera luvya/ke eskansáramos.*

The imperfect subjunctive may express:

♦ An improbable, even impossible wish. Used by itself, the imperfect subjunctive connotes that there is a great distance between the expressed wish and the chances of seeing it fulfilled, hence an unrealistic expectation. The same holds true for *keshke* and *makare*.

♦ Regret. This is expressed by a verb in the imperfect subjunctive since, by definition, it relates to an outcome that did not take place. The same holds true for *keshke* and *makare*.

♦ *If* clauses. Although the imperfect subjunctive is tending to disappear in oral speech, it is still used in writing. One version of the song "*La Serena*" begins: *Si la mar fuera de leche, yo me ariya pishkador...,* and another begins: *Si la mar era de leche, yo me ariya pishkador...*
Note on *ariya:* in oral speech, the form *azeriya* is more frequent (see Lesson 8).

2. Sequence of verb tenses. In Judeo-Spanish, the sequence of verb tenses is hardly ever applicable in oral speech, except in more formal situations. In writing, on the other hand, it always applies. With a verb of command, desire or obligation in the past, the verb in the dependent clause is in the imperfect subjunctive.

Pres.:	*le dize ke venga*	⇨	Past:	*le disho ke vinyera.*
	kero ke venga	⇨		*kije ke vinyera.*
	kale ke venga	⇨		*kaliya ke vinyera.*

If the main clause is in the past, the verb in the dependent clause is, again, in the past:
Present: *lo yama (para) ke venga* ⇨ Past: *lo yamó (para) ke vinyera.*

2. *Tener* + past participle.

Observe: *Ich no tengo ido ayá,* I have never been there. This is a very particular construction, somewhat similar to the present perfect tense in English, but used only to express having had (or never having had) a particular experience in the past. (See Lesson 6A for further comments on this construction.) In this sentence, *ich* simply reinforces the idea. Note how the following examples illustrate the uses of this construction:

Tyenes ido a Selânik?: Have you ever been to Salonika?
No, no tengo ido: No, I have never been there.
Yo tengo ido a Brusa: I have been to Bursa.

CONJUGATION

1. The imperfect subjunctive tense

This tense can easily be formed on the basis of the *they* form of the past tense.

Regular verbs:
♦ Verbs in *-ar*. Model: *kantar. They* form in the past: *kantaron.* Drop the *-aron* ending and add *-ara, -aras,* etc., giving: (*ke*) *kantara, kantaras, kantara, kantáramos, kantarash, kantaran.* Note that the placement of the accent differentiates this form from the future. *Kantará:* he will sing, but (*ke*) *kantara* (accent on the second syllable): (that) he might sing.
♦ Verbs in *-er*. Model: *komer* ⇨ *komyeron,* giving: *komyera, komyeras,* etc.
♦ Verbs in *-ir*. Model: *bivir* ⇨ *bivyeron,* giving: *bivyera, bivyeras,* etc.
Note that the verbs in *-er* and *-ir* take the endings *-yera, -yeras,* etc.

Irregular verbs in the past tense keep the same irregular feature of the root of the third person plural to form the imperfect subjunctive, but sometimes take the ending *-era* instead of *-yera.*

kerer: kijeron ⇨ *kijera.*	*tra(y)er: trusheron* ⇨ *trushera.*
tener: tuvyeron ⇨ *tuvyera.*	*ser/ir: fueron* ⇨ *fuera.*
pueder: pudyeron ⇨ *pudyera.*	*dizir: disheron* ⇨ *dishera.*
estar: estuvyeron ⇨ *estuvyera.*	*aver: uvyeron* ⇨ *uvyera.*
saver: supyeron ⇨ *supyera.*	*azer: izyeron* ⇨ *izyera.*

kantar	estar	ser/ir	komer	azer
kantara	estuvyera	fuera	komyera	izyera
kantaras	estuvyeras	fueras	komyeras	izyeras
kantara	estuvyera	fuera	komyera	izyera
kantáramos	estuvyéramos	fuéramos	komyéramos	izyéramos
kantarash	estuvyerash	fuerash	komyerash	izyerash
kantaran	estuvyeran	fueran	komyeran	izyeran

kerer	tener	traer	dizir	bivir
kijera	tuvyera	trushera	dishera	bivyera
kijeras	tuvyeras	trusheras	disheras	bivyeras
kijera	tuvyera	trushera	dishera	bivyera
kijéramos	tuvyéramos	trushéramos	dishéramos	bivyéramos
kijerash	tuvyerash	trusherash	disherash	bivyerash
kijeran	tuvyeran	trusheran	disheran	bivyera

2. Two irregular verbs with considerable fluctuation:

♦ The verb *muerir/murir/morir* (to die)

Present	Future
muero	**muriré**/mueriré/moriré
mueres	**murirás** /… /…
muere	**murirá**/… /…
murimos/muerimos/morimos	**muriremos**/…/…
murísh/muerísh/morísh	**murirésh**/…/…
mueren	**murirán**/…/…

Imperfect	Past
mueriya/muriya/moriya	**murí**/muerí/morí
mueriyas/…/…	**murites**/muerites/morites
mueriya/…/…	**muryó**
mueríyamos/…/…	**murimos**/muerimos/morimos
mueriyash/…/…	**muritesh**/mueritesh/moritesh
mueriyan/…/…	**muryeron**

Present subjunctive	Imperfect subjunctive	
ke muera	muryera	**Present participle:** muryendo.
ke mueras	muryeras	**Past participle:** muerto.
ke muera	muryera	**Imperative:** muere, muerí(d)/ murí(d)/morí(d).
ke muramos	muryéramos	
ke murásh	muryerash	**Conditional** (like the future):
ke mueran	muryeran	**mueririya**/muririya/moririya
		mueririyas/muririyas/moririyas…

♦ The verb *konsentir/konsintir* (to feel, consent) is conjugated like the verb *sintir* (to hear, feel) (see Lesson 4).

Imperfect: konsintiya/konsentiya, etc. (depending on the infinitive form)	
Past	**Imperfect subjunctive**
konsintí/konsentí	konsintyera
konsintites/konsentites	konsintyeras
konsintyó	konsintyera
konsintimos/konsentimos	konsintyéramos
konsintitesh/konsentitesh	konsintyerash
konsintyeron	konsintyeran
Present participle: konsintyendo.	
Past participle: konsintido/konsentido.	
Imperative: konsyente, konsintí(d)/konsentí(d).	

EXERCISES

Exercise 1: Express the following desires and requests in the form of wishes or regrets.

Ex.: *Kero ke vengan i mos ayuden* ⇨ *Inshallá vengan i mos ayuden!*

Van a vinir i a ayudarmos, inshallá! ⇨ *Makare vinyeran i mos ayudaran.*

1.Kero ke mis ijos se agan doktores.2. Kero ganar munchas parás.3. Kero ke Shemuel se aga bueno ma el doktor pensa ke no ay hayre. 4. Kero ke mi padre me merke una arabá ma no penso ke lo va a azer. 5. Keriya tener ijos ma no tuve. 6. Yo kijera tener una mosa para avlar kon eya. 7. Me plazeriya ke djuguaras al bridj. 8. Kero ke me akompanyes i bayles kon mí. 9. Kero ke me ames ma no me amas. 10. Keriya ke se kazara kon Stella ma se kazó kon su prima. 11. Keriya ke tornara mi marido ma no vino.

Exercise 2: Choose the appropriate word from the list below to fill in the sentences that follow.

afilú si	ya ke	visto ke	madem ki	komo	keshke
makare	afilú si	ma yiné	inshallá	inimás ke	no sea ke

1. … vinyera! 2. No kero komer… la komida se yeló. 3. … keres merkarte una radyo mueva, vate a lavorar. 4. … no me kreyes, no te lo kontaré. 5. … no me demandes la razón ke estó aravyada, mas no te vo a avlar. 6. … si save

ke estás hazino es tan negro ke no va vinir a demandar. 7. Save ke estás hazino … no vyene a demandar. Ké negro ke es! 8. … una persona está hazina, kale ir a vijitarla. 9. Una madre … … pare kulevros, yiné demanda por eyos. 10. … no saves azerlo, lo azeré yo. 11. … no vayas a vijitarlo, mas no te vo a avlar. 12. … toparas la repuesta i ganáramos! 13. … se ambeze a meldar la Ley… digan ke no es buen djudyó. 14. Kale ke sepa la Ley… su nono es haham.

Exercise 3: Based on the information contained in the following sentences, give your advice to the persons concerned (contrary-to-fact situations in present time).

Ex.: *Matilda no se mete prostela i se mancha el fostán.* ⇨
Si te metiyas/metyeras prostela, no te manchariyas/manchavas el fostán.
1. Madam Luiz no toma las kuras i le tuye la kavesa. 2. Shelomó no melda i no se ambeza nada. 3. David no se va al klub i s'está enfasyando. 4. Tant Viktorya kome muncho i se engodra. 5. Mösyö Behar no save avlar en italyano i no puede eskrivir una letra a su haver. 6. No merkó el bileto i no vyeron la pyesa. 7. Berta no melda la gazeta i no save kuálo está akontesyendo. 8. Mi padre no me avre el telefón i no tyene haber de las inyetas. 9. No avla munchas linguas i no está topando echo.

Exercise 4: Translate.

1. Kitaron sarampyón. 2. David Fresko kitava *El Tyempo*. 3. Kon sus krizas, la ija i la mujer lo kitaron loko al padre. 4. No kites estos byervos suzyos de la boka! 5. Me estás kitando alay? 6. Kítale una kupa del armaryo a tu padre ke beva un poko de agua. 7. Ya komimos, puedes kitar los chinís i fregar. 8. De mueve si kitas sinko kedan kuatro. 9. Kitates la leche de la lumbre? 10. En kada anyo, sta kitando grip. 11. Se kitó de la mujer. 12. El diya de la milá, lo kitó el nono. 13. Es la komadre ke me kitó.

Exercise 5: Replace the verb in these sentences with kitar (plus an object, if necessary) and then translate them.

1. Avram León era el gazetero ke estampava el Şalom. 2. Antes los mansevos no diziyan byervo delantre del padre. 3. Alber i Merí s'espartyeron. 4. En Tayland apanyaron el sarilik. 5. Tomí el livro de la kasha para meterlo en el armaryo. 6. Se burla de su ermana i eya se bola de los inyervos. 7. La kura me amahó la dolor. 8. La aspirina abasha la kayentura. 9. Mi madre paryó kuatro kriyaturas.

Exercise 6: *Put the verb in parentheses into the appropriate form.*

1. Tu padre me eskrivyó para ke le (mandar) los livros ke le mankavan. 2. Me disho ke no saviya si (venir) a komer noche de shabad. 3. Makare ke (tornar) antes de la luvya! 4. Si no (echarse) tan tadre duermeriyas mijor. 5. Keshke (tomar) mi ijo en konsiderasyón los konsejos ke le estó dando! 6. Keriya ke me (dizir) lo ke save. 7. La yamí para ke me (ayudar). 8. Si me kijeras, (azer) lo ke te estó demandando. 9. Makare mos (sintir) i mos (avrir) la puerta!

Exercise 7: *Put the following sentences into the past tense.*

1. Me dize ke venga. 2. Kero ke vayas a bushkarlo. 3. Kale ke topes una kaza mueva. 4. Le eskrivo ke me mande los livros. 5. Grito para ke me syentas. 6. Si lo tyenes kale ke me lo des. 7. No keren ke se kaze con él. 8. Le rogo ke me oyga.

El Neder, en el kal de la Adá (Princes' Islands, Istanbul).

Salonikans taking the cure at Karlsbad (Czech Republic), 1919.

Mrs. Kalo making wicks for memorial lamps (Gelibolu, Turkey).

Meza de dolyo: avelim eating olives, cheese, hard-boiled eggs (Gelibolu, Turkey).

READINGS

Proverbos i dichas

De médikos i de hazinos:

Lo ke keda del doktor se lo yeva el endivino
(What the doctor leaves, the soothsayer takes away).
What the doctor can't finish, the soothsayer cures. When someone is ill, the family takes on heavy expenses to care for him/her. First they call upon science but, when all hope is lost, they turn to the irrational out of sheer desperation.

Yerro de médiko la tyerra lo kobija
(An error by the doctor is covered over by the earth).
Clumsy doctors are not punished for their errors.

Doktor Matasanos (Doctor Killhealthy).
This expression is used jokingly for a bad doctor. As a pun, the name *Matatyas* is also taken apart to give *mata tiyas,* Kill-Aunts.

La novya de las syete fustanelas/funtanelas!
(The bride with seven skirts /running sores!).
This is said of someone who never stops complaining about a thousand different health problems. Such a person is likened to the Virgin with seven pains, specific to the churches of Andalusia.

El ke se peda manda el doktor a la muerte
(He who farts sends the doctor to his death).
A fart is a sign of good health. Note that *pishar* (to urinate), *el pishado* (the urine), *pedar* (to fart), are not indecent terms. Only *kagar,* to excrete, calls for a euphemism: *salir de puerpo,* a calque based on the Turkish, literally "to come out of the body".

De hazinuras:

Sta perso hazino (He is lost sick). He is very sick.

Holí i verém. Each of the two terms (one in Hebrew, the other in Turkish) means tuberculosis. This is used to say of a person that he is riddled with illnesses.

De melizinas:

La kura i la milizina
(The cure and the medicine).
These two synonymous words are used ironically to mean "what medicines didn't I take!").

De partes del puerpo:

Ánde el pye ánde la boka
(Where's the foot, where's the mouth).
This is said of two things that have nothing to do with each other, "apples and oranges." Also said: *Del kulo al pulso* (from the arse to the pulse), "cock and bull," utter nonsense.

Todos tenemos dos orejas i una boka para no avlar todo lo ke vemos (We all have two ears and one mouth so as not to repeat to others everything we see).

El ojo ve el korasón dezea
(The eye sees, the heart desires).
This proverb was also widely used throughout the cultures of Medieval Spain.

Boka/ojos por ermozura
(Mouth/eyes for beauty).
This is said of someone who has eyes or a mouth just for decoration—that is, someone who doesn't understand what he sees or who never says anything.

Las bendisyones

Eskapado de mal! (Saved from evil!), expressing a wish that a situation get better.
Refuá shelemá! (H. for Complete health!), a wish for good health.
Sanos i rezyos (ke estén!) ([May you/they be] healthy and sturdy!). This is expressed upon saying goodbye to people; "Stay well/Take care!"
Vidas largas! (Long lives!). A wish expressed on birthdays.

Las maldisyones

Before becoming acquainted with the following curses, remember that *maldisyón sin razón toka a su patrón* (an undeserved or ill-founded curse will fall back upon the person who uttered it).

Kon la sávana ke te vea! (May I see you in your sheet [meaning shroud]).
Ke te pudras en la kama! (May you rot in bed!).
El kapak ke te kayga! (May the lid [of the coffin] fall shut upon you!).
Ke kyeras morir ke no puedas! (May you want to die and not be able to!).
En Ginnam esté su alma! (May his soul be in Hell/May he be cursed!).
Asentado en syete! ([May I see you] seated for seven [days]!). This is a reference to the ritual mourning period when the *avelim* (H. for mourners) sit on the ground for the first week.

The number of curses is impressive and they are filled with the most imaginative sorts of destructive wishes.

Oaths

Atyo, se muryera Kadén or *Badi* (Oh Lord, may Kadén [or Badi] die). Kadén is a popular first name for women. Badi is a common family name. No one knows why Kadén or Badi's life was chosen to be endangered by this oath!

39 🎧 *Djohá ande el karnesero*

La madre de Djohá le mandó al karnesero para ke merkara pachás de kodredo. *"Va,"* le disho, *"ande el karnesero i mira ver si tyene pachás de kodredo."* Fué Djohá i le levantó la pachá del saraguel. Se enkantó el karnesero, ma no dishimos ke era bovo Djohá? Tornó ande la madre i le disho ke no teniya el karnesero pachás de kodredo. Kuando la madre salyó a la tadre a emplear, vido munchas en la butika, i se aravyó. *"De ké me dishites ke no teniya?"* le demandó al ijo. *"Te asiguro mamá ke lo mirí bueno bueno, afilú le alevantí la pachá del saraguel, ma el karnesero no tyene pachás de kodredo, tyene pachás de benadam."*

Glossary
el karnesero: the butcher.
el kodredo: the lamb.
el saraguel: wide-legged trousers.
enkantar(se): to be astonished.
bovo: simpleton.
asigurar: to be certain.
el benadam (H., son of Adam): human being,
   as opposed to an animal, *la hayá.*

9b

Letra

In the letter that received no answer (Lesson 8B), Yontov/León became worried about the health of his brother who couldn't write back. The first paragraph of his second letter is identical to that of the first and has been omitted here.

> *A mi muy kerido ermano Behor.*
>
> *[…]*
>
> *De mas mi kerido ermano me avizates ke tu famiya se topa hazina. El dyo ke la manpare i el Dyo ke le dé la melezina i el Dyo ke le dé la refuá buena i ke esté sana i rezya asigún kere eya.*
>
> *I lo ke keremos mozotros ke sea demaziya. I de tu parte me avizates desrepozado ke te topas por esta kavza es ke te digo ke me mandes la repuesta presto.*
>
> *Mira mi kerido ermano, en el mundo no ay firmeza de punto a punto i de ora a ora.*
>
> *En el mundo el Dyo ke no trayga hazindad […] i el Dyo ke no mos amarge a dingunos de la famiya […].*
>
> *Mas no tengo otro ke sero mi chika letra […]. Selam para ti mi kerido ermano Behor ke syempre penso i pensaré en ti i vos [kero] toparvos sanos i rezyos i haberes buenos sin sar i sin mal. Selam de tu kerido ermano Yontov; repuesta sin falta.*
>
> > *León*

234

Kozikas de kaza

1. El ojo malo o aynará

Suzí: Para el ojo malo aviya aprekantar: "Eda, ija de Ester, te kito el ojo malo el avla mala, todo el sar todo el mal; Eda ija de Ester, ke no tengas ni mal ni sar, todos estos males ke se vayan a las profundinas de la mar."

Bekí: Se pasava la mano por enriva de la kavesa de la ija, Eda dizeremos, kon un punyado de sal; duspués se echava la sal en el kabiné.

Lizá: I kemavan klavikos ensima de la lumbre.

2. Los tres papelikos o las tres kupas i kaviko a la mezuzá

Ester: Se toma un livro de Ley. En un papeliko blanko se mete un poko de asukuar i se mete en la ventana aryentro. Se aroga. A la demanyana, komo estuvo noche entera serka del Dyo, se da a bever la asukuar del papeliko en una kupa de agua o un findján de kavé. Tres noches se toma kon bendisyones. A la ke se kree dizen ke le pasa. Tambyén se aze kaviko a la mezuzá. Yené es papeliko de kavé ke se mete en la mezuzá i se chupa después.

Gentille: Para espanto, debasho de un livro de Ley metes una kupa de agua kon asukuar. Después se dize kidúsh kon esta kupa ayá. Duspués se la das a bever al hazino o mojas una ridaíka i se la metes ande tyene el sikintí. Yo me lo ambezí de mi madre te lo ambezo a ti ke agas este modo. Una aguita kon asukuar, kuálo ay? De esto no vyene danyo.

Glossary

aprekantar: to do incantations (*prekante*).

la mezuzá (H.): small case containing a holy text handwritten on a small roll of parchment, attached to the right doorjamb.

yené/yiné (T.): again.

chupar: to suck.

el kidúsh (H.): prayer recited over a cup of wine on the Sabbath and on holy days, to sanctify the day.

mojar: to wet.

una ridá (T.): a handkerchief.

el sikintí (T.): the worry, problem.

el danyo: the damage, danger.

9b

Me'am Lo'ez (excerpt)

The Me'am Lo'ez *is a commentary on the Bible in Judeo-Spanish. It is addressed to people who can read but who have only a limited knowledge of Hebrew. It follows the weekly passages of the Torah and offers exegetical knowledge of a high level, rules of morality and hygiene, principles of bookkeeping, an encyclopedic knowledge consistent with the period in which it was written, 1730. The author was a rabbi, Jacob Khuli, who was only able to complete the commentary for* Bereshit (Genesis). *Meant to be read on a daily basis at home in the family, the text contains anecdotes and stories and mixes fragments of biblical texts in Hebrew, their translation into Ladino and the commentary in the vernacular language, Judeo-Spanish. This work was continued by others until the beginning of the 20th century, particularly translators who contributed to its widespread distribution.*

Yosef i la mujer de Potifar (muevena perashá), [Gen. 39:1–40:23][17]

I el sar de Yosef fue muncho mas grande del sar ke tuvo Yitzhak en la akedá. "I fué después de las palavras las estas, i alsó mujer de su sinyor a sus ojos i disho: 'yazte kon mí.'" (39-7). I lo fue afalagando kon avlas. I kada diya se mudava buenos vestidos uno mijor ke otro, ke los vestidos de la manyana no los vestiya a medyo diya, i los de medyo diya no los vestiya la tarde, i lo aregalava muncho para ke alsara su ojo a verla. I estuvo rijendo esto munchos diyas asta ke se adolensyó i kayó dolyente en un ondo de kama. Las Mitsriyot, sus amigas, vinyeron a vijitarla, dizyendo:
"Ké es lo ke te manka, ke estás triste i dolyente?"
Eya trusho una partida de etrogim i espartyó uno a kada una de eyas, kon kuchiyo de plata ke los fuera mundando kon su mano, i yamó a Yosef ke estuvyera delantre de eyas. I syendo vyeron su ermozura se kedaron enkantadas i todo su tino teniyan en él, mirándole su kara, a tanto ke se kortaron las manos mundando los etrogim i se embatakaron en la sangre i no se sintyeron. Eya les disho:
"Syendo vozotras por un punto ke lo vistes [sic] ke se vos boló el sezo de la kavesa, ké diré yo ke lo tengo en mi kaza tanto tyempo, i de su (despego) me adolensyé?"

David Gonzalo Maeso and Pascual Pascual Recuero, Me'am Lo'ez,
vol. 1, part 2, Madrid: Gredos, 1970, p. 1010.

---

17. Spelling has been adapted to the norms of this book.

Glossary

el sar (H.): the fear.

la akedá (H.): the binding of Isaac.

alsar: to raise.

yazer: to lie down, stretch out.

afalagar: flatter.

mudar: to change.

aregalar: to treat well, offer gifts.

rijir: to order, command.

un ondo: a deep part, depth.

las Mitsriyot (H.): the Egyptian women.

dolyente: sorrowful.

los etrogim (H.): the citrons.

espartir: to share.

plata: silver.

embatakarse (T.): to get soiled.

sintirse: to feel (in this context).

el sezo: the brain, intelligence.

el tino: the mind.

(despego): detachment. The text states *desfelo* (?).

adolensyarse: to become ill with suffering.

Notes:

1. The intermediary form *vistes* is used here, whereas nowadays the form *vites* has stabilized for the past tense of *ver*. The second person singular form is unexpected here. It could be a printing error.

2. *Las palavras las estas* is a Ladinism, a calque from the Hebrew, used with an emphatic meaning instead of *estas palabras*.

3. *La palavra* has taken on the sense of "speech," or is used in the sense of to give one's word of honor, in modern-day Judeo-Spanish. *Los byervos* is used for ordinary "words."

Questions: *1. Kuálo izo la mujer de Putifar para plazerle a Yosef? 2. Alsó Yosef "sus ojos a elya"? 3. De ké se adolensyó la mujer de Putifar? 4. Kén vino a vijitarla? 5. Ké le disheron las damas? 6. Ké les dyo la mujer de Putifar a las damas? 7. Ké izyeron? 8. De ké lo izyeron? 9. Ké les disho la mujer de Putifar?*

Grammar

The various meanings of *ke*

In Lesson 2A we saw *ke* used as a relative pronoun (who, which, that). We see this usage again in the above text where we have *yo ke lo tengo…, el sar ke tuvo Yosef, ké es lo ke te manka*. We have also seen the use of the conjunction *ke* ("may, that") with the subjunctive in Lessons 3A, 7A and 8A, and its use in conjunctive expressions in Lesson 9A. Further uses found in the above text:

♦ The explicative or causal *ke*, which has the sense of "for, because, indeed" when it comes at the beginning of a clause: *ke los vestidos de la manyana no los vestiya a medyo diya*.

♦ *Ke* can replace *de* in comparisons: *uno mijor ke otro*.

♦ *Ke* can be a shortened version of *para ke* to introduce a subjunctive:

lo yamó ke estuvyera…, espartyó (…) ke los fuera mundando… Ke + subjunctive here has the sense of "so that, in order to…" The sequence of tenses requires the use of the imperfect subjunctive. This construction, where *ke* expresses purpose or result, is frequent. (Note that in English the meaning of these constructions is often conveyed by the infinitive, with the subject of the action expressed as the object of *for*).

Dámelo ke lo munde: [Give it to me so that I peel it] Give it to me so I can peel it *or* …for me to peel it. *Yama a Yosef ke esté delantre de eyas:* Call Joseph (so) that he stand before them *or* for him to stand before them.

Exercise: Translate the following sentences with particular attention to the various uses of *ke*.

1.   Mi madre me disho ke entrates en la universitá. 2. Mi prima es la ke lava las ventanas. 3. Le plaze ke vengan a verlo. 4. Ke trayga yo los boyikos, mamá? 5. Asperimos el diya ke se serró la eskola i le dishimos a la maestra ke no kaliya aharvar a los ijikos, ke esto era muy negro. 6. M'espanto ke se inyerve. 7. M'espanto ke su madre está en el ospital. 8. De ké ke lo diga?! 9. Kuálo tyenes, ke no avlas?

Communication skills

A few expressions:

♦ *syendo ke* + **indicative:** given that, inasmuch as.

syendo […] ke se vos boló el tino.

asta ke + **indicative**. We have already seen *fin a ke* with the same meaning ("until" introducing a verb clause) and pointed out the use of *fasta ke* in Salonika. *Asta ke* is likewise used, although rarely nowadays (*fista ke* is more frequently used). *Asta ke se adolensyó i kayó en un ondo de kama.*

♦ *para ke* + *subjunctive:* so that, in order to: *para ke alsara su ojo a verla:* so that he raise his eye(s) to see her.

♦ *a tanto ke* + *indicative.* To such an extent that: *a tanto ke se kortaron las manos (…) i se embatakaron (…) i no se sintyeron.*

CONJUGATION: *Trayer* and *dizir*

Trayer (to bring, carry).

Future	Conditional
trayeré	trayeriya
trayerás	trayeriyas
trayerá	trayeriya
trayeremos	trayeríyamos
trayerésh	trayeriyash
trayerán	trayeriya

The *Imperfect* forms are regular (see Lesson 7A), with frequent usage of the Bulgarian variant of the imperfect: *traíva, traívas, traíva, traívamos, traívash, traívan.* There also exists an imperfect form in: *trushiya, trushiyas, trushiya, trushíyamos, trushiyash, trushiyan.*

Imperative: traye, trayé(d).

Dizir (to say).

Pres. Subj.	Future	Conditional
ke diga	**diziré**/diré	**diziriya**/dizeriya/diriya
ke digas	**dizirás**/dirás	**diziriyas**/…/…
ke diga	**dizirá**/dirá	**diziriya**/…/…
ke digamos	**diziremos**/diremos	**diziríyamos**/…/…
ke digásh	**dizirésh**/dirésh	**diziriyash**/…/…
ke digan	**dizirán**/dirán	**diziriyan**/…/…

There are two forms of the future and conditional tenses, one regular, *diziré,* more frequently used, and *diré,* as seen in the preceding text. Note that there is even a third form that can often be heard: *dizeré, dizeriya,* perhaps by assimilation to the conjugation of *azer.*

The **imperfect** is regular: *diziya, diziyas, diziya, dizíyamos…*

Imperative: *dize/di, dizi(d).*

Akeyas kantikas del tyempo de la esplendor mos las kantava el padre de una de mis tyas kada dya k'amanese kuando yo era chiko. ("El jajamiko" me yamava porke mas ke todo me plazya meldar livros.) Chastre era, ama se dichya ijo de rey. *David el bueno, salonekli y ijo de rey, desendyente de Espagna*" (…)

"David, le gritavamos, ahora no es tyempo de matarse. Ven a tomar kave y metete el pyjama…"

Se asentava a la meza el chilibi David. Mirava su chini, el kopo de agoua frya ke le tenyamos traydo y el librik kon el kave a la turka ke le plazya kon kaymak y byen asukado. Fina ke mirava a mozotros, ma sin rekonocermos realmente, komo si fuera el un rey deskaydo, la kaveza yena de souegnos, azyendo vigita a unos deskonocidos.

Marcel Cohen, *Lettre à Antonio Saura*, Paris: L'Échoppe, 1997, pp. 51-53.

Notes on spellings that differ from the norms of this book:
tyas, dya, frya, tenyamos, plazya ⇨ tiyas, diya, friya, teníyamos, plaziya.
jajamiko ⇨ hahamiko. souegnos, agoua ⇨ suenyos, agua.
vigita ⇨ vijita.
souegnos, Espagna ⇨ suenyos, Espanya.

Glossary

chastre = shastre: tailor.

ahora = agora.

chilibí (T.): (title) Mister.

el kopo = la kupa.

el librik (T.): copper pot for making Turkish coffee.

el kaymak (T.): fresh cream; here, the foam on Turkish coffee.

asukado = asukarado.

rekonoser, konoser: to recognize.

deskaydo: fallen.

kaveza = kavesa.

Note regarding the **imperfect:** In this text, where Marcel Cohen uses his own personal spelling system, we find still another form of the imperfect—*dishiya*—based on the root of the past tense with imperfect endings: *disho ⇨ dish-iya* instead of *dize ⇨ diz-iya.* Although rare, this form is sometimes found in oral speech as well as in writing.

Questions: *1. Kómo se sirve el kavé a la turka? 2. De ánde es el tiyo David el bueno? 3. Porke lo yamava "jajamiko" a Marcel? 4. Porke los mira a los suyos sin konoserlos?*

Kantika de ijikos

Los dedos de la mano.
(This is said while taking the child's fingers, one by one, beginning with the little finger.)

Chiko miniko
el enaniko
el alto i vano
el eskrivano
el rey de la mano.

Glossary
miniko (T.): tiny.
el enano: the dwarf.
vano: vain.

From M. E. Barzilay, according to his *biznona* (great-grandmother).

41 🎵 *Konseja del sodro i del inyervozo*

Un ombre teniya un haver sodro i él era inyervozo. En el echo saliyan pletos kada diya. Un diya el inyervozo kayó hazino. La mujer del sodro le demandó:

"De ké no vas a vijitar a tu haver? Esto no se aze!"

El marido arespondyó:

"Zaten en el echo no mos damos muncho a entender, yo sodro, él inyervozo. Kuálo ke aga?"

"Haber no se demanda, bre, Hayim?! Un benadamlik no se aze?! Por kudyado no se va?! Es kolay, le vas a demandar: *'Kómo estás?,'* te va a dizir: *'Un poko mijor,'* le vas a dar pasensya, vas a dizirle *'A poko a poko.'* Te vas a interesarte, le demandarás: *'Ké kuras estás tomando?,'* te va a dizir: *'Esto i esto,'* le dizirás: *'Es buena kura.'* Le demandarás: *'Ké médiko te está mirando?,'* te va a dizir *'Fulano,'* le vas a dizir: *'Es buen doktor.'* I ansina, los dos kontentes, te vas a tornar a kaza."

"Tyenes razón," disho el marido. "I se hue ande el haver." Chafteó la puerta, bam, bam! El inyervozo está en el balkón de su kaza, lo vido vinir al sodro i se inyervó muy muncho. Bam, bam, la puerta.

"Ke entre!"

El sodro no syente. Chaftea de muevo. Bam, bam!

"Ke entreee!"

A la fin ya entró.

"Kómo estás?" demanda.

I el inyervozo: "Derrityéndome!"

241

"Eh, a poko, a poko… Ké kuras estás tomando?"

"Medras kon pintas!"

"Es buena kura. Pekí, ké doktor te está mirando?"

"El uerko!"

"Es buen médiko."

Esta vez no puido mas el inyervozo, aydé lo tomó al ombre, lo echó a la kaye.

As told by Mr. Izak Arditi.

Glossary

sodro: deaf.

un haber (T.): some news.

un pleto: a dispute.

aresponder/responder: respond.

zaten/zatí (T.): besides.

el kudyado: the worry.

aydé (T.): come on! up we go!

Fulano: Mr. so-and-so.

chaftear (T.): to knock.

derritirse/derretirse: to melt, come undone.

medras kon pintas: excrement with fly droppings.

el uerko: the devil.

bre!: popular Turkish interjection, "Well, now!"

un benadamlik (H.+ T.): a good moral gesture.

Notes:

1. Medras kon pintas, by repeating two virtually synonymous terms, is an emphatic way of saying "nothing at all," "peanuts"—one of the many ways of expressing failure.

2. Se hue instead of *se fue.* This pronunciation is very common nowadays in Judeo-Spanish. While we recommend that *se fue* be used in writing, be prepared to see *se hue* in various texts.

Vocabulary

Multilingual creativity

Observe: *chaftear, un benadamlik.*

♦ *Çarpt(ır)-mak* (Turkish verb: to push, bump into, hit, knock). This verb came into Judeo-Spanish in its factitive form *çarptır-mak,* due to its emphatic quality. The form was simplified to *çarpt-mak,* and then adapted to the Judeo-Spanish conjugation system by replacing the Turkish infinitive ending *-mak* by the Judeo-Spanish ending *-ear,* thus giving *charpt-ear* (using our spelling norms). Finally, after undergoing the general Judeo-Spanish phonic system, the word was pronounced *chaftear.*

This particular transformation of a Turkish borrowing is complicated but for the most part, with other verbs, the marker for the infinitive in Turkish (*-mak, -mek*) is simply replaced by the equivalent marker in Judeo-Spanish (*-ear*). More recently, because of French influence, the Turkish ending is replaced by *-ar* in the Judeo-Spanish conjugation system.

Dolaş-mak ⇨ *dolash-ear:* to take a walk.
Ugraş-mak, after a further pronunciation change, becomes *urash-ear* or *ogrash-ar:* to make a strong effort, go to great lengths to…
Kullan-mak ⇨ *kulan-ear:* to use, drive (a car).
Boz-mak ⇨ *boz-ear* and especially *boz-d-ear* (intensive form): to break.
Sür-mek ⇨ *sur-ear* (Turkish *ü* is transformed to *u*): to last.

Exercise 1: Find the Judeo-Spanish equivalent for these Turkish verbs.
1. *bat-mak:* to sink.
2. *sar-mak:* to envelope, entwine, hug.
3. *kavur-mak:* to grill, to brown (cooking).
4. *dayan-mak:* to resist, tolerate.

♦ *Un benadam-lik:* Here we have a Hebrew expression, *ben adam:* son of man (literary), which in Judeo-Spanish means "a good person," "a person who does the moral thing." To this has been added the Turkish suffix *-lik,* which is used to make a noun out of another word, usually an adjective, and roughly means the state or act of having a particular characteristic. *Un benadamlik* can therefore mean: having the characteristics of a good person, or an act accomplished by a good person.

Exercise 2: Figure out the meaning of: 1. *un purim-lik,* based on Hebrew *Purim,* the festival of Esther. 2. *el batal-lik,* based on the Hebrew borrowing *batal:* idle, unemployed.

Jewish cemetery in Sarajevo.

The Old Jewish Quarter of Balat (Istanbul)

Former *yahudhane* (see
Lesson 3A), recent view.

*Kazas djudiyas
de afuera Balat.*

La Kanfafaná, a marketing area.

El banyo turko.

Mme Lucie's street, behind the *kal* of Chana.

Jewish women at the Club at Burgaz.

The fish dealer (Heybelí).

Open-air carriages (Heybelí).

Seaside at Burgaz.

Mme Djoya at Heybelí.

Arrival of *el vapor*.

Heybelí—*las tres primikas:* Tracy (New York), Iren (Montreal), and Suzanne (Paris).

Service at the Ahrida synagogue (Balat).

Simantov Sisa, *sanmás*, in front of the *ehal* of the synagogue of Yambol (Balat).

La gayna de Kapará, Kipur, kal de la Adá.

ANTHOLOGY

1. Las tres kozas ke no se pueden guadrar

[...] Kualas son las tres kozas ke no se pueden guadrar?

La primera para nozotros es la pasion del enamorado. El ke ama una jovena, lo aze ver. Komo? Kon su atitud, kon sus palavras, kon sus ojos, kon su komporto. Azer la analiz del individuo ke se topa debaşo de esta pasion es la ovra de los novelistas, no tenemos lugar en nuestras kolonas, ma noventa i nueve por sien de nuestros lektores, kreyemos, pasaron a lo menos en sus juventud por este kamino de flores i de punçones, i no se olvidan en la maturidad los sentimientos felices del pasado—i un poko el ridikul de un sierto komporto de akel tiempo. El enamorado se aze ver, i dezea ke su entorno açeta su amor. No puede guadrar su pasion!

La segunda koza ke no se puede guadrar es el prenyado. Los dos primeros mezes del prenyado (embarazo es kastilyano) se puede guadrar, al treser mes, es mas difisil; la mujer ke lo kiere guadrar al kuatren mes, cuga kon su vida. Dunke, el amor, kavzo psikolojiko, el prenyado (embarazo) kavzo biolojiko son dos efetos ke el ser no puede guadrar.

El treser es el dinero.

El ke izo dinero, el ke gano moneda, kale ke lo amonstre! Komodo? O troka de mujer, o troka de kaza! Si no dezea trokar de kaza ampesa a trokar los vestidos suyos i las vestimientas de su mujer, despues viene el torno a trokar el aparato de una televizion mas grande i un otomobil nuevo para ke los vizinos se enselen de la reuşita materiala ke fue kapaçe de realizar. Ay siertos ke no pueden rezistir a las rogativas de su espoza i la kuvren de coyas; es otra manera de azer la publisita de la fuersa del dinero. Si uno se izo riko i no lo amonstra a kualo sierve lo ganado? Puede ser ke va trokar los mobles de kaza? Solo un entelektual va pensar acustar una biblioteka; si es un nuevo riko ke se kiere pasar por un meldahon, i si por fortuna tiene relasiones, si no amigos entelektuales, va ir al bazar para komprar livros kon kilo ma ke tienen una kuvierta dorada—livros ke no seran nunka meldados, ni tokados solo la mosa de kaza les tomara el polvo una vez al mes –. Komo se puede amonstrar la rikeza? Ay mil i una manera. Bien entendido kada uno es libero de empleyar su dinero komo le gusta, no tenemos el dereço de kritikar kualo ke seya. Ma el dinero si no tiene golor, se ve!

Entre estas tres manifestasiones ke no se pueden guadrar, si mos atadrimos un poko mas sovre el bendiço dinero, es porke tiene una fuersa ke aze kreyer ke puede komprar todo. Deşamos esta apresiasion al juzgamiento de nuestros lektores. El solo denominator komun ke tienen estas tres kozas, son evenimientos ke trokan la manera de bivir entera del ser (ombre komo mujer).

Salamon Bicerano, *Relatos en lingua judeo-espanyola*,
Gözlem, Istanbul, 1997, pp. 300-301.

2. La myel i la fyel - De el tio Yekutiel

Por: Yusuf ALTINTAŞ

Kual Ishak Koen?

Al onoravle Sinyor
Selebre Gazetero
Yusef mi sovrino

[...]
Saves lo ke me vino al tino en las pasadas?

Siguro ke no saves, de ande puedes saver?... Devez en kuando ay kozas ke los selebres gazeteros bile no lo pueden saver, aun ke les parese ke tienen haber de todo lo ke se pasa en el mundo.

En las pasadas me vino al tino los de mizmo nombre i mizma alkunya ke aviya en Hasköy aya alzeman i mos se kariştireyava el meoyo asta ke mos viniya dolor de kavesa para pueder dar a entender custo por ken estamos avlando.

Parati mintiras parami verdad, maz de vente trenta personas aviya aya alzeman en Hasköy ke se yamavan Ishak Koen todos [...] ke si unos kuantos de eyos eran primos, tios i sovrinos el resto no eran de la mizma Mispaha.

Imajinate ke kuando haribi Avram Eskenazi yamava al Sefer diyas de şabat Yaamod Aşem Atov Aadon Anihbad Ishak Koen Likro Batora, alomanko kuatro u sinko personas se alevantavan enpyes i se devraneyavan a kuştureyar a la Teva endereçandosen el Talled ke teniyan en los ombros i la takyayka para ke no se los kayga de la kavesa. Custo en akel momento, Hayimaçi el

Gabay se alevantava enpyes de la Teva i apuntava kon el dedo kual es el ke es yamado komo Koen Aole, i los otros teniyan de tornar a sus lugares i asentarsen, todo en esperando ke vana ser yamados maz despues al Sefer [...].

Enprimero mos paresyo muy kolay de apartarlos sigun la edad ke tienen, i los empesimos a yamar Ishakito Koen, Ishak Koen, Çibi Ishak Koen u Ishakuço Koen. Ama ven veremos a ver ke los mansevos se adultaron, los adultos se envyejesyeron i los ke eran vyejos zaten estavan aya loke parese ke çakteyaron kazik en akel mundo. Biride Ben Porat Yosef kada anyo i anyo unos kuantos de los ke nasiyan en Hasköy se les metiya el nombre de sus nonos ke se yamavan Ishak Koen. Asta ke ya mos se embaranyo el meoyo de no pueder salir içinden.

Kurto te lo azere, no me esto akodrando agora ken era ama, salyo un nasido de vyernes i izo una lista para dar fin a esta curcina todo en dando a kada uno un otro titolo.

Ishak Koen el Yanyali, Ishakuço Koen el Palyarohaci, Ishak Koen el Pramatifta, Ishak Koen el tapetero, Ishakuço Koen el Karkukli, Çibi Ishak Koen de Çiksali, Ishakuço Koen el Berber, Ishak Koen el Tenekeci, Ishakuço Koen del dere, Haribi Ishakuço Koen el Moel, Ishak Koen el Şohet, Ishakito

253

Koen el Sanmas, Çilibi Ishak Koen el Davavekili... I de este modo se kolaylado un pokitiko de pueder apartar el Ishak Koen ke era yamado al Sefer, porke todos mozotros ya mos auzimos de konoserlos i nombrarlos kon estos titolos ke te esto dizyendo.

Ama ven veremos a ver ke la lista ke izo el buen del presyado no era tan kurta. Aya aviya Ishak Koen el Tartamudo, Ishakuço Koen el Korkovado, Ishak Koen el ke se le fuyo la mujer, Çilibi Ishak Koen el Blankuço, Ishak Koen el de las ijas luzyas, Ishak Koen el Hovarda, Ishak Koen el Syego, Ishakuço Koen de la buena parte, Ishak Koen el Borraçon, Ishak Koen el Pişalon, Ishak Koen el Şaşuto, Ishak Koen el Kyulanbi, Ishak Koen el Avlaston, Ishak Koen el Eskaso, Ishakuço Koen el Kifurbaz, Ishakuço Koen ke se le kayo el ijo al pozo, Ishak Koen el Zampara, Ishak Koen el Rikinyon, Ishakuço Koen kazado kon trez mujeres, Ishak Koen el Ronko, Ishak Koen el Kalavasudo, Ishak Koen el Ruvyo, Ishakuço Koen el de la mujer cilveliya... i munços maz ke no me lo esto puedyendo akodrarme agora. Ten nosekualo i yamalos a estos al Sefer kon sus titolos ke todo el mundo los konose este biçin i solo eyos son ke no saven ke se konosen kon estas nombradias.

Acaba dişo yo agora demi parami avera en estos tiempos entre vozotros yene tantos ke se yaman Ishak Koen?

No kreo...
Zaten i si avera bile ya se azeriyan los nombres turkeados komo Izzet Koen, Izel Koen, Ezel Koen, i afilun Iskender Koen. Custo de nosekualo al puso. Ama si keremos avlar lo dereço, si a nada no, a apartar el ke es yamado al Sefer vos yaradeyo el turkearvos los nombres. Basta ke vos akodreş u sepaş por ande es la puerta del Kal.
Neysa Yusef.
Ya la alargimos esta letra maz del karar kon tanta bavajada i çarlina ke no valen ni sinko paras.
Dales saludes a los ke demandan por mi.
I tu sano i rezyo ke me estes, i guadrado ke me seyas de ojo de pato i de samsar.

El Tio Yekutiel.

Yusuf ALTINTAŞ, Şalom, Istanbul, September 1997.

3. Contemporary Poetry

The six writers presented here give witness to the vitality of poetic creativity in Judeo-Spanish. Clarisse Nicoïdski is the author of numerous works in French and of poetry collections in Judeo-Spanish (Sarajevo). Avner Perez and Margalit Matitiahu (Jerusalem and Salonika) publish in Israel and Rita Gabbay Simantov in Greece. D. F. Altabe publishes in the United States while Moshe Ha-Elion's volume of poetry on the Nazi death camps has appeared in Israel. Poetry – along with songs, stories and short chronicles – is the most active literary genre in Judeo-Spanish.

Tia Ester

Kon pasos de vejes, avagarozos,
Dia por dia kaminava tia Ester
Esparziendo la golor del ajo desmenuzado
ke se lo englutia en una vez.
Sovre la siya de paja situada en el koredor
Su puerpo pezgado pozava,
I sus dedos godros sovre su tripa atava.
La solombra eskura igual ke su vestido
Menazava a la pared.

Tia Ester avria los ojos komo ventanas
Por areventar la luz
En el ruido del aire koriente
Se atabafava su boz de ravia
Ke kaiya a los piezes de las kriaturas
Djugando kon djiro.

Oras se kedava asentada,
Avia vezes ke kon sinyo de menaza
Alevantava su dedo ke truviava
Las fachas de los ninyos alegres.
Las tadradas engrandesian su solombra en la pared.
I las noches traian a su puerpo muvimientos de abandono,
A las veses en su kamareta se kedava,
Ma kuando de la vida por siempre se despartio
En la siya de paja su guezmo kedo,
I la pared por su solombra kuntinuava a ser menazada.

Margalit Matitiahu, Alegrika, Kiron (Israel): Eked, p. 23.

Una manu tumó l'otra

una manu tumó l'otra
li dixu di no scundersi
li dixu di no sararsi
li dixu di no spantarsi

una mano tumina l'alma.
mitio un aníu al dedu
mitio un bezu in la palma
i un puniadu di amor

las dos manos si tumaron
alivantarun una fuarza
a cayersi las paredis
a avrirsi lus caminus*

Clarisse Nicoïdski, *Los ojus, las manus, la boca*, Loubressac-Bretenoux: Braad, 1978.

*Note how in the Bosnian dialect the unaccented *e* ⇨ *i* and *o* ⇨ *u* (*ojus, di, dedu*) and accented *e* ⇨ *a* (*fuerza*).

Sarina kanta romansas

Enfrente del yasimin
en su kortijo
Sarina kanta romansas.
Tiene los kaveyos eskuros
i de plata fina l'alma.
Por el rio ke desha
su boz en el aire
vienen los peshes
kon los ojos aviertos
sonyandoseu un esfuenyo.
Se suenyan
de los kavayos del ritmo
ke galopan i korren
sin topar repozo
asta ke yegan
al portal de la romansa
i entran adientro.
Sarina, riendose,
serra las puertas.

Avner Perez, *Verdjel de mansanas*, Maale Adumim (Israel): Yeriot, 1996, p.2.

Shabat

Me accodro de mi nona
cada Viernes por la tadre
como le avlava siempre
a su noguera mi madre

Aide fija regalada
quita te el devantal
metete vistido limpio
que ya yega el Shabat

La comida ya esta pronta
y la mesa se metio
las candelas assendidas
tu marido ya entro

Rita Gabbai Simantov, *Quinientos anios despues*, Athens, Greece, 1992, p. 30.

Pasharos de las kayes

Las palombas inchen las kayes
komiendo lo suzio i deshando el suyo.

Ansianos,
sentados en los bankos,
les echan migas de pan.
las grandes no deshan a las chikas komer
el bokado ke los viejos les dan.
Ma vienen otros pasharos ainda mas chikos
ke les rovan el pan entre la kaye i el piko.

En este mundo dezonesto
no son los grandes ke ganan
ma los mas prestos.

David Fintz Altabe, *Una Kozecha de rimas i konsejas*, Miami: San Lazaro Printings, 2000, p. 27.

Komo komiyan el pan

En los blokos en entrando al retorno del lavoro,
La porsion mas importante –en sus ojos un trezoro–
Resevian: un pedaso de pan preto ke pezava,
Manko de trezientas gramas i a esto s'adjustava,
Un keziko o un dulse i una tasa de bevida.
A sus kamas atornavan karreando la komida.

La bivienda o la supa k'en el dia despartian,
Al momento ke la davan –en segondos la englutian.
Ma el pan se lo komia kada uno a su manera,
Konvensido ke la suya la mijor de todas era,
Ke su ambre d'una parte longamente la kalmava,
I el deskayer del puerpo d'otra parte atadrava.

Uno, kon bukados grandes su porsion la eskapava,
Ke va akonteser mas tadre –por un punto no pensava.
Mudriskava el pan kon fuersa, agostava del konducho,
Konsintir la boka yena –esto le plazia mucho.
Kon estomago enchido se sintia mas kontente,
S'enreziava en su puerpo i no manko –mentalmente.

Otro, kon bukados chikos ke mashkava avagariko,
Su porsion se la komia. Sovre kada pedasiko,
Kuando lo aparejava, la mirada la fiksava,
Komo si tambien sus ojos ke s'afarten dezeava.
En ovrando d'esta forma su eskopo akomplia,
Kon komer de okuparse lo mas longo ke puedia.

Otros, de sus pan komian una parte solamente,
I el resto lo deshavan para el dia el siguente.
Fin estonses lo metian sea en sus pantalones,
O adientro de sus mangas por guadrarlo de ladrones.
D'estos, uno komo el primo, kada parte la mashkava,
Otro, komo el segundo, avagar la eskapava.

No mankavan i otras formas de komer el pan ke davan,
Modos viejos los deshavan i mas muevos empleavan.

Yo k'eskrivo estas linias i k'estuve en este estado,
D'una koza me akodro en pensando al pasado:
No emporta kuando i komo la porsion de pan komia,
Mi estomago de ambre sin se apozar djemia.

Moshe Ha-Elion, *En los kampos de la muerte*,
Instituto Maale Adumim (Israel), 2000, pp. 33-39.

4. Tio Bohor i su mujer Djamila: "Se levanto i disho la mangrana"

This dialog between Uncle Bohor and his wife Djamila is excerpted from a 1940 issue of the Mesajero, *a Salonika newspaper (no. 5, p.1344).*

BOHOR: Ke balabaya, ansina se desha las kozas de ley arastando por enriva el lavamano?

DJAMILA: Bonora ke mos gwadre, tu ke desharias algún livro komo ya lo uzas a deshar kon los entojos adyentro, ay safek ke syempre mos palavreamos por esto.

BOHOR: No es livro, bre fija. Figúrate ke esta manyana, komo del frio no avres ventana agora, vide un bulto en un chiniko de enriva el lavamano. Kreendo ke era un tajiko de pruna de estos ke es-hweles a fazer tu, komo el bovo me lo echí en una ala boka. Ma para lo kitar kon enguyos chekín bilir, ke salyera por tajiko, Djamila? Saves endivinar?

DJAMILA: No.

BOHOR: La kameá tuya. Parese ke te mudates, no te akantidó, la deshates arastando por ande te vino.

DJAMILA: Mas bovo ke te vea. Ke manera, no vites ke era la kameá mia ?

BOHOR: Andá endivinar ke tu ias a deshar arastando la kemeá… Embaldes no es ke estas oras vas kon nyervos, si bweno te favlo, negro me respondes.

DJAMILA: Adyó, dezvanesido ke te vea Bohor. De la kameá le dyo la tose al gato. A mi ya me se avren las reynes del yelor, tu me sales kon la kameá.

BOHOR: Avré ninya, es kon ridjá grande i kon dos éremas koreladas ke te la tomí del dervish agora dyes anyos. Ay safek ke de kwando yevas la kameá ke no tyenes bostejadero ni dolor de sejas.

DJAMILA: Balabáy regalado, la kameá ay sinko anyos ke no la ave vistido, i si no era tu nwera ke me aremishkava la kasha esta semana para ke le dyera la samara del kirim mio ke se kyere fazer yaká para el palto, ainda ia estar al fondo de la kasha aí komo la metí. La kasha no bosteja, ni tyene dolor en las sejas ke no tyene.

BOHOR: Kyere dizir ke no la aves vistido ay tyempo?

DJAMILA: Seguro, porke la dimos a meldar kon el veziniko de ariva i vimos ke avia eskrito mil patranyas ke se las lambe el gato. Kon esto, mi alma Bohor, la kameá es la idea dela persona.

BOHOR: Ansina te parese a ti. Yo se ke un sovriniko mio ke tenia tomadura, eskapó kon una kameá.

DJAMILA: Bweno agora, una vez ke tyene valor esta kameá, vate al eshpital, mira ver kyen sufre de dolor de sejas i bostejos, véndela i mérkame la ashuré para noche de djweves.

BOHOR: Es verdad, Djamila. Se kyere pasado por ande el vinyatero ke mos

258

mande el vino de hazaká dela shuré de kada anyo. Mira, kítame la gemareka ke tengo kon los livros para dezir las berahod.

DJAMILA: Onde la vo ir a estampar i aremishkar todo? Ya no las se yo de kavesa?

BOHOR: Dilas kwando veo.

DJAMILA: Para la noche dela shuré.

BOHOR: No, mo las pasaremos beraber.

DJAMILA: De akodro, syente.

Se levantó i disho la mangrana
Kolorada komo la mansana:
"Yo ke en el árvol kresko,
Ke se diga ya meresko,
Kon kavaná i empyés,
La berahá: Boré peri aés."

Disho la míshpola i asorva,
I kon eyas la harova,
La almendra i pinyón,
Tyenen esta opinyón:
Ke del pasto a su manera,
Dan leche ala kriadera,
I todos en una kon djilvés,
Dizen el boré perí aés.

Disho el tramuziko blondo,
Des.hachado i redondo:
"Por mi dizen kon hohmá,
El boré berí aadamá."

BOHOR: Dime, Djamila, tyenes en tino komo se dize berahá de vino?

DJAMILA: Sí, kyes ke te lo diga a ti el boré atov ve ametí?

BOHOR: Muy hamzira sos, Djamila. Te veré para noche de djweves, kyero kon akel mezmo garip ke me kantates las noches de la hupá ke me kantes las berahod delos frutos dela shuré.

DJAMILA: Ah! Bohor mi alma, akel tyempo tenia kyef, porke era fruto mwevo el kazamyento. Agora pay kuku. Tu estás enkojido komo un figo i yo komo une míshpola…

BUNIS, David M., *Voices from Jewish Salonika, Selections from the Judezmo Satirical Series* Tio Ezrá I Su Mujer Benuta *and* Tio Bohor I Su Mujer Djamila. Jerusalem: Misgav Yerushalayim – The National Authority for Ladino Culture – The Ets Ahaim Foundation of Thessaloniki, 1999, pp. 408–410.

I

לה גרולייה (לייליק קושו)

און דיאה איל חוג׳ה אפ׳ירו אונה גרולייה אי לה
טרושו אין קאזה, ב׳יינדולה גראנדי לי קורטו איל ביקו אי
לוס פייס אי לה אסינטו אין און לוגאר אלטו.

‒ אה ! דישו איל, אגורה טי איזיטיס פאשארו.

2

פיידרייו סו איספ׳ואינייו אי ב׳ה אה טופ׳ארלו
איל חוג׳ה, אונה נג׳׳, טו טוב׳יינדו איספ׳ואיניו
סאלייו אה מידיה נג׳׳ אי איסטוב׳ו קאמינאנדו פור לה קאלי.
און פוליס אינקונטראנדולו פור איל קאמינו לי דימאנדו :

‒ סיניור, קי בושקאס איסטואס אוראס פור לאס
קאליס ?

‒ מי סי פ׳ולייו איל איספ׳ואיניו אי סאלי אה
בושקארלו, לי ריספונדייו איל חוג׳ה.

3

קאלדו די פאלאמאס

און דיאה, נאסרידין ב׳ידי אין און ג׳יקו ריאו 4
אה 5 פאלאמאס קי אזיאן באנייו, אסטה קי איל חוג׳ה
פ׳ואי פארה אפאניארלאס אילייאס סי פ׳וליירון.
איל חוג׳ה, סי אסינטו אל באדרי דיל ריאו קיטו
פאן דיל סאקו קי טיניאה קון סי, אי אימפיסו אה
אונטאר אין איל אגואה אי אה קומיר.

אין איסטו, פאסו און אומברי די פור אלי, אי
ב׳יינדו לו קי אזיאה איל חוג׳ה, לי דימאנדה :

‒ קי איסטאס קומיינדו ?

‒ איסטו קומיינדו קאלדו די פאלאמאס, ריספונדייו
איל חוג׳ה.

Excerpt from *La Vida de Nasredin Hodja*, collection of stories, published by *El djugeton*, Istanbul, 1923.

I
La gruya (leylek kuşu)

Un día el Hodjá aferó una gruya i la trusho en kaza, vyéndola grande le kortó el biko i los pyes i la asentó en un lugar alto.

"Ah! disho él, agora te izites pásharo."

2
Pyedrió su esfuenyo i va a toparlo

El Hodjá, una noche, no tuvyendo esfuenyo salyó a medya noche i estuvo kaminando por la kaye. Un polís enkontrándolo por el kamino le demandó:

"Sinyor, ké bushkas estas oras por las kayes?"

– Me se fuyó el esfuenyo i salí a bushkarlo, le respondyó el Hodjá.

3
Kaldo de palazas

Un día, Nasredín vido en un chiko río 4 a 5 palazas ke azían banyo, asta ke el Hodjá fue para apaníarlas eyas se fuyeron.

El Hodjá, se asentó al bodre del río kitó pan del sako ke tenía kon sí, i empesó a untar en el agua i a komer.

En esto, pasó un ombre de por ayí, i vyendo lo ke azía el Hodjá, le demanda:

"Ké estás komyendo?"

"Estó komyendo kaldo de palazas, respondyó el Hodjá."

Transcription by Gaëlle Collin, Jeanne Laedlein and Anne Perrin

Ven, Sarika, ven,
dame un poko d'agua. (repeat)
Ay, Sarika,
linda i ermozika,
yo te vo tomar
sapatos d'Unkapán,
chizmés de Djibalí.

Agua de la fuente,
no te puedo dar. (repeat)
Sto deskalsa,
ay rosiyo enbasho,
mc se yela el pye.

Ay, Sarika, ay,
linda i henozika. (repeat)
Ay, Sarika,
dame un poko d'agua,
yo te vo merkar
sapatos d'Unkapán,
chizmés de Djibalí.

No me prime a mí,
ke me merkes tú. (repeat)
Tengo un padre
merkader muy grande.
El me va tomar
sapatos d'Unkapán,
chizmés de Djibalí.

43 ⊛ Excerpts from two recorded songs:

Koplas de Avram Avinu.
La Serena (Dame la mano palomba).

Excerpted from *La Boz de Oriente* (monthly), anyo 5, 1936, Istanbul.

8. La novya Aguná*

This passage is excerpted from the first chapter of La Novya Aguná, *a novel published in 1922 by Eliya Karmona, an Istanbul novelist and journalist. The action takes place in the heart of the Jewish community of Istanbul in the 18ᵗʰ century.*

Ke avia esta noche en esta kaza? Avia un espozoryo. Chibi Yaakov el Gevir tenia una ija regalada. Anke muy riko, el no bushkava a darla a algun ijo de riko. Si no ke, el avia eskojido por yerno al ijo de Rabi[1] Aaron el Hasid[2], haham akaal[3] de akel tyempo en Balat, i avia dezinyado la noche de Purim komo noche de despozoryo.

Djusto alas oras dos ala turka[4], un moso vinia informar ke Rabi Aaron el Hasid lya vinia kon su ijo.

Un chiko remeneamyento se sintyo entre todos los asistyentes i elyos rondjavan sus ojos sovre la puerta del salon por ver entrar al novyo.

Rabi Aaron entrava kon su ijo Shimón en dizyendo:

"Purim tov mevorah[5]!"

Todos se levantavan i davan lugar en la kyoshe[6] al Si'[7] rabino ke se asentava en tomando a su ijo alado.

Konversaron de aki i de alya myentras algunos puntos i el espozoryo empeso en estos terminos:

Shimón se levantava i se prezentava en pyes delantre un otro rabino. Este ultimo le tomava la mano en estos terminos:

"Tu Shimón, ijo de Rabi Aaron el Hasid, tomas aki djuramyento ke no puedes espozarte, ni apalavrarte, ni tener ojo kon ninguna ija de Israel[8] afuera de Hana ija de Chibi Yaakov B. K. R.[9] el Gevir, i me das la lesensya de eskrivir los papeles de espozoryo sigun akordo ke tenesh los dos."

---

1. Master.

2. Pious, generous, charitable.

3. Wise man, community rabbi.

4. Meaning "Turkish style," "Middle-Eastern style," as opposed to *ala franka*, "European style." Two o'clock *ala turka* corresponds roughly to about 8 o'clock P.M.

5. A Purim wish: "A good and blessed Purim."

6. Corner, that is, "make room for."

7. Abbreviation for *sinyor*.

8. *Ija de Israel*, "daughter of Israel, of the Jewish people," meaning "a Jewish girl, woman."

9. From the Hebrew, abbreviation for *ben kavod rabi*.

El joven se retirava en dando lugar a Hana su novya ke el rabino dizia los mismos byervos.

Kuando esta operasyon se eskapo, el novyo bezo la mano de su padre i se prezento a bezar la mano de su esfuegro i esfuegra.

Kuando el Gevir espandyo la mano a su yerno para ke se la bezara, el le disho:

— Mira mi ijo, lyo so byen riko i si lyo keria, puedia tomar un yerno mas riko de mi. Ma lyo proferi tomar por yerno un talmid[10] de yeshiva[11] komo ti, mi ija es regalada i todos mis byenes te apartyenen, tu no vas azer ningun echo i vas a meldar[12] kada dia en la yeshiva kon mi ija Hana. Lyo tuve el kuyidado[13] de embezar a mi ija tambyen la santa Ley de Moshe. Kon esto desde oy tu sos mi ijo komo Hana es mi ija.

La seremonia de los despozoryos se eskapo i empesaron a ofrir[14] dulsuryas i diblas[15] por kavod[16] de Purim.

Akea noche entera estuvyeron komyendo i bevyendo i no fue ke serka la manyana ke los ombres se retiraron por ir al kaal[17] a dizir tefila[18].

Gaëlle COLLIN, "*La Novya Aguná*: présentation, translittération et édition d'un roman judéo-espagnol d'Eliya Karmona" in *Neue Romania* 26, Judenspanisch VI, Berlin, 2002, pp. 2–132.

(*) Aguna kere dizir una mujer ke no se puede kazar porke su marido se aogo en la mar i no se topo el kuerpo del muerto.

---

10. Pupil.

11. An advanced Talmudic school.

12. Archaism meaning "to read, study."

13. Care. The more common form is *kudyado*.

14. To serve.

15. Purim pastries.

16. Honor.

17. Synagogue. More often referred to as *kal* in Judeo-Spanish.

18. Prayer.

9. Bula Satula

The chronicles of Bula Satula (Madame Satula), written by Moïse Soulam, a young Judeo-Spanish journalist originally from Salonika, appeared in the New York weekly, La Vara, *from 1922 to 1934. The chronicle below is excerpted from* La Vara *no. 10, November 1922.*

Regalada Vara de mi korason:

Ni el navo se aze ravano ni el ravano se aze navo[1]. Esto propyo estamos vyendo kon una partida de nuestras mujeres. Tesabea la tadre ke es el dia grande[2] se van a meter la mano a la kavesa i van a pensar del eremo luso ke estan azyendo, de las modas ke tomaron i del mal avlar, yevar i traer entre las unas kon las otras.

Si tantiko disho una mujer una koza a la otra ya se espande la novedad i de una pulga le azen un gameo[3]. Las babas[4] nuestras estan metidas para karear[5] engreshos[6] i embrolyos. Es desgrasya por amor del Dyo, non ay ke dizir elyas son kapaches[7] de azer un ijo sin padre ni madre i mandarlo a la eskola[8].

Este mal de estas mujeres se esta espandyendo un poko mas kada dia, i esta devenyendo una hazinura apegadoza[9]. Shashmak sheydir[10] onde estan metidas elyas i en kualo se les va el tyempo. En lugar de mirar el hal de sus kazas, de sus ijos, del gizado i del lavar, elyas pyedren oras olvidadas[11] del dia en indo i kontando todo loke non ay i tuvyendo en la boka a todo el mundo.

---

1. *Ni el navo se aze ravano ni el ravano se aze navo*, proverb: "He who is born stupid will remain so."
2. *Tesabea la tadre ke es el dia grande*, expression: "at an indeterminate time, some time way off in the future."
3. *De una pulga azer un gameo*, expression: "to exaggerate the facts."
4. *Geese,* "people who talk who have nothing to say."
5. To provoke.
6. Imbroglios, trouble among friends.
7. Capable.
8. *Azer un ijo sin padre ni madre i mandarlo a la eskola*, expression: "to make up something totally untrue and tell it with great conviction."
9. Contagious.
10. *Shashmak sheydir* (T.), "an incredible thing."
11. *Oras olvidadas,* "hours spent doing nothing."

Yo por mi me empostemo dela kavesa fin los pyezes, kuando las syento avlar mal de la djente, sin ser i sin porke[12], sin razon, i sin ley.

Kale ver regalada Vara a estas mujeres, en medyo los strites[13], kontando i rekontando postemas de otras, kuestyones de famia, i mizmo lo ke nuestra ley, mos enkomenda de non avlar.

Es koza kuryoza regalada Vara al verlas avlar kon los dedos i las manos, kon los pyes i la kavesa lo ke parese ni mas ni manko ke es shimi[14] ke estan baylando. I despues de un largo moabet[15], despues de sorear[16] toda la eskupina i despues de komersen un sako entero de indyanats[17], las nuestras azen el gud bay[18] ala amerikana i se esparten alegres de alma i buenas de korason por aver avlado mal de las otras i esbafado lo ke avia i non avia i tomando los mas emprestado[19]. Estas mujerikas i balabayas la van a entender komo la entendyo Djoha, kuando estiro las pachas[20], kon la kuala kedo, tu

Bula Satula

Gwenaëlle COLLIN, *"Bula Satula et Ham Avraam": L'immigration judéo-espagnole à New York à travers les chroniques de Moïse Soulam dans l'hebdomadaire* La Vara *(1922-1934)*, Master's Thesis, Paris: INALCO, October 2002.

---

12. *Sin ser i sin porke*, "without any reason whatsoever."

13. From the English "streets."

14. From the English, "the shimmy," a American dance style in which dancers shook their shoulders rhythmically, in style around 1920.

15. Conversation.

16. To waste.

17. From the English "Indian nuts," cashew nuts.

18. "Good bye."

19. *Tomar emprestado*, "to add even more, to invent."

20. *Estirar las pachas [to stretch out one's legs]*, "to die."

10. Komunikado del Beth Din Atsedek

El Beth Din Atsedek se aze un dover de traer a la konosensya del onorado publiko los akavidos siguentes:

1. La orasyon por el taanit de los berohot tiendra luguar dia de vyernes 10 Nisan 1998 a las horas 7.45 de la manyana en las Keilot: Şişli – Neve Şalom i en Cadde-bostan alas horas 7.30.
2. El biur Hametz (keriendo dizir ke no se puede komer hamets) alas horas 9.43.
3. La matsa este anyo es vendida en kutis serrados yevando la marka de Kaşerut del gran Rabbinato 5758–1998.
4. La matsa molinada Kaşer es fabrikada soto el kontrol del Gran Rabbinato, eya es vendida en papeleras de naylon de un kilo donde las bokaduras son serradas i yevan en el lado la marka de Kaşerut.
5. El vino Kaşer kontrolado por el Gran Rabbinato es akel ke yeva el Siyo de "Kaşer Le Pesah."
6. Dulsuryas Kaşer de Pesah se venden solo en la butika del Sinyor A. Bardavit (Serpil) en Şişli.
7. Este anyo tanbien ay dos jeneros de kezo, kezo blanko i kezo kaşkaval Kaşer Lepesah fabrikado soto el kontrol del Gran rabbinato; el kezo blanko kaşer, sera vendido en kutis serrados de 2 kg. i el kezo kaşkaval en ambalaj de medyo kilo yevando el siyo del Gran rabbinato i la eskrita Kaşer Le Pesah.
8. El restorante kaşer Merit sera avyerto 8 diyas de Pesah solo en las noçes kon komidas paskuales.
9. Los regalos aprontados de parte del ospital Or Ahayim i de la Ovra Mişne Tora (ÖYD) son tanbien Kaşer Le Pesah.
10. Şarkuteriya Kaşer Le Pesah se topa en la botika del kasap Yusuf, lado de el orno de Matsa en Şişhane.
11. La firma Robelyu en Göztepe, i la ovra Ihtiyarlar Yurdu este anyo tyene servisyo de komidas Kaşer Le Pesah a las kazas.

Non duvdamos ke Israel Kedoşim se akavidaran en todo lo susdiço i kedamos bendizyendovos kon un buen MOADIM LESIMHA.

Por el Beth Din Atsedek.

Announcement by the Beth Din in *Şalom*, March 25, 1998–5758.

268

ANSWER SECTION

Lesson 1A

Exercise 1: 1. Kómo te yamas? 2. Kuántos anyos tyenes? 3. De ké alkunya sos? 4. Ké echo azes?

Exercise 2: Me yamo x, tengo x anyos, so elevo de djudyó...

Exercise 3: 1. El chay está tivyo. 2. La kaza es vyeja. 3. Mi amigo es chiko. 4. El kuaför es aedado. 5. El boyiko está yelado/friyo. 6. Su mujer es manseva.

Exercise 4: Roza es la mujer de Salvo. Salvo es el marido de Roza. Roza i Salvo son el padre i la madre de Blanka, Sará i David. Blanka i Sará son las ijas de Roza i Salvo. Son las ermanas de David. David es el ijo de Roza i Salvo. Es el ermano de Blanka i Sará.

Exercise 5: 1. Su ija es grande. 2. Sus ermanos son aedados. 3. El chay está kayente. 4. Albert es aedado. 5. Rika es manseva. 6. Sus amigas son vyejas. 7. La skola es franseza. 8. Los boyikos están yelados. 9. Sus ijas están buenas. 10. Los pyanós son fransezes.

Exercise 6: 1. Estó kon (las) amigas de la skola. 2. Es la ija del kuaför. 3. Da lisyones. 4. Komemos boyikos i bevemos chay. 5. Tyenen ijos. 6. Es el marido de la ermana de Rika. 7. Son los ermanos de Albert.

Exercise 7: 1. Son muestras amigas. 2. Es sus pyanó. 3. Es mi madre. 4. Es su mujer. 5. Son vuestros boyikos. 6. Son tus ermanas. 7. Es tu chay. 8. Es su kaza. 9. Son muestros ijos. 10. Es vuestro pyanó. 11. Son mis ijas.

Exercise 8: 1. Kén es tu primo? 2. Ké/kuálo aze tu primo? 3. Ande está tu kuaför? 4. Ké edad/kuántos anyos tyene Alp, tu ijo el bohor? 5. De ké alkunya sos? 6. Kómo se yama tu ermana? 7. Ké haber? 8. Kén da lisyones de pyanó? 9. Kuántos anyos tyene tu marido? 10. Ké/kuálo keres?

Exercise 9: lavoro – lavoras – lavora – lavoramos – lavorásh – lavoran.

Exercise 10: me ambezo – te ambezas – se ambeza – mos ambezamos – vos ambezásh – se ambezan.

Exercise 11: 1. Los ijos de Luna son aedados. 2. El chay está kayente. 3. Los ijikos están buenos (in good health)/son buenos (are nice). 4. El padre está en kaza. 5. La skola es franseza. 6. Vozós estásh en una skola. 7. Ánde estásh vozós? 8. Madam Dudú i su ija están en el kuaför. 9. Los amigos de Henri son komercheros. 10. Tu sos el marido de Lea. 11. Yo so muy grande. 12. Mozós semos mansevos. 13. Henri es mi ermano. 14. Kén sosh vozós ? 15. Mozós estamos ande Djoya.

Exercise 12: 1. -mos. 2. -s. 3. -sh. 4. -n.

Lesson 1B

Konsejika del sodro: 1. Se yama Hayimachi. 2. Mora en Kulaksiz. 3. No, no es godro, es sodro.

Adding/Subtracting: a) Sinko de dizisésh son onze. b) Katorze i tres son dizisyete. c) Mueve i tres son dodje. d) Syete de vente son tredje. e) Kinze de diziocho son tres. f) Mueve de dyez es uno. g) Onze i kuatro son kinze.

Lesson 2A

Exercise 1: 1 . Tyenes durmidero/durmedero parese. 2. Tyenes meldadero parese. 3. Tyenes alevantadero parese. 4. Tyenes kantadero parese. 5. Tyenes korredero parese. 6. Tyenes empleadero parese.

Exercise 2:

Perla – Shelomó	Mazaltó – Sabetay
Ida	Edí

271

Exercise 4: Djugueves vente de marso, vyernes ventiuno de marso, myérkoles dizimueve de marso.

Exercise 5: 1. So hammal. 2. So moso o mosa. 3. So sarraf. 4. So lavorante. 5. So banker. 6. So kashero. 7. So terdjumán. 8. So gazetero. 9. So fabrikatör. 10. So mimar/architekto. 11. So korredor de kazas. 12. So komerchante/ butikaryo. 13. So patrón. 14. So komerchero. 15. So vendedor/empyegado.

Exercise 6: 1. So panadero. 2. So balukchí. 3. So karnesero. 4. So moso. 5. So taukchí. 6. So zarzavachí. 7. So meyanadjí. 8. So lokantadjí. 9. So bayladora. 10. So kayikchí/ barkero. 11. So pishkador. 12. So kuyumdjí/djoyero. 13. So marangoz. 14. So guertelano/ bahcheván. 15. So samarrero. 16. So lavandera. 17. So kapitán. 18. So bakkal.

Exercise 7: 1. Vo a komer pan. 2. Vamos a bever kavé. 3. Vash a vinir/venir. 4. Vas a entender. 5. Va a darme un livro. 6. Vamos a ver a la vizina. 7. Vo a tornar a kaza. 8. Vash a lavorar. 9. Van a avlar. 10. Vas a saver.

Exercise 8: 1. Konosésh a mi vizina? 2. Vijito los muzeos. 3. Konosko esta fusta. 4. Konosemos al haham/rabino. 5. Vijito a mi es-huegra kada semana i semana/todas las semanas. 6. Ves la kaza de Madam Lucie? 7. Vemos a tu prima ke vyene akí. 8. Veo un gatiko. 9. Ve la eskola de Suzí, ma no <u>la</u> konose *(either the school or Suzí)*. 10. Vo a la eskola a ver a la maestra. 11. A este sinyor, lo ves?

LESSON 2B

Kantikas:

Exercise: 1. So sakadjí. 2. So rubí/melamed. 3. So tanyedor. 4. So shastre. 5. So sapatero/ kunduryadjí. 6. So shohet. 7. So moel. 8. So sanmás/shamásh.

9. So antikadjí. 10. So estudyante/elevo. 11. So profesör/profesora. 12. So kuzandera. 13. So rohets. 14. So hazán. 15. So dayán. 16. So hahambashí. 17. So ateshdjí(ya)/atedjí(ya). 18. So komadre. 19. So kazamentera/o. 20. So ropavejero/paryaruhadjí.

El ayudador del kazamentero: 1. El kazamentero espoza o kaza a los mansevikos i las mansevikas. 2. El ayudador ayuda al kazamentero para kazar a los mansevikos. 3. La novya es ermoza i rika. 4. La novya tyene una korkova.

Entre madre i ijo en el telefón:

Questions: 1. Un ijo i una madre avlan en el telefón. 2. El ijo mora en Israel. 3. La madre mora en Istanbul. 4. El ijo kere ir a Istanbul kon su mujer, sus ijos i su es-huegra. 5. Porké no ay mas kamaretas para durmir i no save ké azer.

Exercise: 1. La beven. 2. Lo dize a su madre. 3. Mi ermano los traye a kaza. 4. Lo bevo. 5. La madre las melda. 6. Los keremos muncho. 7. Mi padre la mira. 8. La nona las echa en la kamareta. 9. El rubí me los da. 10. Yo las sé.

LESSON 3A

Exercise 1: 1. La televizyón está enriva de la meza. 2. El telefón está enriva de la meza. 3. La menorá está aryentro del armaryo de livros/en la biblioteka/al lado de los livros. 4. En el/la sofá/la kanapé. 5. El djarro está en la mezika/enriva de la mezika. 6. El tapet está debasho de la mezika. 7. La meza está enriva del tapet. 8. La siya está al lado de la ventana. 9. El livro está debasho de la mezika, en el tapet/en la biblioteka. 10. La gazeta está al lado de la meza, en el tapet. 11. La lampa está al lado del koltuk/de la poltrona. 12. Las kortinas están delantre de la ventana/al lado de la ventana. 13. El espejo está sovre la pared de la kamareta. 14. El minder está enriva de la kanapé.

Exercise 2:

Exercise 3: 1. Kale ke laves. 2. Kale ke meldes. 3. Kale ke eskrivas. 4. Kale ke komas. 5. Kale ke freges. 6. Kale ke te aspertes. 7. Kale ke bevas agua. 8. Kale ke lo agas.

Exercise 4: a) Ánde se mete(n): 1. La mezuzá se mete en la puerta. 2. El tapet se mete en basho, debasho de la meza, en medyo de la kamareta. 3. El saksí de rozas se mete enriva de la meza. 4. La kama se mete al lado de la puerta/enfrente de la ventana, en la kamareta de echar. 5. El chöp se mete en el mupak/debasho de la pila. 6. Los chinís se guadran en el armaryo, en el mupak. 7. Las kortinas se meten al lado de la ventana i delantre de la ventana. 8. La menorá se mete en la kamareta de estar, en la biblioteka. 9. La leshiya se mete debasho de la pila, en el mupak o en el banyo.

b) Ké azemos: 1. En el mupak gizamos la komida, kozinamos. 2. En el banyo, mos lavamos i mos vestimos kada diya. 3. En la kamareta de echar, durmimos. 4. En la kama, mos echamos, mos arepozamos o durmimos. 5. En el koltuk, mos arepozamos. 6. En el salón, miramos la televizyón, aresivimos musafires i bevemos chay en avlando. 7. En el sofá, meldamos la gazeta o livros, miramos la televizyón; avlamos kon los musafires. 8. En el büró, meldamos i eskrivimos. 9. En el balkón tomamos el aver i miramos ahuera.

LESSON 3B

Konsejika del ashuguar: 1. El sanmás guadra la puerta del kal. 2. No kaza a su ija porke es muy prove i no puede aparejar ashuguar. 3. Le da un konsejo ma se burla de él.

La mujer sorretera: 1. Una sorretera es una mujer ke sale diya entero i ke no está en su kaza. 2. La mujer de Djohá va ande las vizinas. 3. No, no se aravya Djohá.

Street scenes: Memories of a street peddler: 1. Los zarzavachís venden vedrura, legumbres, salata… 2. No, no tyenen butikas i van por las kayes, entrando en las kazas para vender kozas a la djente. 3. Venden a las balabayas de kaza. 4. Se burlan en dizyendo a las mujeres: Madam k'avra (Madam kavra). Estos byervos pueden kerer dizir: Madam, ke avra su puerta o Madam la kavra!!!

LESSON 4A

Exercise 1: 1. A él, le plazen tus amigos. 2. A mozós, no mos plaze el tiyatro. 3. A ti, te plaze la televizyón. 4. A vozós, vos plaze avlar kon las vizinas. 5. A mí, me plazen las kantikas. 6. A mi madre, no le plazen las kamaretas chikas. 7. A tu es-huegro, le plaze tu kaza.

Exercise 2: 1. Me plaze englenearme mirando la televizyón o avlando kon amigos. 2. Me plaze arepozarme enriva de mi kama/echado(a) en el sofá… 3.El banyo me plaze kuando está kayente. 4. Me plazen los amigos buenos… 5. No me plaze fregar, dar utí… 6. Me plaze ir al tiyatro o al sinemá. 7. No me plaze ir a la universitá, a la eskola … 8. Me plaze meldar livros i gazetas.

Exercise 3: 1. Estamos djuguando. 2. Están tanyendo mandolino. 3. Estásh komyendo. 4. Se están enfasyando. 5. Estásh avlando muncho. 6. Estamos meldando los haberes. 7. Estó mirando ahuera. 8. Se está arepozando. 9. Te estás lavando. 10. Están durmyendo.

11. Estásh sintyendo la kantika? 12. No estó lavorando. 13. No se están ambezando. 14. Está engleneándose/se está engleneando. 15. Ké estásh azyendo?

Exercise 4: Me estó ambezando en djudyó. Estó meldando livros. Estó sintyendo una kantika mueva. Estó bevyendo chay. Estó komyendo pan i kezo.

Exercise 5: 1. Mi ermana es mas chika de/ke mí. 2. Meldar un livro es mijor de/ke ir al sinemá. 3. La agua del mupak es mas yelada de/ke la del banyo. 4. Su madre es mas aedada de/ke su padre.

Exercise 6: 2. Está mirando la televizyón i está avlando kon las amigas/está bevyendo kavé… 3. Está durmyendo. 4. Está bevyendo chay/está djuguando kartas… 5. Está vendyendo/está avlando kon su haver… 6. Están avlando/están espajando/están kozinando/están azyendo borrekas … 7. Está ambezándose en ivrit/está djuguando un tiyatro/está baylando…

Exercise 7: Kero ke komas – kero ke bivas – kero ke durmas – kero ke lavores – kero ke meldes la gazeta – kero ke barras la kaza – kero ke te laves – kero ke freges los chinís – kero ke djugues – kero ke te ambezes en inglés.

Exercise 8: 1. Van a vinir. 2. Van al banyo turko. 3. Dizen ke sos bovo/la djente dize(n) ke sos bovo. 4. Dizen/la djente dize(n) munchas kozas. 5. Ande eyos, se kanta toda la noche. 6. Para Roshashaná eskrivimos/se eskriven letras. Para Roshashaná la djente eskrive(n) letras. 7. En el klub se kantan kantikas. 8. Se dize/la djente dize(n) "nochada buena" kuando se va(n) a echar. 9. Dizen/dize(n) la djente ke va(n) a avrir las eskolas en enverano. 10. Beven rakí. 11. Ande mí, miramos muncho la televizyón.

LESSON 4B

Kantika de novya: 1. La novya s'está peynando, vistyendo, afeytando. 2. La está yamando su es-huegra. 3. El novyo la está asperando. 4. Kale ke sirva a su marido.

Kantika de aliyá: 1. Avla un ijo kon su madre. 2. El ijo kere irse a Palestina. 3. Porke es syonisto. 4. Los drohim yaman a la mansevéz djudiya. 5. Kale ke deshe a su madre, a su mujer i a sus ijos. 6. Se van a aunar rogando la salvasyón al Dyo. 7. La madre yora porke nunkua mas no lo va a ver a su ijo.

Un artíkolo sovre la lingua: 1. Para dar ayudos i tomar desizyones. 2. Tyene ke ayudar/kale ke ayude a los investigadores, a los eskrivanos, a los poetas, i a los kompozitores en djudyó. 3. Deskutyendo kon todos i dando ayudos i haberes. 4. Están lavorando para avansar i enrejistrar la lingua i la kultura judeo– espanyola. 5. Porke están izolados i biven kada uno en su luguar. 6. Biven en la Evropa, en la Turkiya, en la Amérika i en Israel i otros modos de luguares.

Kómo mos engleneávamos en chika: 1. Se djuga kon findjanes i un kimuriko. Se aboltan los findjanes i debasho de uno se mete el kimuriko. Duspués kale toparlo ande está. 2. Noche de alhad, se eskapó shabad i se arekojen las famiyas para englenearsen. 3. Se salta kon una pyedrizika empushando la pyedra kon el pye.

LESSON 5A

Exercise 1: 1. Está tres i un kuarto. 2. Toma kuarenta i sinko puntos para ir a mi kaza. 3. Vo a lavorar por la manyana a las ocho i medya. 4. Me alevanto a las syete manko un kuarto. 5. Me vo a lavorar kon arabá/kon otobüs… 6. Un pan kosta kuatro frankos i trenta. 7. Una arabá mueva está a sesenta mil frankos. 8. Un litro de agua peza un kilo.

Exercise 2: a) Está ocho i kuarenta i sinko de la demanyana/mueve manko un kuarto. b) Son las dodje i (un) kuarto (de medyodiya). c) Es la una manko un kuarto de la demanyana (matrana), es medyanoche pasada de kuarenta i sinko puntos. d).Es la una i trenta i sinko de la medyodiya (de la tadre) (duspués de midí). e) Son las dyez djustas de la nochada (de la noche). f) Son las ocho i ocho de la noche (de la tadre). g) Es medyanoche. h) Son las dyez i medya de la manyana. i) Es medyodiya/midí. j) Son las syete i ventisinko de la tadre.

Exercise 3: 1. Kuánto kosta?/kuánto es? 2. Kuánto mezura? 3. Ké ora es/ké ora está/ké ora tyenes? 4. A kuánto está? 5. Kuánto peza? 6. Kuánto ay? 7. Ké karar metes/kuánto se mete? 8. Kómo vas ayá? 9. A ké ora te alevantas/te echas/vas al echo?… 10. Kuánto se kere?

Exercise 4: La siya está delantre/debasho de la ventana. El telefón está a la (i)syedra del armaryo. La poltrona está delantre del armaryo. La lampa está a la derecha del armaryo. La televizyón está enfrente del armaryo…

Exercise 5: a) Dozyentos mil frankos. b) Syetemil (i) kinyentas kuarenta i ocho markas. c) Dos milyones trezyentas sikuenta mil sheshentas (i) setenta i kuatro liras. d) Seshmil trezyentos ochenta i mueve dolares. e) Kinyentas (i) trenta i syete mil novesyentas ventisinko pesetas. f) Trezyentos sesenta i sinko mil (i) dozyentos noventa i tres dukados.

Exercise 6: 1. Vo al charshí para merkar dos metros de ropa/teshido para azer una fusta. 2. Kale topar una butika de oras. 3. – Kuánto kosta? – Dozyentos frankos un metro. – Está karo/es karo! 4. – Kuánto peza? – Dos kilos i medyo. – Kero la meatá(d). 5. Esta karne es/está barata amá no es buena. 6. Este es mijor amá kosta vente liras mas. 7. Dosmil i kinyentas markas? Es de baldes!

Exercise 7: A. Dízeme kómo vo a ir… 1. Kale ir por la kaleja del kal a mano syedra salyendo del kal ir derecho, i tomar la primera kaleja a la (i)syedra. 2. Se va derecho por la kaleja del banyo/a mano derecha salyendo del banyo. 3. Kale tomar la kaye de la djamí a la syedra i la kaleja del kal a la derecha fin a la kaleja del vapor i a bashar a la derecha fin a la guerta del gazino. 4. Kale tomar la kaleja de enfrente la kaza de Madam Sará, pasar delantre de la meshkita i kaminar fin a la kaleja del banyo, tomar a la syedra i pasar enfrente de la kaleja del kal, kontinuando la kaleja del banyo fin al orno. 5. Está muy serka. Salyendo de la skala del vapor kale tomar a la syedra i kaminar derecho fin a la guerta.

B. Ánde está… 1. Está a la punta de la kaleja del banyo, a la syedra. 2. Está en la kyushé de la kaleja de la djamí i de la kaleja del kal . 3. Está en la kyushé de la kaleja del banyo i la kaleja del kal, enfrente de la kavané. 4. El orno está a la punta de la kaleja del banyo, a la derecha, enfrente del banyo, duspués del balukchí. 5. Está enfrente de la kavané en la kaleja del kal, al lado de la kaza del doktor Kurtarán, enfrente de la skola djudiya… 6. Está en la kyushé de la kaleja del kal i la kaleja del banyo, enfrente (de) la kaza del rav Shimón i enfrente (d)el balukchí, está duspués del kal, kaminando a la syedra…

LESSON 5B

Konsejika del merkader de teshidos: 1. El merkader vende teshidos, hasé. 2. Le demanda munchas demandas para karishterearle el meoyo/para arovarle teshido. 3. Son los números ke son emportantes. 4. La mujer no entendyó nada porke se embevesyó avlando de su famiya.

Una demanda de matematika: 1. Egzisten la regla de tres derecha i la regla de tres arevés. 2. Las kuentas son las kozas ke se tyenen ke kontar *(the things or quantities to be counted);* el kuento es lo ke es kontado *(the addition, sum).* 3. Lo ke enchikese es el tyempo.

Exercise 1: *Izí:* Onkl Shemuel kóntale lo ke me kontates a mí el otro diya… Te rogo… *Izí:* Balat es la mallé ande moravas… Ma no me dishites ke teniyas una kavané ayá?

Exercise 2: See the verb charts at the end of the book for the correct forms.

Exercise 3: Antes kuando era un mansevo de vente anyos me alevantava … porke lavorava… Me iva al echo…, komiya i beviya en mi büró i tornava a kaza… Teniya munchos amigos i kon eyos mirava la televizyón, iva al match…, djuguava… En vezes ívamos al sinemá, bevíyamos un chay…, nunkua no mos peleyávamos. Eramos buenos amigos, mos aveníyamos, mos engleneávamos i esto era tener buena vida.

Exercise 4: 1. bivíyamos. 2. aviya-ivan. 3. saviya-kantava-teniya. 4. ke biviyas – estavash. 5. diziyash – era. 6. meldávamos – se ambezava/mos ambezávamos. 7. me plaziya – no puediya – no keriya. 8. avlávamos – savíyamos.

Exercise 5: See verb charts.

Exercise 6: 1. fui. 2. komimos i avlimos – se fue. 3. bivyó – se ambezó. 4. mos kazimos – kijimos ir – no mos deshó: disho. 5. yoró – ampesí – tuve. 6. meldimos – topimos. 7. lavorí – ize – no me plazyó – me empyegí. 8. deshó – tuvo. 9. estuvo – se izo.

Exercise 7: M'alevantí a las syete i me fui al echo kon otomobil. Kuando salí del echo, kuando eskapí, merkí rozas i me fui a vijitar ande Flory. Su madre me izo un kavé i Flory i yo avlimos en el salón. Mos peleyimos porke eya kijo/keriya ir al tiyatro i a mi no me plazyó. A la fin fuimos al restorán i mos topimos kon amigos. Fueron todos los mansevos al mezmo bar. Sintyeron muzika ingleza, avlaron, bevyeron vino, yo me durmí un poko i tornimos tadre a kaza. La madre de Flory no estuvo kontente.

Exercise 8: 1. Antes los tulumbadjís vistiyan kalsados livyanos i korriyan mas presto. 2. Me akordo ke un diya estávamos asentados en la puerta, en súpito vino un ombre i disho ke aviya fuego en una mallé muy leshos. 3. Mozós lo mandimos a dar haber a la kavané de al lado. 4. Presto se alevantaron tres mansevos, entraron aryentro i salyeron enteramente vistidos. 5. Estos tres fueron a bushkar a los otros. 6. Mozós mirimos kómo yevavan la tulumba i el fener i ampesavan/ampesaron a korrer. 7. En dos puntos estavan/estuvyeron a la punta de la kaleja i se esparesyeron. 8. Mozós kedimos enkantados. 9. A la noche kuando tornaron, kontaron ke el fuego se amató/se aviya amatado kuando yegaron.

Exercise 9: (*Complete these statements…*) 1. Estava durmyendo…/se aviya durmido… 2 …kuando uvo un fuego grande ke estruyó la sivdad. 3. Lo estava nombrando… 4. … mos kedimos en kaza. 5. … vide a madam Dudú en la kaleja del kuaför. 6. Me fui a la biblioteka… 7. Kuando estava en su kaza… 8. Fui a vijitar ande eya… 9. … ma no estava en kaza.

Exercise 10: 1. I am studying math as well as literature. 2. I too am a Jew/even I am a Jew. 3. She too wants to go to the movies. 4. The husband and wife fight a lot, that's no way to live. 5. We waited for them the whole night but they didn't come. 6. Eli wanted to buy shoes but he didn't come to my shop, and yet I do have very attractive shoes. 7. Mr. Nahum was not only a moel, but also a shohet. 8. You come too. 9. —Why didn't you say hello to him? —I didn't even see him.

Exercise 11: Here is their true story: Marko era de Estambol i Ester Fresko, nasida de Estambol, biviya en Varna. Su padre i su madre vinyeron a morar a Estambol i ayí konosyó a Marko, se espozaron i se kazaron. El teniya una butika i merkó una kaza en Galatá, ke era una ermoza mallé djudiya. Se keriyan muncho byen.

Vyajaron a Fransya, a Israel, a todo modo de luguares. No pudyeron tener ijos. I a poko a poko se izyeron vyejos i, guay de mí, se muryeron (en Ganedén estén sus almas). En la mansevéz, él aviya sido makabisto i eya aviya meldado en la eskola de l'Alyansa.

LESSON 6B

Delgadiya: Aviya un rey de Fransya ke teniya tres ijas. Se enamoró de la mas chika ke se yamava Delgadiya. Ama eya no kijo. Su padre fraguó un kastiyo i la metyó aryentro sin agua ni pan. Delgadiya yamó a su madre i le demandó agua porke se muriya de sed, ma su madre no le dyo porke s'espantava del rey. La ermana no le dyo agua tampoko i Delgadiya se (d)esmayó, kuando le trusheron agua, estava muerta/s'aviya muerto.

Memoryas de un tulumbadjí: 1. No, teniyan otros echos, eran hammales, zarzavachís, barkeros, balukchís, esetra… 2. Asperavan el fuego asentados en la kavané de la mallé. 3. Perendeoğlu era un tulumbadjí djudyó, un kabadayí, orta de boy i blondeado. 4. Los patronos de las kazas ke se kemavan pagavan a los tulumbadjís. 5. El reis suyo les merkava (los) sapatos. 6. No, no ganavan muncha pará; los tulumbadjís eran proves, i por modo de esto teniyan otro echo.

LESSON 7A

Exercíse 1: 1. Inchelas. 2. Méteselo. 3. Mérkatelo. 4. Mirála/miradla (miralda). 5. Méldamelos. 6. Kortásela/kortadsela. 7. Kántasela. 8. Échasela.

Exercise 2: 1. Syénteme. 2. Dame la mano. 3. Ambézaselo. 4. Mirávos/ miradvos en el espejo. 5. Méldame estos livros. 6. Kóntaselo. 7. Dizíselo/dizídselo. 8. Kántamelo. 9. Areséntalos en el plato. 10. Sérrame la televizyón.

Exercíse 3: Lava las domates, múndalas i kórtalas en dos, kita lo d'en medyo i las pipitas. Apronta el gomo. Inche las domates i apreta el gomo kon el dedo. Untalos en la arina i el guevo i fríyelos bueno en la azete. Aeséntalos en un paylón, echa por enriva la azete ke kedó, kaldo de domate kon sal i asukuar, tapa i desha kozer. Kome kayente.

Exercise 4: No avrásh el frijider! No metásh los dedos en la priz! Asentávos/asentadvos! No komásh bombones! No bevásh agua yelada/bevé(d)… Mirá(d) la televizyón/No mirésh… Azé(d) el lavoro de la skola/no agásh… Meldá(d) las lisyones! Eskriví(d) una letra a la tiya Malka! No djuguésh kon top en kaza! No saltésh enriva de la kanapé! No vos abokésh por la ventana!

Exercise 5: 1. Echa al chöp, no eches nada en basho. 2. Amata tu sigaro, no bevas sigaro. 3. Pasa enfrente, no asperes. 4. No avles, kaya, no agas bruido. 5. Aspera, no pases enfrente, no korras. 6. No tokes, aze dikat. 7. Aze atansyón (dikat), no korras.

LESSON 7B

Djohá ande la novya: 1. Djohá se fue a vijitar ande la novya; va a komer a kaza de la novya. 2. Su madre le akonseja ke no koma demaziya, ke se komporte komo benadam. 3. A Djohá no le sirven los konsejos de su madre porke es bovo i no save adaptarlos a la situasyón.

El gid para el pratikante.

Questions: 1. No se puede/es defendido esprimir uvas, kozer pan, asar, friyir, buyir, pozar una koza serka de la lumbre. 2. En Shabad es defendido (de) lavorar, tokar lumbre, azer echo, esetra… No se kuze tampoko. 3. Puedemos azer salata i esprimir limón aryento la komida i puedemos asukar limones para azer limonada. 4. Devemos (de) arepozar, meldar la Ley, ir al kal.

Exercise 1: 1. No sirve. 2. Sirve. 3. Sirve. 4. No sirve. 5. No sirve. 6. Sirve.

Exercise 2: a) tú. Aze salata i eskoje las ojas buenas, desha las pudridas. Múndalas para akeya seudá. No aprontes ni mundes las ojas para otra seudá. No esprimas uvas. Esprime limón en la komida o aryento la agua. Asuka limones para azer limonada. No kozgas pan. No pozes un guevo serka de la lumbre. No ases, no friyas, no buyas. **b) vozós**. Azé salata i eskojé las ojas buenas, deshá las pudridas. Mundaldas para akeya seudá. No aprontésh ni mundésh las ojas para otra seudá. No esprimásh uvas. Esprimí limón en la komida o aryento la agua. Asuká limones para azer limonada. No kozgásh pan. No pozésh un guevo serka de la lumbre. No asésh, no friyásh, no buyásh.

El aharosi de Pesah: 1. Es agro i dulse. 2. Reprezenta el chimento kon ke los Djudyós apegavan las pyedras de las fraguas. 3. Para ke no se aga preto o para ke se espesee.

Los yaprakitos de karne de Tant Ester: 1. No porke si se echan en la agua se espedasan. 2. No se echa en este modo de yaprakitos porke no sirve. 3. Para gizar armí se eskoje(n) domates koloradas i se kita el mijo; duspués se korta(n) las domates pedasikos pedasikos i se meten a kozer kon azete, sevoya kortada, sal i maydanó i kon asukuar, siguro. 4. Se mete asukuar porke la domate es agra i kale adulsarla, asukarla. 5. Se kita el kuero i el mijo, lo de aryentro, las pipitas.

LESSON 8A

Exercise 1: 1. Puede ser ke está echado. 2. Puede ser ke no sepan ánde ir. 3. Puede ser ke vengan/van a vinir. 4. Puede ser ke topésh otobüs/vash a topar. 5. Puede ser ke semos lokos. 6. Puede ser ke seamos lokos. 7. Puede ser ke va a meldar este livro. 8. Puede ser ke melde este livro.

Exercise 2: 1. Mis amigos venirán/vernán/vendrán alhad. 2. Mi nona salirá/salrá/ saldrá/sarlá del ospital. 3. Iremos al tiyatro. 4. Diziré/diré la berahá. 5. Tenerésh/ tendrésh/ternésh/tenrésh un muevo haham. 6. Azerás/arás la kolada? 7. Komeremos endjuntos. 8. Azerá/ ará luvya. 9. Beverésh un kaviko. 10. Se alevantarán.

Exercise 3: 1. viniriya/vendriya. 2. saveriyas. 3. iriya. 4. azeríyamos/aríyamos. 5. Dariya – meldariyas. 6. Saliríyamos/saldríyamos/sarlíyamos i mos iríyamos – se kizderearia/ kizdriyariya.

Exercise 4: 1. He told me his father would come. 2. You must have known it already. 3. They told you I would go to Jerusalem. 4. If he/she gave us permission, we would take a trip. 5. I'd give you today's paper, but you must have read it already. 6. We would go out (of the house) and we'd go to the movies with you, but Mom would get angry.

Exercise 5: 1. I'm afraid that (because) we don't have any news. 2. They were afraid he wasn't coming. 3. Weren't you worried that I didn't call you? 4. We are worried because he is coming by car. 5. They are scared because he has a knife. 6. They are afraid he may not have a knife. 7. He is afraid his mother may be sick. 8. I was scared because I didn't know the lesson and that the teacher was going to get angry. 9. I'm scared I/he/she won't know the lesson and that the teacher is going to tell everybody. 10. I'm afraid he may not know where he/it is and that he may go somewhere else. 11. He's afraid I'm not going to find the answer/because I'm not going to find the answer.

Exercise 6: 1. M'espanto de él. 2. Mos espantimos ke se rompa la kupa. 3. M'espanto ke tus ermanos no van a eskolar antes de las syete. 4. Se espanta/vos espantásh ke me vayga? 5. Vos espantatesh ke aviya bruido. 6. M'espanto no komásh todo. 7. S'espantó ke yorava. 8. M'espanto no me keme.

Exercise 7: 1. Shall we have a coffee? 2. Now I'm going to close the window. 3. They shall lift the plate with the matzah from the table and shall say the blessing. 4. Tomorrow we'll go to the synagogue. 5. Next year we will visit Spain. 6. Let's wait and see. 7. Shall I call the doctor? 8. Now let me tell you that the king's daughter was engaged. 9. If you (really) are going to come, we' ll get the bedroom ready. 10. Let's sit down!

Exercise 8: 1. Ya la trayeriya. 2. Teneriya unos sikuenta (anyos). 3. Si no lo ivas a kontar ya te lo dizeriya/diriya. 4. Kostariya karo. 5. Ya le eskriviríyamos, ma no saverá/savrá meldar muestra letra en fransés. 6. Mos pruntatesh/demandatesh si azeríyamos/aríyamos la aliyá ma teneríyamos/tendríyamos menester de konsejos. 7. Sin la ayuda de él/su ayuda, el vyejo haham no komeriya kada diya i diya.

Exercise 9: (some possible statements) 1. Estará mirando heshbón. 2. Estará propozando una novya. 3. Estará ambezándose las lisyones para el egzamén. 4. Estará sintyendo a la profesora de fransés. 5. Estará vendyendo ropa. 6. Estará trezladando un artíkolo de la gazeta. 7. Estará kozinando para shabad. 8. Estará eskrivyendo un artíkolo. 9. Estará merkando oro. 10. Estará mirando un ijiko hazino.

LESSON 8B

La chosa del dezesperado: 1. El dezesperado yora, beve las lágrimas de sus ojos, konta sus males i kere matarse. 2. Entizna su kaza/chosa porke tyene negros penseryos, está triste i merekiyozo, no kere ver blanko porke es kolor de alegriya, de vida, de luz. 3. Para saver si son mas munchos de los suyos, porke kree ke él es el mas grande desmazalado en el mundo.

Letra: 1. Su ermano le mandó una letra kon syen frankos. 2. El ermano Behor bive en la Fransya. 3. Se gustó ke se topavan todos sanos i rezyos. 4. Está en kudyado porke su ermano no le responde. 5. Se está keshando porke no tyene haber de su ermano i él no demanda kómo se topa. Está solo diyas de moedes i diyas de shabad. 6. No, no tyene dingún paryente afuera de este ermano bohor i sus inyetos ke no konose. 7. Sus sovrinikos ivan a vinir.

El gid para el pratikante: la ravya: 1. La ravya i la sanya akurtan la vida, destruyen i derokan kazas i famiyas, danyan al kuerpo/puerpo i a la alma. 2. No, el baragán es el ke save detenerse en ora de ravya. 3. Peka porke no respekta a dinguno, no konose padre i madre, no los onra, i kafra en el Dyo de Israel.

La agadá de Pesah: 1. El teksto konta lo ke disho el Dyo a Avram. 2. Es la tyerra de Ayifto (Mitsraim). 3. El Dyo djuzgará al puevlo ke los afriyó i ke sirvyeron durante kuatrosyentos anyos. 4. Los Djudyós sirvyeron a Paró. 5. Moshé rabenu los kitó de Ayifto. 6. Tuvyeron por ganansya la tyerra de Israel.

LESSON 9A

Exercise 1: 1. Inshallá mis ijos se agan doktores – Makare ke se izyeran doktores. 2. Inshallá ke gane munchas parás – Ganara munchas parás! 3. Inshallá se aga sano Shemuel – Makare ke se izyera sano, ma el doktor pensa ke no ay hayre. 4. Inshallá mi padre me merke una arabá – Makare me merkara una arabá mi padre, ma no kreo ke lo va a azer. 5. Makare tuvyera ijos, ma no pude! 6. Tuvyera yo una mosa para avlar kon eya! – Makare tuvyera… 7. Makare ke djuguaras al bridj! 8. Inshallá me akompanyes i bayles kon mi. 9. Makare ke me amaras! 10. Makare ke se kazara kon Stella! 11. Makare tornara mi marido!

Exercise 2: 1. Makare vinyera! 2. No kero komer ya ke/visto ke la komida se enfriyó. 3. Madem ki keres merkar una radyo mueva, vate a lavorar. 4. Madem ki no me kreyes, no te lo kontaré. 5. Komo no me demandes la razón ke estó aravyada, mas no te vo a avlar. 6. Afilú si save ke está hazino es tan negro ke no va a vinir a demandar. 7. Save ke estás hazino, ma yiné no vyene a demandar. Ké negro ke es! 8. Si una persona está hazina kale ir a vijitarla. 9. Una madre afilú si pare kulevros, yiné demanda por eyos. 10. Madem ki/si/ya ke/visto ke no saves azerlo, lo azeré yo. 11. Komo no vayas a vijitarlo, mas no te vo a avlar. 12. Makare toparas la repuesta i ganáramos. 13. Inshallá se ambeze a meldar la Ley, no sea ke digan ke no es buen djudyó. 14. Kale ke sepa la Ley inimás ke su nono es haham.

Exercise 3: 1. Si tomaras las kuras no te tuyiriya la kavesa/si tomavas… no te tuyiya… 2. Si meldaras te ambezariyas/si meldavas, te ambezavas. 3. Si te fueras al klub, no te enfasyariyas/estariyas enfasyando/si te ivas… no te enfasyavas… 4. Si no komyeras tanto no engodrariyas/si no komiyas tanto, no engodravas. 5. Si supyerash avlar en italyano puederiyash eskrivirlc/si saviyaslı… puediyash eskrivirle. 6. Si merkaras el bileto uvyéramos visto/veíyamos la pyesa/si merkavas… ívamos a ver… 7. Si meldaras la gazeta saveriyas kualo está akontesyendo/si meldavas… ivas a saver… 8. Si me avriyeras el telefón, teneriyas/tendriyas haber de las inyetas/Si me avriyas… ivas a tener… 9. Si avlaras munchas linguas topariyas echo/si avlavas… topavas…

Exercise 4: 1. They had the measles. 2. David Fresko used to publish "El Tyempo." 3. With their fits of nerves, the daughter and mother drove their father crazy. 4. Don't say those dirty words! 5. Are you making fun of me? 6. Take a glass out of the cupboard for your father so he can drink a little water. 7. We've finished eating, you can clear the dishes and wash them. 8. If you take five from nine you get four (four remain). 9. Did you take the milk off the fire? 10. Every year he catches the flu. 11. He got divorced from his wife. 12. On the day of his B'rit Mila, his grandfather sponsored him (did the honors). 13. It was the midwife who brought me into the world.

Exercise 5: 1. Avram León era el gazetero ke kitava el Şalom (Avram León was the newspaperman who used to publish Şalom). 2. Antes los mansevos no kitavan byervo de la boka delantre del padre (Before, young people would not say a word in front of their father). 3. Alber i Merí se kitaron (Alber and Merí got divorced). 4. En Taylanda kitaron sarilik (They caught malaria in Thailand). 5. Kití el livro de la kasha para meterlo en el armaryo (I took the book out of the box to put it in the closet). 6. Le kita alay a su ermana i la kita loka (She/he makes fun of her/his sister and drives her crazy. 7. La kura me kitó la dolor (The medicine made my pain go away). 8. La aspirina kita la kayentura (Aspirin makes fever go away). 9. Mi madre kitó al mundo a kuatro kriyaturas (My mother gave birth to four children/brought four children into the world).

Exercise 6: 1. para ke le mandara. 2. si veniriya/viniriya/vendriya. 3. Makare ke tornara. 4. Si no te echaras/echavas. 5. Keshke tomara. 6. ke me dishera. 7. para ke me ayudara. 8. azeriyas/ariyas/ya aziyas. 8. Makare mos sintyera i mos avriyera la puerta!

Exercise 7: 1. Me disho ke vinyera. 2. Keriya ke fueras a bushkarlo. 3. Kaliya ke toparas una kaza mueva. 4. Le eskriví ke me mandara los livros. 5. Grití para ke me sintyeras. 6. Si lo teniyas/tuvyeras kaliya ke me lo dyeras. 7. No keriyan ke se kazara kon él. 8. Le rogí ke me oyera.

LESSON 9B

Me'am Lo'ez:

Questions: 1. Para plazerle a Yosef lo afalagó kon avlas, se mudó kada diya buenos vestidos, lo aregaló. 2. No, no alsó sus ojos a elya/eya, no la miró. 3. La mujer de Putifar se adolensyó porke amava a Yosef i Yosef no la mirava. 4. Las Mitsriyot, las mujeres de Ayifto, sus amigas, vinyeron a vijitarla. 5. Las damas le demandaron la razón de su desrepozo, de su dolensya, de su tristeza; la kritikaron. 6. La mujer de Putifar dyo a sus amigas etrogim i kuchiyos de plata para ke los mundaran eyas. 7. Se kortaron las manos, se embatakaron en la sangre i no se sintyeron. 8. Porke se kedaron enkantadas kuando vyeron a Yosef i su ermozura les izo pyedrer/peryer el tino; se les bolό el sezo de la kavesa. 9. Les amostró komo eyas kedaron enkantadas i pyedryeron/peryeron el tino kon verlo solo un punto i komo sufriya eya ke lo veíya kada diya i diya, para ke la entendyeran.

Exercise: 1. My mother told me that you've started college. 2. My cousin is the one who washes windows. 3. He/she is happy that (people) come to see him. 4. Shall I bring the *boyikos*, mom? 5. We waited for the day when school ended and we told the teacher that she should not hit children, that this was very bad. 6. I'm afraid he may get angry. 7. I'm worried because his/her mother is in the hospital. 8. Why should I say it? 9. What's the matter, you aren't talking.

David el bueno: 1. Se sirve kon una kupa de agua friya/yelada i el kavé kale ke tenga kaymak i ke sea byen asukado. 2. El tiyo David es de Selanik. 3. Lo yamava hahamiko porke le plaziya muncho meldar, era meldahón. 4. Porke kon el kavé se akodra del tyempo pasado, de Selanik, i tyene la kavesa yena de es-huenyos.

Konseja del sodro i del inyervozo:

Exercise 1: 1. batear. 2. sarear. 3. kavurear. 4. dayanear.

Exercise 2: 1. a Purim gift. 2. idleness.

VERB CHARTS

kantar *(to sing)*

INDICATIVE

Present	Imperfect	Past	Future	Pluperfect
kanto	kantava	kantí	kantaré	aviya kantado
kantas	kantavas	kantates	kantarás	aviyas kantado
kanta	kantava	kantó	kantará	aviya kantado
kantamos	kantávamos	kantimos	kantaremos	avíyamos kantado
kantásh	kantavash	kantatesh	kantarésh	aviyash kantado
kantan	kantavan	kantaron	kantarán	aviyan kantado

SUBJUNCTIVE

Present	Past	Conditional	Imperative
kante	kantara	kantariya	kanta
kantes	kantaras	kantariyas	kantá(d)
kante	kantara	kantariya	
kantemos	kantáramos	kantaríyamos	
kantésh	kantarash	kantariyash	
kanten	kantaran	kantariyan	

PARTICIPLES

Present
kantando

Past
kantado

komer *(to eat)*

INDICATIVE

Present	Imperfect	Past	Future	Pluperfect
komo	komiya	komí	komeré	aviya komido
komes	komiyas	komites	komerás	aviyas komido
kome	komiya	komyó	komerá	aviya komido
komemos	komíyamos	komimos	komeremos	avíyamos komido
komésh	komiyash	komitesh	komerésh	aviyash komido
komen	komiyan	komyeron	komerán	aviyan komido

SUBJUNCTIVE

Present	Past	Conditional	Imperative
koma	komyera	komeriya	kome
komas	komyeras	komeriyas	komé(d)
koma	komyera	komeriya	
komamos	komyéramos	komeríyamos	
komásh	komyerash	komeriyash	
koman	· komyeran	komeriyan	

PARTICIPLES

Present
komyendo

Past
komido

bivir *(to live)*

INDICATIVE

Present	Imperfect	Past	Future	Pluperfect
bivo	biviya	biví	biviré	aviya bivido
bives	biviyas	bivites	bivirás	aviyas bivido
bive	biviya	bivyó	bivirá	aviya bivido
bivimos	bivíyamos	bivimos	biviremos	avíyamos bivido
bivísh	biviyash	bivitesh	birivésh	aviyash bivido
biven	biviyan	bivyeron	bivirán	aviyan bivido

SUBJUNCTIVE

PARTICIPLES

Present	Past	Conditional	Imperative	
biva	bivyera	biviriya	bive	**Present**
bivas	bivyeras	biviriyas	biví(d)	bivyendo
biva	bivyera	biviriya		
bivamos	bivyéramos	biviríyamos		**Past**
bivásh	bivyerash	biviriyash		bivido
bivan	bivyeran	biviriyan		

aver *(to have)* [used as an auxiliary with other verbs]

INDICATIVE

Present	Imperfect	Past	Future	Pluperfect
	aviya	(uve)*	avré/averé	aviya avido/uvido
	aviyas	(uvites)	avrás/averás	
(ay)	aviya	uvo	avrá/averá	
	avíyamos	(uvimos)	avremos/averemos	
	aviyash	(uvitesh)	avrésh/averésh	
	aviyan	uvyeron	avrán/averán	

SUBJUNCTIVE / PARTICIPLES

Present	Past	Conditional	Imperative		
ayga/aya	uvyera	avriya/averiya	(Not used)	**Present**	avyendo/uvyendo
aygan/ayan	uvyeras				
	uvyera				
(Not used	uvyéramos			**Past**	avido/uvido
in other	uvyerash				
persons)	uvyeran				

*Forms in parentheses are no longer used.

azer *(to do)*

INDICATIVE

Present	Imperfect	Past	Future	Pluperfect
ago	aziya	ize	azeré/aré	aviya echo
azes	aziyas	izites	azerás/arás	aviyas echo
aze	aziya	izo	azerá/…	aviya echo
azemos	azíyamos	izimos	azeremos/…	avíyamos echo
azésh	aziyash	izitesh	azerésh/…	aviyash echo
azen	aziyan	izyeron/ azyeron	azerán/…	aviyan echo

SUBJUNCTIVE / PARTICIPLES

Present	Past	Conditional	Imperative		
aga	izyera	azeriya/ariya	aze	**Present**	azyendo
agas	izyeras	azeriyas/…	azé(d)		
aga	izyera	azeriya/…			
agamos	izyéramos	azeríyamos/…		**Past**	echo
agásh	izyerash	azeriyash/…			
agan	izyeran	azeriyan/…			

dar *(to give)*

INDICATIVE

Present	Imperfect	Past	Future	Pluperfect
do	dava	di	daré	aviya dado
das	davas	dates	darás	aviyas dado…
da	dava	dyo	dará	
damos	dávamos	dimos	daremos	
dash	davash	datesh	darésh	
dan	davan	dyeron/daron	darán	

SUBJUNCTIVE

Present	Past	Conditional	Imperative	PARTICIPLES
dé	dyera	dariya	da	
des	dyeras	dariyas	dad/desh	**Present**
dé	dyera	dariya		dando
demos	dyéramos	daríyamos		
desh	dyerash	dariyash		**Past**
den	dyeran	dariyan		dado

dizir/dizer *(to say)*

INDICATIVE

Present	Imperfect	Past	Future	Pluperfect
digo	diziya	dishe	diziré/dizeré/diré	aviya dicho
dizes	diziyas	dishites	dizirás/…/…	aviyas dicho
dize	diziya	disho	dizirá/…/…	aviya dicho
dizimos	dizíyamos	dishimos	diziremos/…/…	avíyamos dicho
dizísh/dizésh	diziyash	dishitesh	dizirésh/…/…	aviyash dicho
dizen	diziyan	disheron	dizirán/…/…	aviyan dicho

SUBJUNCTIVE

Present	Past	Conditional	Imperative	PARTICIPLES
diga	dishera	dizeriya/diziriya/diriya	dize/diz/di	
digas	disheras	dizeriyas/diziriyas/diriyas	dizí(d)	**Present**
diga	dishera	dizeriya/…/…		dizyendo
digamos	dishéramos	dizeríyamos/…/…		
digásh	disherash	dizeriyash/…/…		**Past**
digan	disheran	dizeriyan/…/…		dicho

entender* *(to understand)*

INDICATIVE

Present	Imperfect	Past	Future	Pluperfect
entyendo	entendiya	entendí	entenderé	aviya entendido
entyendes	entendiyas	entendites	entenderás…	aviyas entendido…
entyende	entendiya	entendyó		
entendemos/entyendemos	entendiyamos	entendimos		
entendésh/entyendésh	entendiyash	entenditesh		
entyenden	entendiyan	entendyeron		

SUBJUNCTIVE — PARTICIPLES

Present	Past	Conditional	Imperative	Present
entyenda	entendyera	entenderiya	entyende	entendyendo
entyendas	entendyeras	entenderiyas	entendé(d)	
entyenda	entendyera	entenderiya		
entendamos/entyendamos	entendyéramos	entenderíyamos		**Past**
entendásh/entyendásh	entendyerash	entenderiyash		entendido
entyendan	entendyeran	entenderiyan		

*This verb has tended towards a regular conjugation based on the infinitive *entyender*.

estar *(to be)*

INDICATIVE

Present	Imperfect	Past	Future	Pluperfect
estó	estava	estuve	estaré	aviya estado
estás	estavas	estuvites	estarás	aviyas estado
está	estava	estuvo	estará	aviya estado
estamos	estávamos	estuvimos	estaremos	avíyamos estado
estásh	estavash	estuvitesh	estarésh	aviyash estado
están	estavan	estuvyeron	estarán	aviyan estado

SUBJUNCTIVE — PARTICIPLES

Present	Past	Conditional	Imperative	
esté	estuvyera	estariya	(estarse)	**Present**
estés	estuvyeras	estariyas		estando
esté	estuvyera	estariya	estate	
estemos	estuvyéramos	estaríyamos	estavos	**Past**
estésh	estuvyerash	estariyash		estado
estén	estuvyeran	estariyan		

ir *(to go)*

INDICATIVE

Present	Imperfect	Past	Future	Pluperfect
vo	iva/iya	fui	iré	aviya ido
vas	ivas/…	fuites	irás	aviyas ido
va	iva/…	fue	irá	aviya ido
vamos	ívamos/…	fuimos	iremos	avíyamos ido
vash	ivash/…	fuitesh	irésh	aviyash ido
van	ivan/…	fueron	irán	aviyan ido

SUBJUNCTIVE

Present	Past	Conditional	Imperative	PARTICIPLES
vaya/vayga	fuera	iriya	va	**Present**
vayas/…	fueras	iriyas	[andá(d)]	yendo/indo
vaya/…	fuera	iriya		
vayamos/…	fuéramos	iríyamos		**Past**
vayásh/…	fuerash	iriyash		ido
vayan/…	fueran	iriyan		

kerer *(to want, to like)*

INDICATIVE

Present	Imperfect	Past	Future	Pluperfect
kero/kyero	keriya	kije	kereré/kerré	aviya kerido
keres/kyeres	keriyas	kijites	kererás/kerrás…	aviyas kerido…
kere/kyere	keriya	kijo		
keremos/kyeremos	keríyamos	kijimos		
kerésh/kyerésh	keriyash	kijitesh		
keren/kyeren	keriyan	kijeron		

SUBJUNCTIVE

Present	Past	Conditional	Imperative	PARTICIPLES
kera/kyera	kijera	kereriya	kere	**Present**
keras/kyeras	kijeras	kereriyas	keré(d)	keryendo
kera/…	kijera	kereriya		
keramos/…	kijéramos	kereríyamos		**Past**
kerásh/…	kijerash	kereriyash		kerido/kirido
keran/…	kijeran	kereriyan		

konoser *(to know, be acquainted with)*

INDICATIVE

Present	Imperfect	Past	Future	Pluperfect
konosko	konosiya	konosí	konoseré	aviya konosido
konoses	konosiyas	konosites	konoserás	aviyas konosido
konose	konosiya	konosyó	konoserá	aviya konosido
konosemos	konosíyamos	konosimos	konoseremos	avíyamos konosido
konosésh	konosiyash	konositesh	konoserésh	aviyash konosido
konosen	konosiyan	konosyeron	konoserán	aviyan konosido

SUBJUNCTIVE

Present	Past	Conditional	Imperative
konoska	konosyera	konoseriya	konose
konoskas	konosyeras	konoseriyas	konosé(d)
konoska	konosyera	konoseriya	
konoskamos	konosyéramos	konoseríyamos	
konoskásh	konosyerash	konoseriyash	
konoskan	konosyeran	konoseriyan	

PARTICIPLES

Present
konosyendo

Past
konosido

muerir(se)/murir(se)/morir(se) *(to die)*

INDICATIVE

Present	Imperfect	Present participle
muero	mueriya/muriya/moriya	muryendo
mueres	mueriyas/…/…	
muere	mueriya/…/…	**Past participle**
murimos/muerimos/morimos	mueríyamos/…/…	muerto/murido
murísh/muerísh/morísh	mueriyash/…/…	
mueren	mueriyan/…/…	

Future	Past	Pluperfect
muriré/mueriré/moriré	murí/muerí/morí	aviya muerto/murido
murirás/…/…	murites/muerites/morites	aviyas muerto/murido…
murirá/…/…	muryó	
muriremos/…/…	murimos/muerimos/morimos	
murirésh/…/…	muritesh/mueritesh/moritesh	
murirán/…/…	muryeron	

SUBJUNCTIVE

Present	Past	Conditional	Imperative
muera	muryera	mueririya/mururiya/moririya	muere
mueras	muryeras	mueririyas/…/…	muerí(d)/murí(d)/morí(d)/
muera	muryera	mueririya/…/…	
muramos	muryéramos	mueriríyamos/…/…	
murásh	muryerash	mueririyash/…/…	
mueran	muryeran	mueririyan/…/…	

pueder/poder *(to be able)*

INDICATIVE

Present	Imperfect	Past	Future	Pluperfect
puedo	puediya	puide/puedí	puederé	aviya puedido,
puedes	puediyas	puidites/puedites	puederás	aviyas puedido…
puede	puediya	puido/puedyó	puederá	
puedemos/podemos	puedíyamos	puidimos/puedimos	puederemos	
puedésh/podésh	puediyash	puiditesh/pueditesh	puederésh	
pueden	puediyan	puidyeron/puedyeron	puederán	

SUBJUNCTIVE

Present	Past	Conditional	Imperative
pueda	pudyera	puederiya	[Not used]
puedas	pudyeras	puederiyas	
pueda	pudyera	puederiya	
puedamos/podamos	pudyéramos	puederíyamos	
puedásh/podásh	pudyerash	puederiyash	
puedan	pudyeran	puederiyan	

PARTICIPLES

Present
puedyendo/
pudyendo

Past
puedido/podido

pyedrer/peryer/pedrer *(to lose)*

INDICATIVE

Present	Imperfect
pyedro/ peryo	pyedriya
pyedres/ peryes	pyedriyas
pyedre/ perye	pyedriya
pyedremos/ peryemos/pedremos	pyedríyamos
pyedrésh/ peryésh/pedrésh	pyedriyash
pyedren/ peryen	pyedriyan

Present participle
peryendo/pyedriyendo/pedriyendo

Past participle
pyedrido/peryido/pedrido

Future	Past	Pluperfect
pyedreré/peryeré	peryí/pyedrí/pedrí	aviya pyedrido
pyedrerás/peryerás	peryites/pyedrites/…	aviyas pyedrido…
pyedrerá/…	peryó/pyedriyó/…	
pyedreremos/…	peryimos/pyedrimos/…	
pyedrerésh/…	peryitesh/pyedritesh/…	
pyedrerán/…	peryeron/pyedriyeron/…	

SUBJUNCTIVE

Present	Past	Conditional	Imperative
pyedra/perya	peryera/pyedriyera/pedriyera	pyedreriya/peryeriya	perye/pyedre/pedre
pyedras/…	peryeras/…/…	pyedreriyas/…	peryé(d)/pyedré(d)/
pyedra/…	peryera/…/…	pyedreriya/…	pedré(d)
pyedramos/…	peryéramos/…/…	pyedreríyamos/…	
pyedrásh/…	peryerash/…/…	pyedreriyash/…	
pyedran/…	peryeran/…/…	pyedreriyan/…	

salir *(to go out, leave)*

INDICATIVE

Present	Imperfect	Past	Future	Pluperfect
salgo	saliya	salí	saliré/salré/sarlé/saldré	aviya salido
sales	saliyas	salites	salirás/salrás/sarlás/saldrás	aviyas salido
sale	saliya	salyó	salirá/…/…/…	aviya salido
salimos	salíyamos	salimos	saliremos/…/…/…	avíyamos salido
salísh	saliyash	salitesh	salirésh/…/…/…	aviyash salido
salen	saliyan	salyeron	salirán/…/…/…	aviyan salido

SUBJUNCTIVE — PARTICIPLES

Present	Past	Conditional	Imperative	
salga	salyera	saliriya/salriya/sarliya/saldriya	sale	**Present**
salgas	salyeras	saliriyas/…/…/…	salí(d)	salyendo
salga	salyera	saliriya/…/…/…		
salgamos	salyéramos	saliríyamos/ …/…/…		**Past**
salgásh	salyerash	saliriyash/ …/…/…		salido
salgan	salyeran	saliriyan/…/…/…		

saver *(to know)*

INDICATIVE

Present	Imperfect	Past	Future	Pluperfect
sé	saviya	supe	saveré/savré	aviya savido
saves	saviyas	supites	saverás/savrás	aviyas savido
save	saviya	supo	saverá/…	aviya savido
savemos	savíyamos	supimos	saveremos/…	avíyamos savido
savésh	saviyash	supitesh	saverésh/…	aviyash savido
saven	saviyan	supyeron	saverán/…	aviyan savido

SUBJUNCTIVE — PARTICIPLES

Present	Past	Conditional	Imperative	
sepa	supyera	saveriya/savriya	save	**Present**
sepas	supyeras	saveriyas/savriyas	savé(d)	savyendo
sepa	supyera	saveriya/savriya		
sepamos	supyéramos	saveríyamos/…		**Past**
sepásh	supyerash	saveriyash/…		savido
sepan	supyeran	saveriyan/…		

ser *(to be)*

┌─ INDICATIVE ───

Present	Imperfect	Past	Future	Pluperfect
so/se	era	fui	seré	aviya sido
sos	eras	fuites	serás	aviyas sido
es	era	fue	será	aviya sido
semos	éramos	fuimos	seremos	avíyamos sido
sosh	erash	fuitesh	serésh	aviyash sido
son	eran	fueron	serán	aviyan sido

├─ SUBJUNCTIVE ───────────────────────┬──── PARTICIPLES ────

Present	Past	Conditional	Imperative	
sea/seya	fuera	seriya	sé	**Present**
seas/seyas	fueras	seriyas	sed	syendo
sea/…	fuera	seriya		
seamos/…	fuéramos	seríyamos		**Past**
seásh/…	fuerash	seriyash		sido
sean/…	fueran	seriyan		

sintir/sentir *(to hear)*

┌─ INDICATIVE ───

Present	Imperfect	Past
syento	sintiya	sintí/sentí
syentes	sintiyas	sintites/sentites
syente	sintiya	sintyó
sintimos/sentimos	sintíyamos	sintimos/sentimos
sintísh/sentísh	sintiyash	sintitesh/sentitesh
syenten	sintiyan	sintyeron

Future	Pluperfect	Imperative	
sintiré/ sentiré	aviya sintido/aviya sentido	syente	**Present Participle**
sintirás/ sentirás	aviyas sintido/…	sintí(d)	sintyendo
sintirá/ …	aviya sintido/…		
sintiremos/ …	avíyamos sintido/…		**Past Participle**
sintirésh/ …	aviyash sintido/…		sintido/sentido
sintirán/ …	aviyan sintido/…		

├─ SUBJUNCTIVE ──

Present	Past	Conditional
syenta	sintyera	sintiriya/sentiriya
syentas	sintyeras	sintiriyas/…
syenta	sintyera	sintiriya/…
sintamos/syentamos	sintyéramos	sintiríyamos/…
sintásh/syentásh	sintyerash	sintiriyash/…
syentan	sintyeran	sintiriyan/…

sirvir/servir *(to serve)*

INDICATIVE

Present	Imperfect	Past
sirvo/syervo	sirviya/serviya	sirví/serví
sirves/syerves	sirviyas/…	sirvites/servites
sirve/syerve	sirviya/…	sirvyó
sirvimos/servimos	sirvíyamos/…	sirvimos/servimos
sirvísh/servísh	sirviyash/…	sirvitesh/servitesh
sirven/syerven	sirviyan/…	sirvyeron

Future	Pluperfect	Imperative	
sirviré/ serviré	aviya sirvido/aviya servido	sirve/syerve	**Present Participle**
sirvirás/…	aviyas sirvido/…	sirví(d)/serví(d)	sirvyendo
sirvirá/ …	aviya sirvido/…		
sirviremos/ …	avíyamos sirvido/…		**Past Participle**
sirvirésh/ …	aviyash sirvido/…		sirvido/servido
sirvirán/ …	aviyan sirvido/…		

SUBJUNCTIVE

Present	Past	Conditional
sirva/syerva	sirvyera/servyera	sirviriya/serviriya
sirvas/syervas	sirvyeras/…	sirviriyas/…
sirva/syerva	sirvyera/…	sirviriya/…
sirvamos	sirvyéramos/…	sirviríyamos/…
sirvásh	sirvyerash/…	sirviriyash/…
sirvan/syervan	sirvyeran/…	sirviriyan/…

Tener *(to have, own, possess)*

INDICATIVE

Present	Imperfect	Past	Future	Pluperfect
tengo	teniya/tiniya	tuve	teneré/terné/tendré	aviya tenido/tinido/tuvido
tyenes	teniyas/tiniyas	tuvites	tenerás/…/…	aviyas tenido/tinido/tuvido…
tyene	teniya/…	tuvo	tenerá/…/…	
tenemos	teníyamos/…	tuvimos	teneremos/…/…	
tenésh	teniyash/…	tuvitesh	tenerésh/…/…	
tyenen	teniyan/…	tuvyeron	tenerán/…/…	

SUBJUNCTIVE — PARTICIPLES

Present	Past	Conditional	Imperative	
tenga	tuvyera	teneriya/tenriya/tendriya	ten	**Present**
tengas	tuvyeras ·	teneriyas/…/…	tené(d)	tenyendo/tuvyendo
tenga	tuvyera	teneriya/…/…		
tengamos	tuvyéramos	teneríyamos/…/…		**Past**
tengásh	tuvyerash	teneriyash/…/…		tenido/tinido/tuvido
tengan	tuvyeran	teneriyan/…/…		

Trayer/traer *(to bring/carry)*

INDICATIVE

Present	Imperfect	Past	Future	Pluperfect
traygo	traíya/traíva	trushe	trayeré/traeré	aviya trayido
trayes/traes	traíyas/...	trushites	trayerás/...	aviyas trayido
traye/trae	traíya/...	trusho	trayerá/...	aviya trayido
trayemos/...	traíyamos/...	trushimos	trayeremos/...	avíyamos trayido
trayésh/...	traíyash/...	trushitesh	trayerésh/...	aviyash trayido
trayen/...	traíyan/...	trusheron	trayerán/...	aviyan trayido

SUBJUNCTIVE

Present	Past	Conditional	Imperative
trayga	trushera	trayeriya/traeriya	traye
traygas	trusheras	trayeriyas/...	trayé(d)
trayga	trushera	trayeriya/...	
traygamos	trushéramos	trayeríyamos/...	
traygásh	trusherash	trayeriyash/...	
traygan	trusheran	trayeriyan/...	

PARTICIPLES

Present
trayendo

Past
trayido

Venir/vinir *(to come)*

INDICATIVE

Present	Imperfect	Past	Future
vengo	veniya/viniya	vine	veniré/viniré/verné/vendré
vyenes	veniyas/...	vinites	venirás/vinirás/vernás/vendrás
vyene	veniya/...	vino	venirá/vinirá/verná/vendrá
venimos/vinimos	veníyamos/...	vinimos	veniremos/.../.../...
venísh/vinísh	veniyash/...	vinitesh	venirésh/.../.../...
vyenen	veniyan/...	vinyeron	venirán/.../.../...

Pluperfect	Imperative	
aviya venido/vinido	ven	**Present participle:** vinyendo
aviyas venido/vinido...	viní(d)	**Past participle:** venido/vinido

SUBJUNCTIVE

Present	Past	Conditional
venga	vinyera	veniriya/viniriya/verniya/vendriya
vengas	vinyeras	veniriyas/.../.../...
venga	vinyera	veniriya/.../.../...
vengamos	vinyéramos	veniríyamos/.../.../...
vengásh	vinyerash	veniriyash/.../.../...
vengan	vinyeran	veniriyan/.../.../...

Ver *(to see)*

INDICATIVE

Present	Imperfect	Past	Future	Pluperfect
veyo/veygo/veo	veíya	vide	veré	aviya visto
ves/vees	veíyas	vites	verás	aviyas visto
ve/vee	veíya	vido/vyo	verá	aviya visto
vemos/veemos	veíyamos	vimos	veremos	avíyamos visto
vesh/veésh	veíyash	vitesh	verésh	aviyash visto
ven/veen	veíyan	vyeron	verán	aviyan visto

SUBJUNCTIVE

PARTICIPLES

Present	Past	Conditional	Imperative	
veya/veyga/vea	vyera	veriya	ve	**Present**
veyas/veygas/veas	vyeras	veriyas	ved	vyendo
veya/.../...	vyera	veriya		
veyamos/.../...	vyéramos	veríyamos		**Past**
veyásh/.../...	vyerash	veriyash		visto
veyan/.../...	vyeran	veriyan		

JUDEO-SPANISH
VOCABULARY

A

abafar: to steam (cooking).
abashada (la): the cold (illness).
abashar: to lower, go down.
abastar: to suffice, be enough.
abokarse: to bend over, lean out.
aboltar: to turn around.
abrigo (el): the shelter, protection.
achilear (se) (T.): to open up oneself to, to become informed.
adá (la) (T.): the island.
adisyón (la) (F.): the restaurant check.
adjilé (T.): quickly.
adjuntar: to add, join.
adjustar: to adjust, complete.
adolensyarse: to fall ill, be in pain.
adovar: to repair.
aedado, a: aged, elderly.
afalagar: to flatter.
aferrar: to catch, grasp.
afeytado (el): makeup, ornaments.
afeytarse: to put on makeup, ornaments.
afilú (H.): even (if).
afinar: to let (someone) starve.
afitar: to happen, take place.
afriyir: to deprive, persecute, torment.
agora/aora: now.
agradar: to please, give pleasure.
agristada (la): a lemon sauce.
agro (el): the vinegar.
agro, a: sour.
agua (la): the water.
aharvar (H.): to hit, beat.
ahuera (de): outside.
ajeno, a: foreign, alien.
akavidarse: to act cautiously
akear: to do this and that.
akedá (la) (H.): the Biblical sacrifice of Isaac.
akel, akeya: that (over there).
akel (el): the "thingy," so-and-so.
akí: here.
aklarar: to make clear.
akodrarse: to remember.
akonteser: to happen, take place (general sense).
akurtar: to shorten.

al lado de…: next to…
alargar: to make longer.
alavado, a: praised.
albóndiga (la): the meatball.
alesharse: to move off at a distance.
alegrarse: to become happy.
alegre, a: happy.
alegrete: joyous.
alegriya (la): the joy.
alhad (el) (Sp. Ar.): Sunday.
alimanyas (las): wild beasts.
aliyá (la) (H.): the going up; azer su aliyá: emigrate to Israel.
alkunya (la) (Sp. Ar.): the family name.
alkuruto: endlessly.
alma (la): the soul.
almenara (la) (Sp. Ar.): the chandelier, lighting fixture.
almendra (la): the almond.
alsar: to raise (up).
alto, a: tall, high.
aluenga (la): the tongue.
alzemán (S./ H.): formerly, once upon a time.
amá (T.): but.
amahar (Span. Arabism): to heal, relieve, cure.
amanyana: tomorrow.
amanziyarse: to take pity on.
amar: to love.
amargar: to embitter, sadden.
amargo, a: bitter.
amariyo, a: yellow.
amatar: to extinguish.
ambar (el) (T.): the storeroom, attic, cellar.
ambezar (se): to teach (to learn).
ambre (la): hunger.
amerikana (la): cotton cloth.
amigo, a (el, la): the friend.
amor (el): the love.
amostrar: to show, display.
ampesar/empesar: to begin.
ande: where; at the house of…
ánde?: where?
andjeló (el): the angel.
aní (H.): poor.
aniyo (el): the ring (for finger).
aniyo de kidushim: engagement ring.

ansí, ansina: thus, in this way.
ansya (la): the worry, anxiety.
antes: before.
antikadjí (el) (T.): the antique dealer.
anyada (la): the year.
anyo (el): the year.
apalavrado, a: engaged, spoken for.
apanyar: to catch.
aparejar: to prepare.
apartar: to put aside, separate.
apenas: scarcely, hardly.
apiyadarse: to take pity on.
apozar: to set, pose.
aprekantar: to make incantations.
apretado, a: tight.
aprontar: to prepare.
apurarse: to wear oneself out.
arabá (la) (T.): the car, automobile.
a(r)rapado, a: shaved.
a(r)regar: to water.
a(r)rematar: to burst, die.
a(r)rovar: to rob.
aravyarse: to become angry.
ardor (el): the ardor, passion.
aregalar: to treat well, give, offer a gift
  (= *dar regalo*).
arekojer: to gather, pick.
arelumbrar: to shine, gleam.
arenadjí (el) (T.): seller of scrubbing
  sand.
arepozarse: to rest.
aresentar: to place, pose, set up.
aresivir: to receive.
arevés: backwards, reversed.
areyevar: to take, hold, absorb.
arina (la): the flour (*and see* **farina**).
armaryo (el): the closet, cupboard.
armí (el): dish based on tomato purée.
arogar: to supplicate, beg.
arrastar: to drag behind.
arroz (el): the rice.
artar (se): to satisfy hunger.
arto, a: full, sated.
arvolé (el): the tree.
aryentro (de): in, inside (of).
asar: to roast, grill.
asararse (H.): to take fright.
asender: to light (a fire), turn on the
  light.
asentar: to seat.

aserrar: *see* **serrar**.
ashuguar (el): the trousseau.
asigún: as, according to.
asolar/asoladar: to ravage, destroy.
asperar: to wait.
aspertarse: to wake up.
asugurar/asigurar: to assure, make
  certain.
asukar: to put sugar in.
asúkuar (la): the sugar.
asuvir: to climb, go up.
atabafarse: to suffocate, be smothered.
atemar: to exterminate.
ateshdjí, -ya/atedjí, -ya (el, la) (T.):
  person who lights the fire on Shabad.
atyó!: oh, Lord!.
auflar: to swell, swell up.
aunarse: to join together, unite.
avagar avagar: slowly and carefully.
avel (el) (H.): the person in
  mourning.
avenirse: to get along well.
aver (el) (H.): the air.
aver: to have.
aveyana (la): the hazelnut, filbert.
avlar: to speak.
avokato (el) (F., T.): the lawyer.
avrir: to open.
ayá: there, over there.
aydé (T.): let's go, let's get a move on.
ayegar: to arrive, have something sent
  to (someone).
ayer: yesterday.
ayí: here.
Ayifto: Egypt.
aynará (el) (H.): the evil eye.
ayre (el): the wind.
ayudador (el): the assistant, helper.
ayudar: to help.
ayudo (el): the help, aid.
azer: to do, make; *azerse pishmán*
  (T.): to miss, feel regret; *azerse
  preto:* to turn black.; *azerse djudyó:*
  to convert to Judaism.
azete/azeyte (la): the oil.
azno (el): the donkey, ass.

B

babá (T.): papa.
bahcheván (el) (T.): the gardener.
bakkal (el) (T.): the grocer.
balabay, a (el, la) (H.): master, mistress of the house.
Balat: Jewish neighborhood in Istanbul on the Golden Horn.
baldes (de): free of charge, "a steal."
balta (la) (T.): the axe.
balukchí (el) (T.): the fish dealer.
bamyas (las) (T.): okra.
banker (el) (T.): the banker.
baragán: see *barragan.*
barka (la): small boat.
barkero (el): boatman.
barminán (H): how terrible!, Heaven protect us!; adj., bad, evil.
barmizvá: see mizvá.
barragán: strong, powerful.
barrer: to sweep.
barro: clay, earthen.
baruhu baruh shemó (H): blessed be His name.
barva (la): chin.
basho (en): below, on the ground.
bashustuné (T.): at your service.
batal/batlán (H): idle.
batalik (el) (H & T): idleness.
batar(se)/batirear (se) (T): to sink (for boats).
batear (la puerta): to knock (at the door).
batir (el): the beating (of the heart, for ex.).
bava/vava (G): granma, old woman.
bavajada (la): nonsense, foolishness.
bayladora (la): the dancer (fem.).
bayle (el): the dance.
beemá (la) (H.): the animal, beast, head of cattle.
benadam (H.): (lit.: son of man) a good human being, a respected man, grown up.
bendicho, a: blessed.
berahá (la): the blessing.
berendjena (la): the eggplant, aubergine.
berit (el) (H.): the circumcision ritual.

bever: to drink; *bever sigaro:* to smoke (a cigarette).
beyenearse (T.): to like each other.
bezar: to kiss.
biko (el): bird's beak.
bilé (T.): even.
bimuelera (la): pan for frying doughnut-like pastries.
biskocho (el): a kind of pastry.
bivdo, a: widowed.
bivir: to live.
bivo, a: alive, lively.
biznona (la): great grandmother.
biznyeto (el): great-grandson.
blando, a: soft, tender.
blanko, a: white.
blondeado: fair-haired.
blu: blue.
bodre (el): the edge, rim.
bohor (H.): (noun or adj.): eldest son.
boka (la): the mouth; *la boka del korasón:* entry to the stomach.
bokal (el): the pitcher, carafe.
bolar: to fly.
bolarse: to fly off, disappear, die; boil over (milk).
bombones (los): the pieces of candy.
bonbonyera (la): the candy dish.
bonete (el): the bonnet.
bo(r)racho, a: drunk.
borreka (la) (T.): stuffed pastry.
bovo, a: foolish, idiotic.
boy (el) (T.): the age, size.
boyiko (el): little stuffed turnover.
boyo (el): stuffed salted pastry.
boz/bos (la): the voice; in T.: *ses.*
bozdear (T.): to break.
braso (el): the arm.
brit milá (la) (H.): the circumcision ritual.
bruido (el): the noise.
bueno, a: good.
buey (el): the ox, steer.
bulisa/bula: lady, madam.
burakar: to make a hole.
burako (el): the hole.
burla (la): the joke.
burlarse: to make fun of.
büró (el): the office, desk.
bushkar: to look for, seek.

butikaryo (el): the shopkeeper, store owner.
buyir: to boil.
buz (T.): ice, icy.
buzyera (la): the ice-box.
byervo (el): the word.

Ch

chadir (T.): the umbrella, tent.
chan (el) (T.): the bell.
chanta (la) (T.): the purse, bag.
charshí (el) (T.): the covered bazaar, market place.
chay (el) (T.): the tea.
chiko, a: little; child.
chimento (el): the cement, mortar.
chiní (el) (T.): the dish, chinaware.
chöp (el) (T.): the garbage, trashcan.
chosa (la): the hut.
chupar: to suck.

D

dado (el): the die (dice).
dainda: encore.
dantist(o) (F): dentist.
danyar: to harm, damage.
danyo (el): the harm, damage.
dar: to give; **dar haber** (T.): to give news, inform; **dar el get** (H.): to grant a divorce; **dar utí** (T.): to iron, press.
datil (el): the date (fruit).
dayán (el) (H.): the rabbinical judge.
dayanear (T.): to resist
debasho: below, beneath.
dedo (el): the finger.
defekto (el): the defect.
degoyar: to slaughter, slit the throat.
delantre de: before, in front of.
demanda (la): the question.
demandar: to ask questions.
demanyana (la): the morning.
demanyana matrana: early in the morning.
demaziya: surplus quantity, too much.
demet (el) (T.): the bouquet.
derecha (la): the right side.

derecho, a: straight, simple.
derokar: to overturn, destroy.
desde… fin a…: from… to… (time expression) [In Salonika **fasta**, **fista** are used instead of **fin a**).
deshar: to leave, let.
deskaminante: lost in one's journey.
deskutir: to discuss.
desmayarse/dezmayarse/ezmayarse: to faint.
desmudo/dezmudo, a: naked.
despartirse (de): to take leave of.
despedasar: to break into pieces.
después: see **duspués**.
desrepozado, a: tired.
destruyir: to destroy.
detenerse: to restrain oneself.
detrás: behind.
desvaneser(se): see **esvaneser(se)**.
devantal (el): the apron.
devda (la): the debt.
dever: to owe.
dever (el): the duty.
dezeyar: to desire.
dicha (la): the saying.
dicho, a: said.
diferensya (la): the difference.
dikat (el) (T.): the care.
dinguno, dinguna, dingunos, dingunas: none; no (adj. masc. & fem., sing. & plu.).
divizyón (la): the division.
diya (el): the day.
diyamante (el): the diamond.
diz (el) (T.): the knee.
dizido: said (variant of **dicho**).
dizir: to say.
djanim (T.): my soul (term of affection).
djarro (el): the pitcher.
djaspe (el): the jasper.
djente (la): the people.
djinoyo (el) (I.): the knee.
djoya (la): the jewel.
djoyero (el): the jeweler.
djudyó/djidyó (el): the Jew; Judeo-Spanish (language).
djueves/djugueves (el): Thursday.
djuguar: tp play.
djumba (la) (T.): the bay-window.

djusto, a: correct, exact.
djuzgar: to judge.
dodje: twelve.
doktor (el): the doctor.
dolap (el) (T.): the closet, cupboard.
dolashear (T.): to stroll.
dolmúsh (el) (T.): group taxi, jitney.
dolor (la): the pain.
dolyente: suffering.
dolyo (el): mourning.
domate (la) (T.): tomato.
donzeya (la): the young lady.
dos: two.
dota (la): the dowry.
dovletlí, -liya (T.): well-to-do.
drohim (los) (H.): Young Zionists.
dublar: to bend.
dueler/dugueler: to hurt, ache.
dukado (el): the ducat (old coin).
dulse: sweet, sugary.
dulse (el): sweet preserves.
durera (la): constipation.
durmir: to sleep.
duspués/después: after.
dyente (el /la): the tooth.
dyez: dix.
dyezén, a: quantity of ten, tenth.

E

echar: to throw, put to bed; **echar
  guayas:** to wail and scream.
echarse: to go to bed, throw oneself.
echas (las): the deeds.
echo (el): the work.
echo: past participle of *azer.*
echos (los): business; **echos buenos!:**
  have good business!
egzempyo (el): the example.
egzistir: to exist.
ehal (el) (H.): the ark of the Torah
  scrolls.
elektrik (el) (T.): electricity.
elevo, -a (F.): student, pupil.
embasada (la): the embassy.
embatakarse (T.): to get soiled.
embatako (el): muddy area, muck.
embeveserse: to be distracted,
  absorbed by something.

embirrarse: to get angry.
embrenear (se): to be delighted,
  entranced.
empesar: to begin.
emplear: to use, to go shopping.
empyegado: employee.
empyegarse: to get a job.
enamorarse: to fall in love.
enano (el): the dwarf.
enchikeser: to shrink, become small.
endagora: right now; starting now.
enderechar: to straighten out, put
  right.
endechadera (la): the hired mourner.
endivino (el): the soothsayer, wizard.
endjunto: together.
enfasyarse: to get bored.
enforkar: see **forkar.**
enfrente: in front, across from.
englenearse (T.): to have fun.
enhaminar (H.): to braise, steam.
enkantado, a: astonished.
enkantarse: to be astonished.
enkolgar: to hang.
enmentar: to mention.
enreynar/areyenar: to stuff (cooking).
enrikeser: to become rich.
enriva de…: on, at the top of…
ensanyarse: to become enraged.
ensegida: immediately.
enshaguar: to rinse.
enshavonar: to wash with soap.
enshemplo (el): the example.
enshuguar: to dry off, wipe up.
ensima (de): on, on top of.
entender/entyender: to understand,
  to hear.
enteresante: interesting.
enteresar: to interest.
entezarse: to become stiff, frozen.
entiznar: to cover with ashes, blacken.
entrar: to enter, introduce; *entrar en
  el mes:* to go into the (last) month of
  pregnancy; *entrar a la mar:* to swim
  in the sea.
entre: between, among.
enverano (el): the summer.
erensya (la): the heritage.
ermana (la): the sister.
ermano (el): the brother.

ermozo, a: handsome, beautiful.
ermozura (la): the beauty.
ermuera (la): the daughter-in-law.
esetra: etc.
es-huegra (la): the mother-in-law.
es-huegro (el): the father-in-law.
eskaldar: to scald.
eskansar: to rest.
eskapar: to finish, to escape.
eskarinyarse: to long for, to miss.
eskaso, a: stingy.
eskojer: to choose.
eskola (la): see **skola**.
eskolar: to get out of school.
eskonder: to hide.
eskova (la): the broom.
eskrita (la): a writing, notation.
eskritor (el): the writer.
eskrivano (el): the writer.
eskrivir: to write.
eskurrir: to drip.
eskuchar: to listen.
esmayar: see **desmayar**.
espajar: to clean up, straighten out.
espalda (la): the back (body).
espander: to hang up to dry.
espantar: to scare.
espantarse (de): to be afraid of.
espareser(se): to disappear; to appear.
espartimyento (el): division, share.
espartir: to divide, share.
espartirse: to take leave of.
espedasar (se): to tear up (be torn to bits).
espejo (el): the mirror.
espesearse: to thicken.
espidir: to digest.
espinaka (la): the spinach.
espondjar: to mop the floor.
espozado, a: fiancé, fiancée.
esprimir: to squeeze.
esuenyo/esfuenyo/es-huenyo (el): the sleep.
estampador (el): the printer, publisher.
estar: to be, to be present.
estrechura (la): the narrowness, distress.
estrenas (las): gifts offered on new occasions.

estruir (se)/destruyir (se): to destroy (be destroyed).
esvaneserse/desvaneserse: to lose consciousness.
etrogim (los) (H.): citrons.
ezmayarse/esmayarse: see **desmayarse**.

F

fabriká (la): the factory
fabrikatör (el): the industrialist.
faltar: to omit, miss, fail to do…
familya (la): the family.
fanela (la) (T.): (flannel) undershirt.
farina/arina (la): the flour.
fasha (la): baby's wrap.
fashadura (la): the layette, baby's trousseau.
fasil: easy.
feguzya (la): faith, confidence.
fener (el) (T.): the lantern.
findján (el) (T.): the cup.
finyir: to knead.
firida (la): the wound.
firir: to wound.
firir (el): the blow, beating.
flecha (la): the arrow.
flor (la): the flower.
flosho, a: loose, limp.
forkar/enforkar: to hang.
forsar: to force.
fostán (el) (T.): the dress.
fragua (la): the building, construction.
fraguar: to construct.
fransés (el): French (language).
fransés, -za: French.
fregar: to scrub, do the dishes.
fregón (el): dish-cloth, scrubber.
frente (la): the forehead.
fresko, a: fresh.
freza (la): the strawberry.
frijider (el): the refrigerator.
friyir: to fry.
friyo (el): the cold, shiver.
friyo, a: cold.
fuego (el): the fire.
fuersa (la): the force.

fuerte: strong, difficult.
fumo (el): the smoke.
fusta (la) (T.)**:** the skirt.
fustanela (la): the slip, underskirt.
fyel (la): the gall, spleen.
fye(r)ro (el): iron (metal).

G

gameyo (el): the camel.
ganansya (la): the profit, reward, salary.
ganar: to earn, win.
ganedén (el) (H.)**:** Paradise.
garato (el): salted fish (sliced).
garón (el) (H.)**:** the neck.
gato (el): the cat.
gayna (la): the hen.
gayo (el): the rooster.
gazeta (la): the newspaper.
gazetero (el): the journalist.
gazino (el): outdoor cafe with music.
gerra (la): the war.
get (el) (H.)**:** the divorce.
ginnam (el) (H.)**:** Hell.
gitarra (la): the guitar.
giyar sovre: to supervise, guide (someone).
gizar: to cook
godro, a: fat.
golor (la): the smell, odor.
gomitar: to vomit.
gomitó (el): the vomit.
gomo (el): the stuffing (cooking).
gongosha (la): the nausea.
gostar: to taste.
gostijo (el): portion of a cooked dish sent over for neighbors to taste.
gota (la): the drop.
gozar: to enjoy.
gramos (los): the grams.
grande: big, adult.
grip (la): the flu.
gritar: to shout.
grito (el): the shout.
gruya (la): the crane.
guadrar: to keep, put in order.
guay de…!: poor (so and so)!
guay de mí!: woe is me!, how sad!
guaya (la): cry of despair; *fazer/echar*

guayas: to wail in despair.
guerta (la): the garden.
guertelano (el): the gardener.
guevo (el): the egg.
gustarse: to take pleasure in, be happy.
guzano (el): the worm, insect.

H

haber (el) (T.)**:** news.
hach (el) (T.)**:** the cross (Christian).
haham (el) (H.)**:** the rabbi; *el haham bashí* (H./T.): the grand rabbi.
Halich (el) (T.)**:** the Golden Horn (Istanbul).
haloshentos, as… : a heap of, lots of…
hamallik (T.)**:** porter's job.
haminado (H.)**:** steamed, braised.
haminar (H.)**:** to steam, braise.
hammal (el) (T.)**:** porter, loader.
hamor (el) (H.)**:** the donkey, ass.
handrajo (el): the rag, dustcloth.
hanum (la) (T.)**:** term of affection, dear one.
hap (el) (T.)**:** the pill.
has ve shalom! (H.)**:** God forbid!
hasé (el) (T.)**:** cotton fabric.
hastané (la) (T.)**:** the hospital.
haver (el) (H.)**:** partner, comrade.
havrá (la) (H.)**:** the school, association.
hayá (la) (H.)**:** the animal, beast (pl.: *las hayot* or *las hayás*).
hayre (el) (T.)**:** profit, positive result.
hazán (el) (H.)**:** the cantor.
hazindad (la): see **hazinura**.
hazino, a (Span. Arabism)**:** sick.
hazinura (la): the illness, disease.
hazir (el) (H.)**:** the pig.
heshbón (el) (H.)**:** the accounts.
henozo, a (H.)**:** gracious.
hinzir (el) (T.)**:** the pig (insult).
hupá (la) (H.)**:** wedding ceremony.

I

ich (T.)**:** not at all.

igo (el): the fig.
ijada (la): urinary infection.
ija (la): the daughter.
ijo (el). the son; *el ijo regalado:* the only son.
inat (el) (T.): stubbornness; *meter inat:* to become stubborn.
inchir: to fill, stuff.
indjenyero (el): the engineer.
indjideyar (T.): to hurt, harm, wound.
indyana (la): the turkey.
inshallá: God willing, provided that.
interesarse: see **enteresarse**.
investigador (el): the researcher.
invyerno (el): the winter.
inyervarse/inyerveyarse: to become irritated.
inyeto, a (el, la): the grandson, granddaughter.
ir: to go. **irse:** to go away, leave.
isportadjí (el) (T.): street peddler.
istorya (la): History.
isyedra/istyedra (la): the left side.
itfayé (el) (T.): the fireman.
ivrit (el) (H): Hebrew (modern language).

J

jurnalisto (el): the journalist.

K

kabadayí (el): the bandit, swaggerer.
kabiné (el): the bathroom, toilet.
kafrar (H.): to blaspheme, reject.
kagar: to excrete (fam.).
kaji/kaje: almost
kal (el) (H.): the synagogue.
kal (la): the whitewash.
kaldera (la): the cooking pot.
kaldo (el): the sauce, gravy.
kaleja (la): the street.
kaler: to have to (impersonal).
kalsa (la): the sock, stocking.
kalsado (el): the shoe, footware.
kama (la): the bed.
kamareta (la): the room; *la kamareta*

de echar: the bedroom.
kaminar: to walk.
kamino (el): the road, way.
kamiza (la): the shirt.
kampo (el): the field.
kanapé (la) (F.): the couch.
kaniya (la): the ankle.
kansado, a/kanso, a: tired.
kantadero, a (el, la): the singer.
kantar: to sing.
kantika (la): the song.
kantón (el): the corner, angle.
kanyo (el): the mud, muck.
kapak (el) (T.): the cover, lid, cap.
kapará (la) (H.): the sacrifice.
kapachitá (la) (I.): the capacity.
kapitán (el): the captain.
kara (la): the face.
karar (el) (T.): the quantity.
karga (la): the load.
karika (la): the cheek.
karishtrear/-terear/-triyar: to mix, mix up; *karishterear el meoyo:* confuse one's mind.
karkanyal (el): the heel.
karne (la): the meat.
karnesero (el): the butcher.
karo, a: dear.
karta (la): playing card.
kasap (el) (T.): the butcher.
kasavet (el) (T.): melancholy.
kasha (la): the box, cashregister.
kashero, a (el, la): the cashier.
kasherola (la): the cooking dish.
kashka (la): the skin (of fruit).
kashón (el): the drawer.
kasta (la): the family, family race.
kastanya (la): the chestnut.
kat (el) (T.): the floor (of house or building).
katorze: fourteen.
kavané (la) (T.): the café.
kavar: to dig.
kavás (el) (T.): the guard.
kavayo (el): the horse.
kavesa (la): the head.
kaveyo (el): the hair.
kavra (la): the goat.
kavretiko (el): the little goat, kid.
kavurear (T.): to roast, sauté.

kavzante: that which causes.
kavzo (el): the case, event.
kayar: to be quiet.
kaye (la): the street.
kayente: hot.
kayentura (la): the heat, fever.
kayer: to fall (*kaygo, kayes…*) .
kayik (el) (T.): the small boat.
kayikchí (el): the boatman.
kaza (la): the house.
kazado, a: married.
kazamentero, a (el, la): the marriage arranger.
kazar: to marry.
ke: that, which, whom, because.
ké?: what?
kedar: to stay, remain; *kedar en kudyado:* to be worried.
kemado, a: burned, burnt.
kemarse: to burn, burn up.
ken: who, whom.
kén?: who, whom?
kenar (el) (T.): the edge, rim.
kerer: to want, wish, like, love.
kerido, a: dear, darling.
kesharse: to complain.
keshke (T.): provided that.
ketubá (la) (H.): the marriage contract.
kezo (el): the cheese.
kilo (el): the kilo (2.2 pounds).
kimuraná (la) (T.): the coal cellar.
kinyentos, as: five hundred.
kinze: fifteen.
kirbá (la) (T.): the water-skin.
kishada (la): the jaw.
kishlá (la) (T.): the barracks.
kitá (la) (T.): the team, brigade.
kitar: to remove; *kitar alay* (T.): to poke fun at.
kitarse: to get divorced.
kito, a: divorced.
kizdereyar/kizdriyar (T.): to anger, irritate.
klavina (la): the carnation.
klavo (el): the nail; *el klavo de komer:* the clove (spice).
koches (los) (T.): jacks (children's game).
kocho, a: cooked.
kodredo (el): the lamb.

kolada (la): the wash, laundry.
kolay (T.): easy.
kolcha (la): the mattress.
kolor (la): the color.
kolorá/kolora (la): the anger.
kolorado, a: red.
koltuk (el): the armchair.
komadre (la): the mid-wife, godmother.
komedor (el): the dining room.
komer: to eat.
komerchante (el): the merchant, shop owner.
komerchero (el): the customs clerk.
komida (la): the food.
komo: how, how much.
kómo?: how?
komportarse: to behave.
kompozitor (el): the composer.
kondesa (la): the countess, the rival woman.
konfite (el): the candy.
konoser: to know, be acquainted with.
konseja (la): the tale, little story.
konsejo (el): the advice.
konsentir/konsintir: to feel.
konsograr: to become related to another family through the marriage of one's child.
kontar: to tell, recount.
kontente: contented, happy.
kontino (de): continuously.
konvidado (el): the guest.
koraje (el): the courage.
korasón (el): the heart; *tener korasón:* to have a heart condition.
korkova (la): the hump (of a hunchback).
korolado, a/korelado, a: red.
korredor (el): the hallway.
korredor de kazas (el): real-estate agent.
korrer: to run.
kortar: to cut.
kortijo (el): the patio, courtyard.
kortina (la): the curtain.
kostar: to cost.
kosuegra (la): a mother in relationship to the parents of her child's spouse.

kosuegro (el): a father in relationship to the parents of his child's spouse.

kovdo (el): the elbow.

kovijar/kuvijar: to cover, cover up.

kovre (el): the copper.

koza (la): the thing.

kozer: to cook.

kozina (la): the bathroom (in Salonika, the kitchen).

kozinar: to cook.

kreser: to grow, become older.

kreyer: to believe.

Kriyador (el): the Creator.

kriyar: to nurse, bring up, raise.

kriyatura (la): the baby, child.

krudo, a: raw.

kuafòr (el) (T): the hairdresser, coiffeur.

kuálo?: which, what?

kuantitá (la): the quantity, size.

kuarto: quarter.

kuatrén, a: fourth.

kuatro: four.

kuatropeas (las) (L.): the quadrupeds.

kuchara (la): the spoon.

kucharada (la): the spoonful.

kuchiyo (el): the knife.

kudyado (el): care, worry.

kuenta (la): the number.

kuento (el): the addition, sum.

kuero (el): the skin, leather.

kuerpo/puerpo (el): the body.

kueshko (el): the pit, seed.

kufa (la) (T.): the basket.

Kulá (la): the Galata Tower and neighborhood.

kulanear (T.): to use; *kulanear arabá:* to drive a car.

Kuledibí (T.): Jewish quarter around the Galata Tower.

kulero (el): the diaper.

kulevro (el): the snake, serpent.

kulo (el): the arse, derrière.

kunyado, a (el, la): the brother-in-law, sister-in-law.

kupa (la): the drinking glass.

kura (la): the medicine.

kuyumdjí (el) (T.): the jeweler.

kuzandera (la): the seamstress.

kuzir: to sew.

kyushé/kyöshé/köshé (la) (T.): the street corner.

kyuprí (el) (T.): the bridge.

L

lado (al): beside, next to.

ladrón (el): the thief, robber.

lágrima (la): the tear (weeping).

lampa (la): the lamp.

lavandera (la): the washerwoman.

lavar: to wash.

lavorante (el): the workman.

lavorar (I.): to work.

lavoro (el) (I.): the work.

leche (la): the milk.

legumbre (el): the vegetable.

Lchlí, Lehliya (T. for Polish): Ashkenazi Jew.

lentejas (las): the lentils.

lenya (la): wood for burning.

leona (la): the lioness.

leshiya (la): the wash, bleach.

leshos: far.

levadura (la): the yeast.

levanim (los) (B. with H. pl.): Bulgarian money/white coin.

Ley (la): the Law (the Torah, Pentateuch).

likorino (el): smoked mullet (fish).

limón (el): the lemon.

limonada (la): the lemonade.

limpyeza (la): the cleanliness, housekeeping.

limpyo, a: clean.

lingua (la): the language.

lisensya (la): the license, permission.

lisyón (la): the lesson (pl. *las lisyones*).

litro (el): the liter.

livro (el): the book.

livyano, a: light (not heavy).

lokantadjí (el) (T.): the restaurant owner.

loko, a: crazy.

lonso (el): the bear, fool, "heavy" person.

loor (la): praise.

luguar (el): the place, the cemetery.

lumbre (la): the fire (in the hearth, source of heat).

luna (la): the moon.
lunes (el): Monday.
luvya (la): the rain.
luzido, a: handsome, pretty.
luzyo, a: handsome, pretty.

M

ma: but.
machukuar: to crush.
madam (la): the lady, madam.
madem ki (T.): since, inasmuch as…
madrasta (la): the step-mother.
madre (la): the mother.
maestro, a (el, la): the teacher.
magazén (el): the store, shop.
mahzén (el) (T.): the warehouse.
majar: to crush.
makare + subj. (G.): oh, if only…!
mákina (la): the machine.
mal (el): the harm, evil (pl. *los males:* the ills).
maldisyón (la): the curse.
malah amavet (el) (H.): the angel of death.
mallé (la) (T.): the neighborhood, quarter.
malo, a: bad, wicked.
mamzer (el) (H.): the bastard.
mandamyento (el): the commandment.
mandar: to send.
manifatura (la): clothing shop.
manifaturadjí (el) (du T.): hosier, clothier, fabrics dealer.
manko: less, minus.
mankura (la): the need, lack, shortage.
mano (la): the hand.
mansana (la): the apple.
mansevéz (la): youth.
mansevo,a: young, young man/woman.
manteka (la): the butter.
manyana (la): the morning.
manziya (la): the pain, affliction, loss.
mar (la): the sea.
marangoz (el) (T.): the woodworker, cabinet maker.

marido (el): the husband.
marinero (el): the sailor, seaman.
martes (el): Tuesday.
mas: more.
masa (la): the dough.
masá (la) (H.): (= matsá) unleavened bread.
mashallá (T.): Thank the Lord!
matar (se): to kill (oneself).
matropikar: to multiply.
matropikasyón (la): the multiplication.
mauvyar: to complain, miscarry, abort (influence of *mauyar:* to howl, meow).
maví (T.): blue.
maydanó (el) (G.): the parsley.
mazalozo, a (H.): lucky.
meatá (la): half.
medjidiyé (el) (T.): old Ottoman coin.
médiko (el): the doctor.
medyanoche: midnight.
medyo, a: half-.
medyodiya: noon.
melón (el): the melon.
meldahón (el): a person who reads all the time (said ironically).
meldar: to read, study, recite the prayers.
menear: to stir, shake.
menester (el): the need; *tener menester:* to need.
menesterozo, a: needy, poor; necessary.
menorá (la) (H.): the candle-holder.
menudo, a: small, minute.
meoyo (el): brains, the mind.
merekiyarse (T.): to worry about.
merekiyozo, a (T.): worried.
merkader (el): the merchant.
merkar: to buy, purchase.
mesklar: to mix together.
meter: to put; *meter inat* (T.): to be obstinate; *meter tino:* to pay attention, be determined.
metro (el): the meter.
meyaná (la) (T.): the tavern.
meyanadjí (el) (T.): the tavern keeper.
mez (el): the month.

meza (la): the table.

mezé (el) (T.): hors-d'oeuvre dish.

mezmo, a: same.

mezuzá (la) (H.): the mezuzah

midí (la) (F.): noon.

mijo (el): the soft inside of bread or vegetables; a grain of millet.

mijor (de): better than.

mijorar: to feel or make better, improve.

mil (inv.): a thousand.

milá (la) (H.): the circumcision ceremony.

milyón (el): (the) million.

mimar (el) (T.): the architect.

minder (el) (T.): the cushion, pouffe.

miniko, a (T.): tiny.

minudo: *see* **menudo.**

minyán (el) (H.): a group of at least ten of the faithful needed to hold prayer service.

mirar: to look, look at, observe.

Mitsriyot (las) (H.): the Egyptian women.

mizvá (la) (H.): the Bar Mitzva ceremony; a good moral act.

mobilya (la) (T.): the furniture.

muchiguar: to increase, multiply.

modrer: to bite.

moed (el) (H.): the religious holiday.

moel (el) (H.): the circumcisor, *mohel.*

mojado, a: wet, moist.

mojar: to wet, moisten.

moler: to grind, chop.

molinar: to grind, mill.

montanya (la): the mountain.

moradero, a/morador, a: inhabitant, resident.

morar: to reside, live.

morir: to dic.

moro, a: Moor.

mortero (el): the mortar (for cooking).

moso, a: servant, valet, maid.

mösyö/ musyú (F.): mister.

muchiguar: to increase, multiply.

mudar: to change.

mudayas (a las): in Salonika = **a las mudeskas.**

mudeskas (a las): making gestures like a deaf-mute.

muerto, a: dead.

mueve: nine.

muevén, a: ninth.

muevo, a: new.

muez (la): the walnut.

mujer (la): the woman, wife.

muncho, a: much, a lot.

mundar: to peel.

mundo (el): the world.

mupak (el) (T.): the kitchen.

murir/morir/muerir: to die.

mursá (H.): unpleasant person, pouter.

musho (el): the lip.

myedo (el): the fear; *tener myedo:* to be afraid.

myel (la): the honey.

myérkoles (el): Wednesday.

N

na (T.): here, see this.

nada: nothing.

nalga (la): the buttock.

nalo, nala, nalos, nalas (T.): here it is, here they are, etc.

namorozo, a: sweetheart, man or woman in love.

narandja (la): the orange.

nariz (la): the nose, nostril.

naser: to be born (*nasko, nases…*)

naylón (el) (T.): plastic bag (for carrying).

neder (el) (H.): the vow.

negro, a: bad, mean, evil.

noche (la): the night.

noguera (la): see **ermuera.**

nona (la) (I.): the grandmother.

nono (el) (I.): the grandfather.

nümeró (el): the bathroom, toilet.

nunkua/nunka: never.

O

ochén, a: eighth.

ocho: eight.

ograshar (T.): to strive, put oneself out.

oja (la): the leaf.

ojo (el): the eye; *a ojos a ojos:* impatiently.

olvidar: to forget.

ombre (el): the man.

ombro (el): the shoulder.

ondo (un): a deep place.

onestetad (la): honesty.

onze: eleven.

ora (la): the hour, clock, watch; o'clock.

oreja (la): the ear.

orno/forno (el): the oven.

oro (el): the gold.

ospital (el): the hospital.

otobüs (el) (T.): the bus.

otonyo (el): the autumn.

otro (el), otra (la): other (noun and adjective).

oveja (la): the ewe, sheep.

oy: today.

P

pachá (la) (T.): the leg.

padre (el): the father.

paga (la): the salary.

pagar: to pay (in general).

pala (la): the shovel.

palavra (la): the word.

palaza (la): the duck.

palo (el): the wood, stick.

palomba (la): the dove.

pan (el): the bread.

panadero (el): the baker.

papel (el): paper; money (fam.)

papelera (la): paper bag, paper cone.

papú (el): granpa, old man.

par (el): the pair.

pará (la) (T.): coin, money.

para: for, in order to.

paré(d) (la): the wall (in Bulgaria, *la pader*).

parida (la): woman who has just given birth.

parido (el): the husband of *la parida*.

parir: to give birth to.

párparo (el): the eyelid.

parra (la): climbing (grape) vine.

partir: to leave, depart.

paryaruhadjí/palyaruhadjí (el) (G.): the rag dealer.

paryenté (la): blood relation.

paryentes (los): relatives.

pasar: to pass, spend (time).

pasar de: to go beyond.

pashá (el) (T.): pasha, term of affection.

pasharó (el): the bird, flying 'insect.

pasiko (el): the piece, small piece.

pastera (la): the washtub.

pasuk (el) (H.): verse from the Bible.

patata (la): the potato.

pato (el): the goose.

patrón (el): the boss, master, CEO.

pavora (la): the fear, terror.

payla (la): the wash-basin, dishpan.

paylón (el): the large dish, tray.

paz (la): peace.

pechar: to pay (a tax).

pecho (el): the chest, breast.

pedar(se): to fart.

pedaso (el): the morsel, crumb.

pedo, pedado (el): the fart.

pekado (el): the sin.

pekar: to sin.

pekí (T.): very well.

pelegrino, a: pilgrim, wanderer (noun & adj.).

peleyar(se): to fight, to have a dispute.

pena (la): the pain, suffering.

pensar: to think, to worry.

penseryo (el): the worry.

penseryozo, a: worried.

peor: worse.

pera (la): the pear.

perashá (la) (H.): the Torah reading portion of the week.

perdido, a/pyedrido, a/pedrido, a/peryido, a: lost.

pereshil (el): the parsley.

perikolozo, a (I.): dangerous.

perkurar (a or de): to try to.

permetido, a/permitido, a: permitted, allowed.

perro, a (el, la): the dog.

persona/presona (la): the person.

peryer: to lose.

Pesah (el) (H.): Passover.

peshe (el) (in Salonika): *see* pishkado.

peshín/pishín (T.): immediately.

pestanya (la): the eyelash.

peynado (el): the coiffure, hair style.

peynarse: to comb oneself.

pezar: to weigh.

pezo (el): the weight, the scale.

pidyón (H.): the "purchase" of the first-born.

pikar: to mince, sting.

piko (el): unit of measure.

pila (la): the sink.

pimyenta (la): the pepper.

pino (el): the pinetree, cypress.

pinya (la): the pine cone.

pipino (el): the cucumber.

pishado (el): the urine.

pishar: to urinate.

pishkado (el): the fish.

pishkador (el): the fisherman.

pishmán (azerse): to miss, regret.

pirón (el) (G.): the fork.

piska (una): a pinch.

piskueso (el): the nape, back of the neck.

piskuzar: to look into.

pita (la): small round bread.

piyutim/piyutimes (los) (H.): religious songs (sing.: *un piyut*).

plata (la): silver.

plato (el): the plate, dish.

plazer: to please.

plazer (el): the pleasure.

pleto (el): the dispute.

poder (el): the power.

poeta (el): the poet.

pokitiko (un): just a little bit.

poko: small amount, a little.

polis (un) (T.): a policeman.

polvo (el): the dust, powder.

por modo de: because of, for the reason that.

porké: because.

portakal (la): the orange.

povereto, -ta (el, la) (I.): the poor dear (man or woman).

povre (el): the poor man; *see* prove.

poyo (el): the chicken.

pozar: to put down, set down.

pozo (el): the well.

pranso (el): the meal, banquet; *meter pranso:* to serve a meal.

prasa (la) (T.): the leek (vegetable).

prekante (el): the charm, incantation.

prenyada (la): the pregnant woman.

prenyado (el): the pregnancy.

presto: quickly, fast.

presyado, a: dear one, "sweetie."

presyo (el): the price.

presyozo, a: precious; precious one.

preto, a: black.

primavera (la): spring (season).

primer/o, a: first.

primo, a (el, la): cousin.

pri(n)sipyo (el): the beginning.

privada (la): the bathroom, toilct.

priz/priza (la) (F. or T.): the electric outlet.

prometer: to promise.

pronto, a: ready.

prostela (la) (G.): the apron.

prove: poor; *prove ani* (S. + H.): very poor.

provecho (el): the profit, benefit.

pruntar: to ask.

pudrido, a: rotten.

pudrir: to rot.

pueder: to be able.

puerko (el): the pig.

puerpo (el): the body.

puerta (la): the door.

pujar: to increase.

pulido, a: polished, polite [old: handsome, pretty].

puliya (la): the moth.

pulso (el): the wrist, pulse.

punchón (el): a thorn, sting.

punta (la): the end of, point.

puntada (la): pneumonia.

punto (un): a minute.

purimlik (un) (H. and T.): a Purim gift.

pye (el): the foot.

pyedra (la): the stone.

pyojo (el): the louse (lice).

R

rakí (el) (T.): anise-flavored liquor, *cf.* Greek *ouzo*.

rana (la): the frog.

rashá (el) (H.): the evil one, enemy, traitor.

ratón (el): the mouse.

rav (el) (H.): the rabbi.

ravanó (el): the radish.

ravya (la): the anger, rage.

rayar/rayer: to grate, grind.

razón (la): the reason.

redoma (la): the bottle.

regalado, a: offered as a gift; an only child.

regalo (el): the gift.

reis (el) (T.): the chief.

remedyo (el): the solution, remedy.

remojar: to soak.

repozar: to repose, rest.

repozo (el): the rest, repose.

repuesta (la): the answer.

resha (la): the grill; type of pastry.

responder: to answer, respond.

resta (la): the necklace, garland.

revedrino, a: grown green again, become young.

revedrido, a: (same as *revedrino*).

rey (el): the king.

rezyo, a: sturdy, in good health.

ridá (la) (T.): the dustcloth, handkerchief.

rijir: to command, put order into.

rikinyón (el): the wealthy man.

riko, a: rich.

riyir: to laugh.

riyo (el): the river.

rizín: newly, recently.

rogar: to ask, pray, supplicate.

rohets (el) (H.): the washer of the dead.

romper: to break.

ropa (la): the merchandise, clothing goods.

ropavejero (el): the rag dealer.

rosh hodésh (H.): the new moon, first of the month.

roto, a: broken.

rovés (a la): on the contrary; inside-out.

roza (la): the flower (sometimes: the rose).

rubí (el) (H.): the rabbi, professor.

rubisa (la) (H.): the rabbi's wife.

ruvyo, a: reddish, russet.

S

safanorya (la): the carrot.

saká (el) (T.): the water carrier.

saksí (el) (T.): the flower pot.

sal (la): the salt.

salado, a.: salted.

salar: to salt.

salata (la) (T.): the salad.

salir: to leave, go out; *salir de puerpo:* to excrete.

salón (el): the living room.

saltar: to leap, jump.

salto (el): the leap, jump.

saludar: to greet.

salvasyón (la): the salvation.

samán (el) (T.): the straw.

samarra (la): the fur, fur coat.

samarrero (el): the furrier.

samur (el) (T.): the sable fur.

sangre (la): the blood.

sanmás/shamásh (el) (H.): the synagogue *shamash*.

sano, a: healthy.

sanya (la): relentless anger.

sapatero (el): the shoemaker, cobbler.

sapatika (la): the slipper.

sapato (el): the shoe, footware.

sar (el) (H,): the fear.

sarampyón (el): the measles.

sarear (T.): to clasp, embrace.

sarilik (el) (T.): the jaundice.

sarnudar: to sneeze.

sarraf (el) (T.): the gold exchanger.

sartén (el): the frying pan.

sávana (la): the bedsheet; the shroud.

saver: to know, know how.

savrozo, a: tasty, delicious.

sed (la): the thirst.

sedaká (la) (H.): charity.

Sefaradim (los) (H.): the Sephardim.
sehorá (la) (H.): the care, worry.
sehorento, a (H.): sad, distressed.
seja (la): the eyelash.
sején, a: sixth.
sekar: to dry, dry out.
seko, a: dry.
sekreter (el, la) (T. from F.): the secretary.
selam (el) (T.): health.
semana (la): the week.
semejante: similar, resembling.
semen (el): the seed, the family line.
sentral: central.
ser: to be, exist.
sereza (la): the sweet cherry.
serrar: to close, end, turn off (appliances).
servir/sirvir: to serve.
sesh: six.
setén, a: seventh.
seudá (la) (H.): the meal, feast.
sevoya (la): the onion.
sezo (el): the mind, brains.
sigaro (el): the cigarette.
sigundo, a: second.
siguro: certain; certainly, of course.
simán (el) (H.): the sign, omen.
sinemá (el) (F.): cinema, movies.
sinkén, a: fifth.
sinko: five.
sintido (el): the mind.
sikintí (el) (T.): the worry, problem, anguish.
sintir: to hear.
sintirse: to feel (ill, etc.).
sinyal (el): the signal.
sinyifikar: to mean, signify.
sirá (la) (T): the row.
sisko (el): the coal-dust.
sitmá (la) (T.): malaria.
sivdad (la): the city.
siya (la): the chair.
siyo (el): the seal (on a document).
skala (la): the dock, embarkation point.
skola (la): the school.
sodro, a: deaf.
sofá (la) (T.): the sofa.
solamente: only.
sonyar: to dream.

sorretero, a (el, la): person who goes out a lot.
sovrina (la): the niece.
sovrino (el): the nephew.
sudar: to sweat, perspire.
suenyo (el): *see* **esuenyo**.
suerte (la): the luck.
suká (la) (H.): the booth erected for the festival of Sukkoth.
Sukot (H.): the festival of Sukkoth.
sumo (el): the juice.
súpito (en): suddenly.
supstraksyón (la) (F.): subtraction.
surear (T.): to last.
suspirar: to sigh.
suzyo, a: dirty, soiled.
syedra (la): the left side.
syego (el): blind man.
syelos (los): heaven.
syempre: still, always.
syen: one hundred (invariable).
syervo, a (el, la): the slave, servant.
syete: seven.

Sh

shabad (el) (H.): Saturday, the Sabbath.
shalvar (un) (T.): wide-legged trousers.
sharope (el) (Sp. Ar.): the syrup, sugar paste.
shastre (el): the taylor.
shavdo, a: pale, insipid, without taste.
shavón (el): the soap.
shilvané (la) (T.): the attic.
shofbén (el) (F.): the water-heater.
shushurella/shushunera (la): diarrhea.
shurup (el) (T.): the syrup.

T

tabaká (la) (T.): the layer.
tadrar: to be late (in doing something).
tadre (la): afternoon, evening.
tadre: late.

taksí (el): the taxi.

taled/tallé (el) (H.): the prayer shawl; *echar taled/tallé:* hold the shawl at the wedding ceremony.

tambyén: also.

taní(d)/taanit (el) (H.): fasting.

tanyedor (el): the musician.

tanyer: to play (a musical instrument).

tapar: to cover, plug up.

tapet (el): the rug, carpet.

tapón (el): the plug, stopper.

tashidear (T.): to carry, transport.

taukchí (el) (T.): the poultry dealer.

taushán (el) (T.): the rabbit.

taván (el) (T.): the roof.

tavla (la) wooden plank, board.

tavlí (el) (T.): backgammon (game).

tefilá (la) (H.): the prayer.

tejado (el): the roof.

teksto (el) (F.): the text.

telefón (el) (T.): the telephone.

temprano: early.

teneké (el) (T.): the tin can.

tener: to have; *tener korasón:* to have a heart condition; *tener chapetas:* to have red cheeks (cold, fever).

terdjumán (el): the interpreter.

terrasa/tarrassa (la): the terrace, porch.

teshido (el): cloth goods, fabric.

teta (la): the breast.

tevá (la) (H.): the rabbi's podium (at the synagogue).

tijera (la): the scissors.

tinaja (la): the jar, pot.

tino (el): the mind, attention.

tivyo, a: warm, tepid.

tiya (la): the aunt.

tiyatro (el) (T.): the theater.

tiyo (el): the uncle.

tokar: to touch.

tomar: to take; *tomar a pasensya:* to endure, bear patiently; *tomar aver:* to go out for some fresh air.

top (el) (T.): the ball.

topar: to find; *toparse bueno:* to find oneself in good health.

tornada (a la): upon returning.

tornar: to return, come back home.

tos/toz (la): the cough.

tósigo (el): the poison.

tradjumán (el) (T.): the interpreter.

travajador (el): the worker.

travar estrechura: to experience difficulties.

trayer/traer: to bring, carry.

tredje: thirteen.

tres: three.

tresalir: to be overjoyed.

treser, a: third.

trezladador (el): the translator.

tripa (la): the stomach, belly.

trokar: to change, exchange.

tú: you (pronoun); **tu:** your (adj.).

tualet (la): the bathroom, toilet

tulumba (la) (T.): the water pump.

tulumbadjí (el) (T): the volonteer fireman.

turar: to last.

Turkino, -a: a Sephardic Jew from the old Ottoman Empire.

tuyir: to hurt, ache.

tyempo (el): time (passage of time); weather.

tyerra (la): the earth.

U

uerfandad (la): being or feeling like an orphan, absence, solitude.

uerko (el): the devil.

umano, a: human.

uno, a: a, an, one.

untar: to grease, dip in oil.

unya (la): the fingernail.

urashear (T.): to make an effort to, strive for.

uva (la): the grape.

V

vaka (la): the cow.

vakif (el) (T): the foundation.

vano, a: vain.

vapor (el): the ship, steamer.

vaziyo, a: empty.

vazo (el): the vase.

vedre: green.

vedrura (la): green vegetables.
vejéz (la): old age.
veluntad (la): the will.
venas (las): the veins.
vendedor (el): the vendor, seller.
vender: to sell.
venir/vinir: to come, come over.
ventana (la): the window.
vente: twenty.
ver: to see.
vestido (el): *see* **vistido**.
vestimyenta (la): the clothes.
vestir(se): *see* **vistir(se)**.
vez (la) (pl.: *las vezes*): the time (once, twice, etc.).
vezindar: to be neighbors with.
vida (la): the life.
videlo (el) (I.): the calf, veal.
vidreriya (la): the glassware.
vidro (el): glass (material).
vijitar: to visit.
vijola (la): ceremony at which the rabbi bestows a name on a new-born girl.
vinagre (el): the vinegar.
vinir: to come.
vino (el): the wine.
viruelika (la): chicken pox.
vishna/vijna (la) (T.): the sour cherry.
vistido (el): the clothing, dress.
vistir(se): to get dressed, put on clothing.
vizino, a/ vezino, a: neighbor.
vuestro, a: your.
vyaje (el): the trip, voyage.
vyejo, a: old.
vyernes (el): Friday.

Y

ya: already.
yaká (la) (T.): the collar.
yamar(se): to call, be called (named).
yaprak (el/la) (T.): leaf (for stuffing).
yasimín (el): the jasmine.
yave (la): the key.
yavedura (la): the lock.
yazer: to lie down, stretch out.
yegar: to arrive.
yelar: to become cold.
yelarse: to catch a chill.
yenar: to fill.
yené/yiné (T.): again, anyway, just the same.
yeno, a: full, stuffed.
yerno (el): the son-in-law.
yerrar(se): to be mistaken.
yerro (el): the error, mistake.
yerva (la): the grass.
yeshivá (la) (H.): Talmudic school.
yevar: to carry, carry off.
yo: I, me.
yorar: to weep, cry.
yoro (el): the weeping.
yukurí (el) (T.): the attic, storeroom.

Z

zarzavachí (el) (T.): the greengrocer, produce seller.
zurzuví: undefinable, ridiculous color.

Bibliography and Discography

Books

Alvar, Manuel. *Poesía tradicional de los judíos españoles.* Mexico City: Porrua, 1971.

Badi, Meri. *250 recettes de cuisine juive espagnole.* Paris: Jacques Grancher, 1984.

Baruh, Izidor N. *Pesah Bayramı hatırası – Haggadah shel Pessah.* Istanbul: Or-Ahayim hastanesi Vakfi.

Behar, Nisim. *El Gid para el Pratikante.* Part 2. Istanbul: Güler Basımevi, 5727 – 1967.

Bicerano, Salamon. *Relatos en lingua judeo-espanyola.* Gözlem gazetecilik basın ve yayın A.Ş., 1997.

Bortnik, Rachel. "Un artikolo sovre la lingua," in *Şalom* (01/15/92).

Bunis, David M. *A Lexicon of the Hebrew and Aramaic Elements in Modern Judezmo.* Jerusalem: Magnes Press, Hebrew University and Misgav Yerushalayim, 1993.

Canetti, Elias. *The Tongue Set Free: Remembrance of a European Childhood.* Trans. from the German by Joachim Neugroschel. New York: Seabury, 1979.

Cohen, Marcel. *Lettre à Antonio Saura.* Bilingual edition [Judeo-Spanish/French]. Paris: L'Echoppe, 1997.

Cohen-Rak, Nicole. "La 'Solidaridad Ovradera,' journal socialiste de Salonique – 1911 – 7 issues ed., translation [into French], various indexes and linguistic considerations." Doctoral dissertation, 2 vols. University of Paris III, 1986.

Collin, Gaëlle, Ed. *Neue Romania – Judenspanish VI:* La Novya Aguna d'Eliya Karmona, no. 26. Berlin, 2002.

Collin, Gwenaëlle. *Bula Satula et Haym Avram: L'immigration judéo-espagnole à New York à travers les Chroniques de Moïse Soulam dans l'hebdomadaire La Vara (1922–1934).* Master's Thesis. Paris: INALCO, 2002.

Crews, Cynthia M. *Recherches sur le judéo-espagnol dans les pays balkaniques.* Paris: Droz, 1935.

Fintz Altabé, David. *Una kozecha de rimas i konsejas: A Harvest of Rhymes and Folktales.* Miami, FL: San Lazaro printers, 2000.

Gabbaï-Simantov, Rita. *Quinientos anios despues.* Athens: 1992.

Gonzalo Maeso, David and Pascual Pascual Recuero. *Me'am Lo'ez: El gran comentario bíblico sefardí.* Biblioteca Universal Sefardí. 4 vols. Madrid: Gredos, 1964.

Ha-Elion, Moshe. *En los kampos de la muerte.* Israel: Instituto Maale Adumim, 2000.

Hemsi, Alberto. *Cancionero sefardí.* Edwin Seroussi, ed., with the collaboration of Paloma Díaz-Mas, José Manuel Pedrosa and Elena Romero, postface by Samuel G. Armistead. Jerusalem: Jewish Music Research Center, Hebrew UP, 1995.

Koen-Sarano, Matilda. *Kuentos del folklor de la famiya djudeo-espanyola.* Jerusalem: Kana, 1986.

_____. *Djohá ke dize?* Jerusalem: Kana, 1991.

_____. *Konsejas i konsejikas del mundo djudeo-espanyol.* Jerusalem: Kana, 1994.

Lazar, Moshe. *Joseph and his Brethren.* Culver City, CA: Labyrinthos, 1990.

_____. *Sefarad in My Heart: A Ladino Reader.* Lancaster, CA: Labyrinthos, 1999.

Levis-Mano, Guy. *Romancero judeo-espagnol.* Paris: GLM, 1971.

_____. *Romancero: Romances populaires d'Espagne,* ed. and trans. [into French]. Paris: Allia: 1994.

Malinowski, Arlene. "Judeo-Spanish in Turkey," in *International Journal of the Sociology of Language,* no. 37, 71-98.

Matitiahu, Margalit. *Alegrika.* Kiron (Israel): Eked, 1992.

Nehama, Joseph. *Dictionnaire du judéo-espagnol.* Madrid: Instituto Arias Montano, 1977.

Nicoïdski, Clarisse. *Los ojus, las manus, la boca.* Loubressac-Bretenoux (France): Braad, 1978.

Passy, Albert Morris. *Sephardic Folk Dictionary: English to Ladino—Ladino to English* (3rd ed.), 1997 (contact the author).

Perahya, Klara, and Suzi de Toledo, Suzi Danon, Fani Ender. *Erensya Sefaradí.* Istanbul: Gözlem, 1997.

Perahya, Klara and Ruti Meranda, Suzi Danon, Regine Sedaka, Çela Zakuto. *Diksyonaryo/Sözlük Judeo-espanyol/Türkçe – Türkçe/ Judeo-espanyol.* Istanbul: Gözlem, 1997.

Perahya, Klara and Elie. *Dictionnaire français/judéo-espagnol.* Paris: Langues & Mondes–L'Asiathèque, 1998.

Perez, Avner. *Siniza i Fumo.* Jerusalem: Sefarad, 1986.

_____. *Verdjel de mansanas.* Maale Adumim (Israel): Yeriot, 1996.

Quintana Rodriguez, Aldina. *"Una informasion de la aritmetica y una muestra de los kuentos"* in *Hommage à Haïm Vidal Sephiha,* eds. W. Busse and M.-C. Varol-Bornes. Bern: Peter Lang, 1997, pp. 295-314.

Salzmann, Laurence and Ayşe Gürsan-Salzmann. *Anyos munchos i buenos, Turkey's Sephardim: 1492–1992.* Philadelphia: Blue Flower Photo Review Book, 1991.

Saporta y Beja, Enrique. *Refranes de los judíos sefardíes.* Barcelona: Ameller, 1978.

_____. *En torno de la Torre Blanca.* Paris: Vidas Largas, 1982.

Sephiha, Haïm-Vidal. *Le ladino (judéo-espagnol calque), Deutéronome, versions de Constantinople (1547) et de Ferrare (1553): Edition, étude linguistique et lexique.* Paris: Eds. Hispaniques, 1973.

_____. *Le Judéo-Espagnol.* Paris: Entente, 1986.

_____. *L'agonie des Judéo-Espagnols.* Paris: Entente, 1977.

_____. *Du miel au fiel: Contes judéo-espagnols.* Paris: Bibliophane, 1992.

Shaul, Eli. *Folklor de los Judios de Turkiya.* Istanbul: Isis, 1994.

Shaul, Moshe and Aldina Quintana Rodriguez, Zelda Ovadia. *El gizado sefaradí.* Zaragoza: Ibercaja, 1995.

Stavroulakis, Nicholas. *Cuisine des Juifs de Grèce.* Paris: Langues & Monde – L'Asiathèque, 1995.

Varol, Marie-Christine. *Balat: Faubourg juif d'Istanbul.* Istanbul: Isis, 1989.

_____. "Le judéo-espagnol d'Istanbul: Etude linguistique." 3 vols. Doctoral dissertation, University of Paris III, 1992.

The Press

Defunct newspapers and journals:

La Boz de Oriente, Istanbul.
La Luz de Israel, Tel-Aviv.
La Solidaridad Ovradera, Salonika.
El Djugeton, Istanbul.
El Telegrafo, Istanbul.
La Vara, New York.

Current journals and reviews

Aki Yerushalayim. P.O. Box 8175, Yerushalayim 91080, Israel. Contact: Moshe Shaul, judeospa@trendline.co.il

Erensia Sefardi. Dr. Albert de Vidas, Ed., 46 Benson Place, Fairfield, CT 06430, USA. Contact: Dr. Albert de Vidas, erensia@aol.com

Ke Haber. David Siman, Sephardi Federation of Palm Beach County, 109 Palomino Dr., Jupiter, FL 33458, USA.Contact: Daisy Allalouf-Newell, DaiJac@aol.com

La Lettre sépharade [in French]. Jean Carasso, F-84220, Gordes, France. Contact: Jean Carasso, Lettre.sepharade@wanadoo.fr

La Lettre sépharade [in English]. Rosine Nussenblatt, 9206 Cedarcrest Drive, Bethesda, MD 20814. Lettresepharade@earthlink.net

Los Muestros. 52 rue Hôtel-des-Monnaies, 1060 Brussels, Belgium. Ed.: Moïse V. Rahmani, 25 rue Dodonnée, 1180 Brussels, Belgium. Contact: Moïse Rahmani, moise.rahmani@sefarad.org. Website: http://sefarad.org

El Pregonero, same address as *Aki Yerushalayim.*

Şalom, Atiye sokak, Polar Apt. 12/6, Teşvikiye, Istanbul, Turkey. Shalom @turk.net

Sefaraires, monthly email. Contact: Luis León, sefaraires@datafull.com

Tiryaki. Tünel, Kumbaraci Yokuşu, 131, Beyoğlu, Istanbul, Turkey. Contact: Moşe Grosman, grosman@superonline.com

Cassette tapes and compact disks

Adama. *Chants et musiques des mondes judaïques.* Adamuzic.

Aguado, Bienvenida "Berta" and Loretta "Dora" Gerassi. *Chants judéo-espagnols de la Méditerranée orientale.* Maison des Cultures du Monde (101 bd Raspail, 75006 Paris, France). Recordings done in Jerusalem and Tel Aviv in 1993 by Pierre Bois and Edwin Seroussi. CD.

Atlan, Françoise. *Romances sefardíes: Noches.* Musique du Monde, Buda Musique (188 bd Voltaire, 75011 Paris, France). CD.

Bessis, Sandra and John McLean, Philippe Foulon, Alain Bouchaux. *Paseando...: Chants judéo-espagnols,* ARB (45 rue Sainte-Anne, 75002 Paris). CD.

Esim, Janet-Jak. *Antik bir hüzün...: Judeo-Espanyol Şarkılar 1492–1992.* Polin Bant Kayıt Sanayi ve Ticaret, IMÇ 6. Blok 6229-6502, Unkapanı, Istanbul. Cassette.

Los Pasharos Sefardis. *Kansionero djudeo-espanyol por Karen Gerşon/Izzet Bana.* Yavuz Hubeş and Selim Hubeş Music, Gözlem Gazetecilik Basın ve Yayın A.Ş. (see *Şalom* address). 3 cassette box.

Jagoda, Flory & family. *La Nona kanta: The Grandmother Sings.* Global Village Music (245 West 29th St., New York, NY 10001), 1992. CD.

Rot, Dina. *Una manu tumó l'otra: Cantando poemas de Juan Gelman y Clarisse Nicoydsky* [sic]. Lcd El Europeo (Jorge Juan, 9, Madrid 28001, Spain), 1997. CD with book of poems.

Weich-Shahak, Susana, *Cantares y romances tradicionales sefardíes de Oriente.* Vol. II. Madrid: Tecnosaga, 1993. CD.

Internet Sites and Addresses

• Ladinokomunita
http://www.sephardicstudies.org/komunita.html. Ladinokomunita is a mailing-list in which the only language of exchange is Judeo-Spanish. To subscribe send a blank email to:
Ladinokomunita-subscribe@yahoogroups.com

• American Sephardi Federation (New York) http://www.asfonline.org/portal/
• Sephardic House (The Cultural Division of the American Sephardi Federation, New York: http://Sephardichouse.org/
• FASSAC – Foundation for the Advancement of Sephardic Studies and Culture (USA). http://www.sephardicstudies.org/
• Şalom, weekly publication of the Jewish community of Istanbul, with articles in Judeo-Spanish. http://www.salom.tr/
• Jewish Museum of Thessaloniki: http://www.jmth.gr/
• Etz-Hayyim Synagogue of Hania, Crete:
http://www.etz-hayyim-hania.org/
• Rhodes Jewish Museum: http://www.rhodesjewishmuseum.org/
• Union of Jews from Turkey in Israel: http://www.turkisrael.org/
This organization puts out a bulletin in Turkish and Judeo-Spanish that can be consulted at: http://www.geocities.com/hitahdut/
• SefarAires, a monthly email publication from Buenos Aires directed by Luis León and written in Judeo-Spanish and in Spanish, with the goal of dissemi-nating Sephardic culture and the Judeo-Spanish language. To receive it, free, contact: sefaraires@datafull.com or sefaraires@hotmail.com
• Sephardim.com, a research tool for Sephardic genealogy:
http://www.sephardim.com
• Oral Judeo-Spanish Literature (Samuel Armistead):
http://flsj.ucdavis.edu/home/
• Corpus de la parole:
http://corpusdelaparole.culture.fr (entendre/langues non territoriales/judéo-espagnol)

INDEX

Photographic Credits

46 • Manuel Varol.

62 • 1-2: Lorenzo Salzmann.
  • 3: Sabetay Varol.

67 • 1-3: Coll. Gérard Lévy.

68 • 1: Coll. G. L.
  • 2: Coll. Faraggi.
  • 3: L. S.

77 • 1: Coll. Anavi.
  • 2: S.V.
  • 3: L. S.

78 • 1-2: Marie-Christine Varol.
  • 3: Joëlle Tiano-Moussafir.

86 • Coll. G. L.

88 • 1-2: M.-C. V.

96 • 1: Paul Veysseyre.
  • 2: Viktor Yenibahar,
  rephotographed by P. V.

98 • 1: M.-C V.
  • 2: L. S.

109 • 1: Coll. G. L.

110 • 1: Coll. G. L.
  • 2: L. S.

113 • 1: Coll. Anavi.
  • 2: L. S.
  • 3: Viktorya Emanüel.

114 • 1: M.-C. V.
  • 2: P. V.

133 • 1-2: L. S.

134 • 1-2: L. S.
  • 3: Coll. G. L.
  • 4: M.-C. V.

138 • Coll. Jeanne Laedlein.

154 • 1-5: S. V.

157 • 1: Coll. Enrico Isacco.
  • 2: Coll. Alice Joachimowicz.
  • 3: Coll. G. L.
  • 4: Coll. S. Amado.

158 • 1: Coll. Maurice Hasson.
  • 2-4: Coll. G. L.

165 • P. V.

166 • M.-C V.

176 • M. V.

183 • 1-2: L. S.

205 • 1-2: L. S.

206 • 1: Coll. Alice Joachimowitz.

214-215 • Court. Vicky Tiano.

216 • 1: L. S.
  • 2: M.-C V.

229 • L. S.

230 • 1: Coll. Dolly Benozio.
  • 2-3: L. S.

243 • Coll. Henri Montias.

244 • 1: V. Y.
  • 2: M.-C. V.

245 • 1: V. Y.
  • 2: P. V.
  • 3: V. Y., rephotographed by P. V.
  • 4: V.Y.

246 • 1-3: M.-C V.

247 • 1-3-4: M.-C V.
  • 2: L. S.

248 • 1-3: L. S.
  • 2: P. V.

Abbreviations used on this page
G. L. = Gérard Lévy.
L. S. = Lorenzo Salzmann.
M.-C. V. = Marie-Christine Varol.

M. V. = Manuel Varol.
P. V. = Paul Veysseyre.
S. V. = Sabetay Varol.
V. Y. = Viktor Yenibahar.

CD RECORD

STUDIES AND TEXTS IN
JEWISH HISTORY AND CULTURE

The Joseph and Rebecca Meyerhoff Center for Jewish Studies
University of Maryland

General Editor: Bernard D. Cooperman

Vol. 1.   *Religion and Politics in the Ancient Near East*
           edited by Adele Berlin.
           ISBN: 1883053242; vi + 150 pp.; 1996.

Vol. 2.   *Freedom and Moral Responsibility: General and Jewish Perspectives*
           edited by Charles H. Manekin and Menachem M. Kellner.
           ISBN: 1883053293; viii + 273 pp.; 1997.

Vol. 3.   *Land and Community: Geography in Jewish Studies*
           edited by Harold Brodsky.
           ISBN: 1883053307; x + 418 pp.; 1997.

Vol. 4.   *A Life in Jewish Education: Essays in Honor of Louis L. Kaplan*
           edited by Jack Fruchtman, Jr.
           ISBN: 1883053383; 291 pp. 1997.

Vol. 5.   *Religious and Ethnic Communities in Later Roman Palestine*
           edited by Hayim Lapin.
           ISBN: 1883053315; xii + 298 pp.; 1998.

Vol. 6.   *Hitting Back: An Austrian Jew in the French Résistance*
           Dolly Steindling.
           ISBN: 1883053536; xxvi + 239 pp.; 2000.

Vol. 7.   *The Jews of Italy: Memory and Identity*
           edited by Barbara Garvin and Bernard D. Cooperman.
           ISBN: 9781883053369 (hard.); 9781934309162 (soft.); 462 pp.;
           2000.

Vol. 8.   *The Six-Day War and World Jewry*
           edited by Eli Lederhendler.
           ISBN: 1883053595; x + 340 pp.; 2000.